CRITICAL
CONDITIONS

CRITICAL
CONDITIONS

Regarding the Historical Moment

**Edited and with a Foreword by
Michael Hays**

University of Minnesota Press
Minneapolis   London

"Us and Them: On the Philosophical Bases of Political Criticism," copyright 1992 by Satya P. Mohanty.

Jonathan Arac, "Hamlet, *Little Doritt,* and the History of Character," reprinted from *South Atlantic Quarterly,* vol. 87, no. 2 (1988), copyright Duke University Press by permission.

Published by the University of Minnesota Press
2037 University Avenue Southeast, Minneapolis, MN 55414
Printed in the United States of America on acid-free paper

Library of Congress Cataloging-in-Publication Data

Critical conditions : regarding the historical moment in critical practice / edited and
    with a foreword by Michael Hays.
        p.   cm.
    Includes bibliographical references and index.
    ISBN 0-8166-2021-0 (alk. paper) — ISBN 0-8166-2022-9 (alk. paper : pbk.)
    1. Criticism. I. Hays, Michael.
    PN81.C837   1992
    801'.95—dc20
                                                                    92-6756
                                                                    CIP

Contents

The Scene and the Unseen of the Critic's Discourse

Michael Hays

In the simple practice of borrowing from the discourse of love, there is . . .
a danger that has to this day not been sufficiently understood. . . . Once
one has opted for this path there remains only the choice of evils.

—Constant, *Adolphe*

In a recent article in the *New York Times* culture section, Richard
Bernstein seeks to comfort his readers about the somehow disquiet-
ing state of academic criticism by announcing that "in the rough and
tumble lit-crit sweepstakes, . . . one school, the New Historicism, has
been gaining considerable notice, perhaps even pre-eminence," primarily
through the work of its "undisputed leader," Steven Greenblatt. The
supposed losers in this struggle seem to be theory—as represented by
deconstruction—and all criticism that would take a political position as
part of its effort to "link the analysis of literature to history."[1] The article
goes on to assure us that the New Historicism has, once again, made
it possible to interweave history and criticism in order to "explain poems,
novels, etc."—without worrying much about the theoretical ground or
the possible political implications of such a practice. Indeed, the author
cites with evident satisfaction Greenblatt's comment that *if* there is any
Marxism in his work it is of "a very renegade sort," and that he has
"become a bit more conservative." The New Historicism is further
described as "a new turn in a recurring cycle," thereby securing historical
criticism safely within the confines of the old and (merely) literary.

This praise of a return to a depoliticized academic milieu, to "facts"
that can simply be noted on the blackboard that figures so prominently
in the title of the article, is, of course, itself a fully politicized trope, a
mainstay in the discourse of the current neoconservative assault on what

has been labeled "political correctness" in the academy. Thus, despite Bernstein's effort to adduce an alternative possibility, when understood in historical context, the essay serves as a further, ironic indication that the institutional functions of the academy are indeed bound up with the political and ideological order of our cultural institutions—precisely *because* there are powerful voices claiming the contrary. However, as in the case at hand, such connections are often obscured by the fore-grounding not of the issues involved, but of the fact of the struggle itself. Different interpretive theories and methods are objectified as winners or losers and derided as insufficient, as out of place, or as *mere* recurring events in "the lit-crit sweepstakes"—without further inquiring after the political or the historical implications of individual practices or even the necessity of this venue of conflict itself.

The language of such gestures can be quite revealing, however, and the sweepstakes image is really quite interesting, since, in combination with the notion of "schools," it embeds the classical paradigm of free (individual) competition in a system of training and supervision in which the "thoroughbreds" in the sweepstakes vie not only for victory but also for the greater profit of their owners and trainers, thereby suggesting a hierarchy in which "lit-crit" operates at the behest of the somewhat more worldly disciplines normally associated with economic and social power. Thus, though the article mystifies its own linkage of the two by lauding "successful" literary criticism for its supposed apoliticality, the terms it employs point beyond this mystification to a clearer understanding of the historical antecedents of this particular mise en scène of criticism— and to a possible understanding of the conditions that gave rise to the institution of criticism as we have inherited and practice it. As the reader will see, opening the way to such understanding is also an aim of this book as a whole. Rather than discuss the essays in this volume in any detail in this foreword, however, I want to return to the sweepstakes metaphor with which I began, since it will help me suggest some reasons for insisting that these individual essays be allowed to speak for themselves.

Central to this metaphor are not the specifics of any critical practices as such, but the competition between them, the critical agon. Nonethe-less, this common ground is not readily visible if we become involved in any of the various "local" disputes within the discipline. From the point of view of the current debates concerning, for example, the "old" and "new" Americanists, or the canon, the struggle occurs elsewhere entirely than between the theories depicted in the *Times* article. But the agon remains—and reappears in each new confrontation between meth-ods, between critics, and even between the critic and the text. The particular historical and ideological implications of each such struggle are, therefore, to be discovered not only by examining the way in which the critic represents the figures put into play in the critical agon, but also by examining the history and the institutional implications of the mise en scène of the agon itself.

It is, of course, no accident that I have used a theatrical metaphor in discussing the production of the critical situation. It is a commonplace of contemporary criticism to seek out and identify the representational aspect of social as well as aesthetic "events." Indeed, the notion of *textual* mise en scène has become one of the terminological meeting points of a number of critical practices in recent years and has been put to use in discussing critical as well as narrative texts, though it is the mise en scène of the latter that has attracted the greatest attention. One finds it put to use profitably in the critical vocabularies of semiotics, deconstruction,[2] speech act theory, reception aesthetics, the New Historicism, and several versions of feminist and psychoanalytic theory, where much has been made of it as a means of escaping the binary logic of referentiality and naive representation.

Mária Minich Brewer discusses this and other theatrical figures that have emerged in the vocabulary of contemporary criticism in her essay "Performing Theory."[3] Brewer identifies the theatrical metaphors operative in current theory and practice and suggests that they *may* be relevant to an understanding of the contemporary critical context, but offers no means of ascertaining that relevance—their place or function in the history of the critical institution. In contrast, what I want to suggest here is how the notion of mise en scène (Brewer prefers the less revealing term *frame*) and specifically the historical situation of the *metteur en scène* can help us understand a fundamental aspect of the development and ordering practice of modern Western criticism. It seems to me that, up to now, the use of such theatrical metaphors has served to mask as much as it has revealed about the genealogy of that development. *Should* we assume that the playful irony that always accompanies such representational metaphorics and so subtly detects the linguistic and ideological order (or disorder) of the texts scrutinized allows the critic to escape from "the ruses of interpretation's need to define meaning" as Brewer claims? I hope to show here that a careful examination of the mise en scène of a critical persona as well as the staging of the critic's commentary can point to an order of meaning that has been a fundamental though unexamined element of the critical institution at least since the late nineteenth century.

In order to discuss this historical ground, I want to look at the way in which mise en scène, as it emerges in contemporary criticism, both names the practice of the critic and blocks access to a larger historical/critical understanding of the institutional context that precedes both the practice and the practitioner—the context that sanctions interpretive control and allows the *metteur en scène* to foreground his/her distance from what we now refer to as "representation" while surreptitiously staging a second level of narrative in which mise en scène empowers its creator at the expense of the public before which it unfolds. I would like to begin this effort by raising some initial questions about the agency involved in staging terms derived from a cultural discourse, and then by looking at an essay by Paul de Man, the critic whose work, perhaps more than that of any other contemporary, shows us the productive as well as the limiting characteristics, the insight and the blindness, operative in the critical institutions we have inherited.

Whoever has read Benjamin Constant's novel, *Adolphe,* no doubt remembers the first awakening to love experienced by the eponymous protagonist of that novel. What is most striking about this awakening is not the event, but the source to which the narrator ascribes it. As in the most banal of romances, Adolphe falls in love with a beautiful young stranger, but this love is not presented as the result of his interaction with her person. Instead it arises from his submission to the very discourse of love to which he has consciously turned in what, from our contemporary point of view, might best be described as an effort to stage a seductive "scene" of love—a scene mounted in order to satisfy his need to represent a completed emotional "self" and enacted by eliciting and shaping the affective response of another.

> Plagued by a vague emotion, I thought to myself, "I want to be
> loved;"... I examined my heart and my tastes; I felt no marked
> preference.... [But, Ellénore], coming into view at a moment when my
> heart needed love and my vanity success,... seemed a conquest worthy of
> me.... My plan... introduced a new interest into my life and enlivened
> my existence to an unaccustomed extent.[4]

When the object of his attentions responds, assimilating the terms and enacting the role assigned by this discourse, Adolphe promptly forgets his initial motivation and understanding of the situation: he himself submits to the scene of love and the discourse that it plays out. "There was no longer any question in my mind of schemes or plans; I was perfectly convinced that I was really in love.... The need to see the person whom I loved and to enjoy her presence dominated me to the exclusion of all else" (24, 72). But as the narrator makes clear, it is actually his engagement with the terms of the scene he has staged, the scene in which love's discourse is put to work as part of an interpretive construct, that enthralls him. The result is an ever greater gulf between Adolphe's expectations concerning his "love" and the quotidian reality constituted by his relationship with Ellénore.

A growing awareness of this contradiction does not lead Adolphe to a self-critical evaluation of the history of his own discourse and practice, though. Instead his recurring acceptance of the intersubjective scene arranged and introduced through his mise en scène produces an ever greater withdrawal from the everyday and from any possibility of linking his interpretation of the scene of love with his position in the social and political world at large.[5] Adolphe finally breaks off this affair, but we learn from a "letter to the publisher" at the close of the novel that he never really manages to understand how his submission to his own mise en scène renders inevitable the failure of his interpretive claims concerning the object and context of his "love" or of his other enterprises.

What is of crucial importance in Constant's rendering of this situation is the distinction he makes between "love" as an anonymous social discourse and the ability of an individual to consciously put such culturally available material to work. This does not mean that Constant assumes Adolphe could have understood or mastered this (or any other) discourse as a general cultural apparatus, or that he had liberated himself from its *emprise*. On the contrary, as the preceding quotation indicates, the discursive order within which Adolphe imagines the possibility of a completed "self" remains outside his ken; he is taken up and defined within it even as he decides to put some of its available artifacts to use. But being acted upon by a discourse in no way prevents him from realizing that such a discursive mode exists, or that he in turn can take up some of its terms and employ them on a local level.

In Constant's novel, then, Adolphe fails to keep in mind or adequately scrutinize not the discourse of love as such, but his own agency, his conscious selection of the terms and gestures that he has borrowed from this discourse and knowingly put into play. He mistakes his own mise en scène for reality, and is to this degree trapped within a context of his own making. It is on this level that Constant suggests it might have been possible for Adolphe to derive from the history of his own interpretive practice a "self-consciousness" that would allow him at the very least to attempt to renegotiate his relations with the others in his lifeworld. But Adolphe never becomes fully aware of the degree to which the inauthenticity of both his involvement with the object of his attentions and his engagement in the world at large are predicated on his willful submission to a discourse initially taken up ironically, as a means of realizing his desire for self-completion by eliciting "institutionalized" amorous responses from an Other. His need of interpretive control combines with forgetfulness to erase the possibility of a fuller critical understanding of the performative nature of this situation.

Constant sums up the effect of submitting to this mise en scène of love's discourse in the following manner:

> [It] takes the place of extended remembrance through a sort of magic. All the other attachments have need of a past: [it] creates . . . and surrounds us with a past. It gives us, as it were, a sense of having lived for years with a being which but lately was almost a stranger to us. (97)

Submission to his mise en scène of "love" interrupts Adolphe's consciousness of his complicity in the fashioning of the scene, his consciousness of the work necessary to grasp the critical linkages between context, language, and action, and binds him instead to a figuration of life-world experience that excludes from its tropes whatever does not reinforce the priority of the powerful affective charge it promises. The result is a "fatuous self-satisfaction" that ultimately even allows Adolphe to turn "self-critical," but only in relation to the effects of the scene he has staged, not the context prior to its staging. Adolphe, as *metteur en scène*, has staged an interpretive scene that grants him both positive and negative "self-recognition," but only at the price of forgetting the historical and institutional contexts from which the artifacts of his mise en scène and his interpretive work derive. The way back to history and to the possibility of an interactive production of the social as well as the amorous is, thus, blocked, but not by the cunning of love's discourse; it is now blocked by Adolphe's inability to forgo the fictions of self-empowerment available in the craft of interpretive mise en scène itself.

How, then, does this tale of the mise en scène of love's discourse lead us to a better understanding of our own critical situation? The crucial moment in Constant's (and my own) allegory is the linkage of discourse and history (historical consciousness or its fictive other) through the notion of mise en scène and the interpretive work of the *metteur en scène*. Understanding the historical roots of the directorial functions espoused by the critic can help us see the scene of criticism as one in which the staging of our discursive relationship to a (textual) other operates in a manner similar to Adolphe's, but within an institutional context that, *unlike* his discourse of love, involves a set of historically bound practices that can be examined both as a means of understanding our individual critical discourses and also in terms of their functional links to the definition and distribution of knowledge and power in the larger cultural and political structures within which the critical institution operates.

An essay by Paul de Man that tries to come to grips with these problems should help me get at this complex set of relations, especially since, along the way, it runs into some of the same difficulties that are confronted in *Adolphe*. The essay in question is de Man's account of the difference between the mimetic and the aesthetic, between the political order of interpretation and the free play of the word revealed in his reading of Kleist's brief text "Über das Marionettentheater."[6] In his essay, de Man seeks to demonstrate how aesthetic practice undermines all efforts at hermeneutic interpretation, and, by extension, any possibility of deriving an interpretive model from the aesthetic work that could serve as a means of articulating a relation between knowledge and action, between the self and others—a means of overcoming historical alienation and fragmentation.

De Man broaches this set of problems by reading Kleist's text as a commentary on Schiller's *Letters on the Aesthetic Education of Man*. According to de Man, Kleist, like Schiller, is concerned with the problematic linkage of the aesthetic and the epistemological, that is, with the possibility of achieving a self-mastering freedom and a knowledge of the world derived from the interpretation of aesthetic works. Kleist, according to de Man, opposes Schiller's notion of aesthetic education and the aesthetic state (his sociopolitical model of the self-conscious individual grounded in the aesthetic). Kleist's essay works to reveal the impossibility of employing formalized aesthetic objects to define and order the world of lived experience—the impossibility of imposing a semantic order on the aesthetic that could unproblematically serve as an enabling device in understanding or unfolding the structures that configure our existence. The importance of this argument, though de Man leaves it to the reader to imagine its full worldly implications, is to associate *all* interpretation with political ideology, since all interpretation involves "codes and systems of inscription" that, while asserting an ideal of (aesthetic) knowledge / freedom, in fact function as exclusionary and repressive structures of knowledge that serve the apparatuses of culture in the state. Thus, the interpretive act becomes an exercise in mystifying the relations between critical practice and institutional order while at the same time serving to reinforce that order. Seen in this light, interpretation is revealed as another version of, a reenactment of, Hegel's construction of the individual as a self-conscious entity within the state.

De Man's essay is on this level an exemplary demonstration of the positive contribution of deconstruction and one of his more powerful renderings of the dangers inherent in the act of interpretation. It supplies emphatic evidence of the importance of our recognizing the ideological ground of any interpretation that ascribes a single meaning or cluster of meanings to a text or other interpretive object. I will not trouble the reader with a rehearsal of all the specific arguments offered by de Man since I am far more interested here in his assertions about the way Kleist *stages* the scenes in which his text engages with these questions of aesthetic education. As de Man correctly points out, "this stress on staging, on the mimesis of the diegetic narratives—the text *shows* people engaged in the act of *telling*—emphasizes the self-consciousness of the representational mode . . . and problematizes the relationship between rhetoric and a hermeneutics of persuasion" (269).

Interpretation is always, whether we recognize it as such or not, an effort at persuasion. It works to convince us of the correctness of the order of meaning it offers. But in this case, thanks to Kleist's *visible* mise en scène, the effort reveals itself as a *scene of persuasion,* and, because one can observe the persuasion as a scene, it becomes a mimesis, a trope of persuasion. By drawing on Kleist's self-conscious rendering of the representational context of the narrative statements in his text, de Man, like other critics who have taken up this theatrical metaphor recently, is able to point out that one can "read" the mise en scène of a narrative in a manner analogous to the ways in which one reads the narrative assertions and arguments contained within such scenes. When de Man proceeds to do this with the "scenes" in Kleist's essay he discovers that there is a profound difference between what is said and what we are now able to "see" in the narrative scene. We "see" that every effort at or assertion of self-conscious mastery of the "meaning" of a textual event is disrupted not only by the now well known (deconstructive) play of language—the rupture between signifier and signified in the diegetic narrative—but also by the fact that the scene itself illuminates and comments on the narrative voices as roles, and thus enacts the subversion of both the life-world authenticity of the narrative and the narrator's authority.

As de Man puts it, the mise en scène introduces another level of diegetic narrative, which "tells the story" of the narrator's effort to stage the authority of his assertions. The result of this very complex analysis is, as I have said, a demonstration of the insufficiency of Schiller's theory of aesthetic education on the one hand, and of all interpretive (and hermeneutic) reading on the other. De Man concludes with a return to Schiller's image of the dance as an emblem of aesthetic education and asserts the necessary violence of all efforts to determine the meaning of a text. "This dance," writes de Man, "regardless of whether it occurs as mirror, as imitation, as history, as the fencing match of interpretation, or as the anamorphic transformations of tropes, is the ultimate trap, as unavoidable as it is deadly" (290). Deadly, that is, for any critic whom the work of art still serves or could serve as a means of returning to history, to a referential relation between the aesthetic object and historical reality. According to de Man, we are all failed critics and teachers who have allowed our assertions to become "canonized," "systematic," or "exemplary" (272), that is, formalized "pedagogical" discourses that begin to function in our culture in a manner analogous to Constant's "discourse of love."

This is not merely an argument on the side of "theory" then, or one merely opposed to "historical" perspectives in criticism; it is, as I have already suggested, an effort to understand how criticism has functioned in the academy and in the state. As de Man says, "the problem is not entirely trivial or self-centered, for the political power of the aesthetic, the measure of its impact on reality, necessarily travels by way of its didactic manifestations. The politics of the aesthetic state are the politics of education" (273). De Man wishes us to consider the way in which our critical activities entail our engagement in a "politics of education" that not only (re)shapes the aesthetic object, but also affects the relations of the participants in the discursive scene (teacher/critics, ephebes, and the public at large) while mystifying the links between this scene and the relations of power and knowledge that inform our sociopolitical perceptions, the "stage" on which we enact our lives.

This aspect of de Man's essay should give pause to anyone interested in the practice of criticism, for it raises fundamental questions about the legitimating claims of all critical points of view, and more especially about the unannounced, even unsuspecting political role of those who espouse these positions. Indeed, one of the purposes of this foreword— and of this book as a whole—is precisely to raise these questions again and to explore them both as theoretical problems of history and critical discourse and as a means of understanding the cultural and institutional implications of the critical practice of critics as disparate as Sacvan Bercovitch, Stanley Fish, Steven Greenblatt, and, of course, Paul de Man himself. As we read de Man's essay, it becomes clear that he believes there is no way out of the ideological dilemma of interpretation. His solution is to "perform" the only alternative that remains for him, his deconstructive refusal to submit to the politics of meaning, the politics of education. But has he really succeeded in freeing himself from this politics, or from what Constant referred to as "the choice of evils?" Can we not both accept the content of his argument and, using some of his own insights, still seek the traces of a history that could open the way to a different and historically grounded understanding and practice of criticism? These are the questions I want to pursue now by looking closely at the way in which de Man stages his ironic refusal of all interpretation.

Early on, de Man suggests that the theatricality of Kleist's text is "centered on agonistic scenes of persuasion, of instruction, and of reading," adding, "it follows that the reading of this text is the testiest of all . . . tests, especially if the reader happens also to be a teacher" (271). Since de Man is a teacher, and most of his readers are either teachers or would-be teachers, it is clear that de Man aims to use this test both to assay his own mettle and to raise serious questions about our own. In the next paragraph de Man asserts that, in fact, "academic as well as nonacademic readers have collectively flunked this test." This claim further notifies us that de Man's interest is not merely in Kleist, Schiller, and the politics of education; these moments in the essay are also the pre-texts for de Man's mise en scène of something else: the demonstration of his readerly mastery over both a text that "our own modernity has not yet been able to confront" (266) and, more importantly, over competing contemporary critics, critics who remain an unnamed but "harassed" collective body of interpreters that operates within the rubrics de Man has set up—Kleist's "agonistic scenes of persuasion, of instruction, and of reading."

At this point it should be clear that the agon is not only in Kleist's text, but, more importantly, between de Man and these unnamed others, and (to reprise de Man on Kleist) "hence [the] necessarily theatrical mode [of de Man's essay], the emphasis on stage and scene; hence also the prominence of its critique of mimetic themes and the variety of its narrative stylistics." That de Man has employed his textual objects in this way may not seem particularly surprising or noteworthy—no more so than the fact that he conceives of the critical scene as agon rather than agora. But if we are to pursue the implications of his mise en scène fully we must remember that this agon, however it is staged, entails the masterly defeat of others, not open-ended dialogic exchange. And as I suggested in the opening section of this foreword, such competition is neither unknown in the critical profession nor necessarily free of the institutional and economic orders that define our culture as a whole. Indeed, de Man's enactment—as well as his description—of the agon of criticism is itself grounded precisely in this situation, as a competition for mastery, for authoritative voice in the critical scene. De Man's mise en scène, like those he critiques, turns out to be a "scene of persuasion, a scene of instruction," one that in its own way mystifies the relation between the critic, the object of the critical discourse, and their mutual histories.

The blindness that has made de Man's insight possible and the grounds for the powerful impact his discourse has generated are most readily discovered if one examines both the problem of discourse and the scene of instruction described in de Man's text *and* the unfolding of the critical language and the subsequent publication of the essay. In the internal scene of instruction (which serves as a model for the problems engendered by the "teacher's" effort to provide the ephebe with a model from which to learn the general integrity of the aesthetic work), the teacher in fact provides only a particular example, one that betrays "the general truth it is supposed to support and convey" (276). The ephebe tries repeatedly and hopelessly to emulate the example provided by the teacher, but he fails—not because of incompetence, but because "the work of art is only a displaced version of the true model, the judgment of authority" that the teacher has instituted by providing the exemplary model in the first place.

The psychology that de Man provides for this scene is quite interesting: the ephebe has submitted to the teacher's instruction out of a desire for (self-)recognition—implemented through the teacher's approval. To this idea de Man adds:

> As for the teacher's motives in accepting to enter into these displacements of identity, they are even more suspect than those of the younger person, to the precise extent that sadism is morally and socially more suspect than masochism. [But, he adds,] their motives are open to the worst of suspicions as well as to the most convincing of excuses, thus making the entire question of intents and motivations a great deal less compelling than the philosophical question from which it derives: the assumed integrity, not of the self, but of the work. (279)

This return to the "philosophical" question of the text prevents any further investigation of motives and excuses or of the structures of authority and power de Man has elicited from Kleist's essay. Instead de Man insists that it is essential to turn again toward the theoretical, that is to "the necessity to decide between the signified and referent, between violence on the stage and violence in the streets" (280). This return allows him to move away from the historical situation he has elicited and conclude his ironic subversion of what he calls "the hermeneutics of signification." But it is precisely at this moment that de Man most powerfully reveals not the difference but the links between the violence on stage (his mise en scène) and the violence in the streets (the historical situation of the critical enterprise). His example of the ephebe and the teacher then becomes a vehicle for examining de Man's own critical practice and, by extension, the mise en scène of the discourse(s) of criticism as we experience it today.

De Man's final deconstructive demonstration of the play of the word and the text purports to show how "the ambiguity of the word . . . disrupts the fluid continuity of each . . . narrative [in a] disjunctive plurality of meanings" (289). But it is also a performative representation of the power of his critical control, his superiority over those guilty of what he refers to as the "carelessness of classical aestheticians who misread Kant." Such comments are, of course, an essential part of the didascalia, the internal stage directions for the mise en scène through which de Man enacts his critical self-empowerment, and the ironic "fall" of interpretation.[7] The gestus of his critique of others, a critique that always claims to be merely a thoughtful reading of the aesthetic play of Kleist's text, also closes out the possibility of de Man's reader entering into any open dialogic meeting with either the text staged or the stage text (i.e., the combination of text and mise en scène that places the reader in the position of submissive spectator attending [to] the interpretation provided by de Man as *metteur en scène*). I will quote at length from this closing section of the essay in order both to show de Man at work as *metteur en scène* of this ambiguity and to reveal the discursive self-deception of the scene he stages:

> And when, by the end of the tale, the word *Fall* has been overdetermined in a manner that stretches it from the theological fall to . . . the grammatical declension of nouns and pronouns (what we call, in English, the grammatical case), then any composite word that includes *Fall* . . . acquires a disjunctive plurality of meanings.
>
> . . . As we know from another narrative text of Kleist, the memorable tropes that have the most success (*Beifall*) occur as mere random improvisation (*Einfall*) at the moment when the author has completely relinquished any control over his meaning and has relapsed (*Zurückfall*) into the extreme formalization, the mechanical predictability of grammatical declension (*Fälle*).
>
> But *Fälle*, of course, also means in German "trap," the trap which is the ultimate textual model of this and of all texts, the trap of an aesthetic education which inevitably confuses dismemberment of language by the power of the letter with the gracefulness of a dance. This dance, regardless of whether it occurs as mirror, as imitation, as history, as the fencing match of interpretation, is the ultimate trap, as unavoidable as it is deadly.

This closing disempowerment of other critical methods and voices does not directly assert the superiority of de Man's own; rather it masks this assertion within the power of the letter, a linguistico-philosophical paradigm that removes Kleist's text and his own from the discursive realms of the intersubjective and the historical by asserting the insufficiency of reference to these realms in the matter of the word and the text. According to de Man, they always outstep the referential dances other critics would make them dance. Thus, de Man's turn to aesthetic play (and violence) draws us into the discourse of his criticism in such a way that there seems no escape; but his critical insight into the usefulness of Kleist's *visible* mise en scène inevitably leads back to the question of his own somewhat less visible staging, and to the recognition that it, too, offers another level of diegetic narrative, one that points to the historical condition of the critical mise en scène, not to the *mise en abîme* of "the dismemberment of language."

On this second semiotic level, the narrative does not necessarily assert itself through direct address or statement; as in the theater, it is the stage set, the decor, and the framing of the entrances and exits that most powerfully establish the rapport between the critic / *metteur en scène* and the text, and, more importantly, the reader / spectator. This set of relationships has a history of its own, one to which I will turn soon, but first I want to examine the lines I quoted above as the closing moment of de Man's critical insight.

Having worked his way through a series of playful disruptions that turn the "case" (*Fall*) in hand into the "trap" set by language, de Man himself clearly expects our applause (*Beifall*) at his success. But—to continue in his manner—his performance can only be regarded as a *Durchfall* (failure), since, despite his claim, *Fälle* does not mean "trap". *Fälle* is the plural of *Fall* (case), while another word, *Falle,* means both "catch" and "trap." It would seem that de Man himself has been caught in this particular trap, and the *Fallbrücke*, the linguistic bridge de Man has tried to build to lead us out of narrative closure back to the aesthetic, has turned out to be a rather prosaic drawbridge whose connecting span is razed. We are, thus, obliged to reverse our course, and in so doing, the expected *Beifall* becomes instead the *Fallbeil* (guillotine) that returns us to history and to the violence of the streets otherwise often associated with theoretical and absolutist claims to *political* mastery.

Whence this blindness, this forgetting of the prosaic reality involved in the work of his own discourse and practice? Obviously, I prefer not to believe that this "error" in de Man's text is due to "mere" carelessness. It would seem rather that the text as we have it demonstrates that not only de Man, who wrote and revised this essay just before his death, but also his editors—former students and acolytes—were so taken by this mise en scène that they found it unnecessary to check the claims of the discourse it stages. If de Man has fallen into his own trap it is because he has submitted, as did Adolphe in Constant's tale, to the power of the scene he has created and to the words it has elicited. His ephebes have in turn played out the role he inscribes for them in his essay.

I want to emphasize, however, that the possibility of the ephebe's endless reprise of the (critical) gestus first suggested by his or her teacher is not just a problem confronted today when reading the diaphanous repetitions found in the work of students of de Man, deconstruction, or both. As de Man's essay suggests, it is a fundamental possibility in modern criticism in general. When confronted by the critical condition of the profession, we need to keep in mind the significance of the relationship between teacher and ephebe as deployed by de Man and to link that psychological rapport to the history of the critic as *metteur en scène* as well as to the mise en scène of history in recent criticism, for, as is demonstrated in Donald Pease's comments on Steven Greenblatt in this volume, a return to history that does not retain de Man's suggestive insights into the ideological implications of the practice of mise en scène will quickly experience its own fall away from dialogic openness into discourse.

The ephebe, we recall, turns to the teacher not merely in order to learn a *profession,* but also, more importantly, to construct a sense of self through the self-recognition that will supposedly come from the teacher's approving gaze—as a return for the student's successful emulation of the proffered model. This seems at first to be much like the effect sought by Adolphe in the allegory I have drawn from Constant's novel: a narcissistic, if not masochistic, project in subjective mise en scène. But whereas Adolphe (or anyone so inclined) can draw on a broadly based, culturally determined discourse of love for self-representation and, thus, carry out an act of conscious agency as well as partake in what might be described (among other possibilities) either as the ideology of eros or eros as social neurosis, the discourse of criticism is neither so broad based nor so historically continuous. Critical mise en scène of the sort I have been describing is no older than its counterpart in Western theater as such: both belong to systems of interpretation and "meaning" production that developed in the second half of the nineteenth century.

Crucial to understanding both is the history of the notion of mise en scène, a term that was officially admitted into use in French only in 1873.[8] Though it may have been in use occasionally before this, the expression acquired the significance we assign to it today only after the appearance of the director/interpreter, the *metteur en scène* who was empowered to mediate between the work of art and a public that gradually learned to accept both the alterity of the work and the need for

such guidance. The development of this new model of aesthetic understanding reached a crucial point around 1880, and although there is no
room here for a lengthy exploration of the process, a few suggestions
may point the way toward a useful linkage of this history with the
institution of criticism as a complementary model for socioaesthetic
"education."[9]

The crucial moments in this rapprochement are to be found in the
new institutional relations established in the nineteenth century between
the audience/reader and the director/critic. It is important, therefore,
to remember that these relations were far more overtly addressed then
than they were later, since, unlike most twentieth-century academic critics
and theorists, their nineteenth-century counterparts were quite conscious
of the political implications of their artistic debates. They also understood
the theater to be a crucial space for enacting the ordering processes of
individual and cultural definition, not merely in terms of the plays performed, but also with regard to the hierarchic relations of class and
knowledge that were organized by the architectural arrangements of the
house and by the rapport between the spectators, the actors, and the
work itself.[10] This is no doubt primarily due to the fact that earlier in
the nineteenth century the right of interpreting and evaluating a play or
a text still belonged in large part to the individual reader or member of
the audience.

As I have shown elsewhere, Byron, Coleridge, Lamb, and others attest
to the vigor and, from their point of view, the unfortunate critical independence of this audience response.[11] By the middle of the century,
Matthew Arnold was more assertive about the task and the primacy of
the critic but nonetheless still granted the general reader or spectator the
right to a first attempt at correctly understanding the "value" of a work.
In his essay "The Literary Influence of the Academies," he proposed the
critic and the academy as arbiters, "a recognized authority, imposing on
us . . . a respectful recognition of a superior ideal. . . . What we seek to
learn is *whether we were right* in being amused . . . and in applauding."[12]
At that same time, the post-1848 government in France was somewhat
more direct in its understanding of the need to create an institutionalized
structure for educating the public and inducing "us" to recognize "a
superior ideal." In 1851, a ministerial decree created two awards of 5,000
francs each, one for the author of the play judged to have "best fulfilled
the conditions necessary for a moral result" and the other to be granted
to a work that "was of a nature to serve in the education of the laboring
classes by propagating healthy ideas and displaying good examples."[13]
It was none other than Sainte-Beuve, the foremost critic and theoretician

of his day, who was given the responsibility for reporting to the com-
mission created to award these prizes, thus signaling ideological and
institutional linkages between the academy and the state that would later
be obscured by the tropes of academic as well as aesthetic freedom.

In England there was substantial change in both Arnold's attitude and
the situation of the audience by the 1880s. For Arnold, it was no longer
the public at large or even the poet, but rather the trained critical reader /
interpreter, who was central to the literary-cultural enterprise.[14] There
was an analogous change in the public's situation in the theater. When
the Deutsches Theater opened in 1883, for example, the audience was
no longer permitted to interrupt the performance by applauding. This
and other such practices were banned because they damaged the aesthetic
mood and "the ideal relationship between the artist and the public."[15]
But the "artist" actually empowered here was not the playwright, it was
the *metteur en scène,* the translator of the "mood," of the ideas and
values of the text, for a public that would now bow to this new master's
disciplined representation of the "economy of the work of art."[16]

One need only compare this empowerment of the masterly theater
director to the emergence of what Paul Bové has called the master reader /
teacher in the academy (and to the disciplinary value of the critical tropes
enacted by this teacher) to see that what is at stake in both realms is a
disciplinary hierarchicalization of the relationship between the public
and the socioaesthetic structure and "values" that are formally enacted
(and confirmed) through the interpretive gestus of the critic / *metteur en
scène.*[17] The force of this interpretive power is again best represented by
an event in the theater: the house lights are extinguished, and the audience
literally finds itself in the dark, no longer in possession of the right or
the means to determine the local or the general significance of the event
unfolding before it. Indeed, this meaning is no longer assumed to be
accessibly lodged in the play's text; rather it can be discovered only
through a prior submission to and careful absorption of the particular
mise en scène staged by the new interpreter.[18]

A very interesting transformation has taken place at this point. The
individual members of the audience, no longer in possession of the right
to produce their own meaning and no longer able simply to assume that
the text has a transparent meaning of its own, are taught that they can
only "see" the meaning of the work (and the life-world order [or disorder]
that it represents to them) by relying on the interpretive diegesis of a
(physically) absent other: the scene of understanding produced by *metteur
en scène.* The interactive, even dialogic scene formerly staged in the
interplay between the work and the public, the informative interplay
between the text performed and an audience empowered to "read" its

meaning, gives way to an agon, a struggle to grasp the order of signi-fication within which the text has been framed. Rather than serving as a scene of intersubjective work and meaning production, this new context demands submission to a monologic order that questions but cannot itself be easily questioned. The task of the reader/spectator at this point turns into a catechetic struggle for self-validation, a struggle first to understand the "discourse" through which the questions of the mise en scène are framed, then to emulate and, ultimately perhaps, to accede to the presence and power—the "answer"—staged by these diegetic tokens of the absent interpretive demiurge.[19]

The most interesting thing about the critical relations structured by this new interpretive order is that, no matter what "text" is proposed as the object of the performance, and regardless of the discursive "style" of the mise en scène, the narrative of the mise en scène always restages the empowerment of the *metteur en scène* as the condition of the reader/spectator's "understanding"—an understanding that entails in its turn an initial self-blinding disempowerment, a fall into discourse that offers a compensatory (though abstract) sense of connection and completion. Even if one rejects the *content* of another's mise en scène, as de Man does in his essay, the signifying *practice* of mise en scène remains in place. It is the diegetics of this performative scene that, as in the scene described by Constant, invade the place of extended remembrance and "through a sort of magic . . . surround us with a past." In lieu of the problematic world of the quotidian and the historical, "it gives us, as it were, a sense of having lived for years with a being which but lately was almost a stranger to us."

In this context, the anxiety revealed by the ephebe in de Man's essay is not surprising. One finds it expressed again in the comments made by the graduate student cited in a recent *New York Times* article con-cerning the Modern Language Association convention. This student, who refers to himself as an "apprentice scholar," pleads for "access to the mind" of someone who will "teach" him the books he wants to read.[20] The possibility of opening his own dialogue with these texts seems not to exist; personal identity (mastery) is equated with an enabling discourse and mise en scène practiced under the gaze of another. But this catechized context can bring with it the possibility only of failure or of endless repetition of the critical gestus. There is no return from *this* scene of mastery to a more fully self-conscious historical critique, to a remem-bering and possible reworking of one's participation in the historical relations between self and text, self and life-world. Here de Man is right in his description of the closure produced by the practices of reading and the institutions of criticism produced by Western modernity. But de

Man is wrong in assuming that the staging devices, the "play" of his own critique for example, cannot be fruitfully examined as a means of returning to the question of history as well as a means of avoiding the dangers of "meaning production"—the monologic closure of interpretation around an ideological order representing the institutions of the state.

If there is a way out of this situation, it cannot be through an "enlightened" countermonologue or a turn to some ideal theater/institution of the past or future. Rather than a still newer criticism, or the countermise en scène of a new historicism, criticism itself must be made to speak and reveal the presence of the *metteur en scène* and the (dis)empowering structures that pervade its scene. Only after this process has uncovered the ideological and institutional implications of the critical agon can the creative work Gramsci assigns to his version of the intellectual demiurge unfold freely. A model for this work is again to be found in his theater criticism, where he praises Pirandello's early dramatic efforts (*not* the mise en scène of the later plays such as *Six Characters*) because of their dialogism—the space allowed to unlettered Sicilian peasants whose voices meet in unresolved, humorous tension.[21]

The essays contained in this volume take up some of the threads of this project. In addition to examining several versions of the critical gestus and the problem of self-reflexivity, they raise questions about the possible grounds for authentic dialogic exchange and the kinds of historical understanding possible between the text and its reader and between the reader and his/her others within and outside the profession.

Paul Bové opens up the question of "oppositional" criticism and its implications for the critic and the institution in an essay on Sacvan Bercovitch and his discussion of the critical practices at work in American studies. Donald Pease elaborates yet another dimension of the political and institutional diegetics of critical practice in his comments on Steven Greenblatt's work. The relation of such practice to the political conditions in contemporary society is central to both these essays. In a slightly different vein, Daniel O'Hara examines the work of Stanley Fish and others in order to focus on the ways in which the literary archive itself can help us understand the potential insufficiency and the exclusionary nature of certain discourses on academic criticism. Each of these essays draws our attention to the tropes of a critical commentary and to its critico-historical implications, thus providing access to the historical situation of the critic as well as the critical institution as such.

Carol Kay and Jonathan Arac approach this same problem from a different direction by examining two specific instances of the way in which historical understanding is modeled by and in the work of reading. Arac outlines the genealogy of a nineteenth-century representation of *Hamlet* that seeks to universalize the play's central figure as a means of defining both the literary and the social "nature" of the individual. Kay, on the other hand, looks at a moment in the transformation of contemporary criticism by reviewing the changes in her own critical understanding of the problem of history as it unfolds in relation to the works of Richardson, Rousseau, Burke, and de Man.

Of course, the question of history as such is fundamental to all of these essays, since, despite the assurances so glibly offered in Richard Bernstein's article, the way from literature to history is neither simple nor direct, no more so than is the status of the term *history* itself. Because of this, Suzanne Gearhart has been impelled to renegotiate the passage between Kant and Hegel in search of a historico-philosophical framework for undertaking the kind of historically grounded criticism sought after in the other essays. She demonstrates that a truly critical history must constantly engage in a self-reflexive search, a search that maintains a tension between thinking history and practicing it.

The contradictions constituting the "subject" who does this thinking and its ability to engage in a dialogue with the world outside itself provide the starting point for Gearhart, and it is again this problematized subject that is at the heart of Satya P. Mohanty's essay. He posits a minimal notion of rationality that would enable the monologic and agonistic voices of cultural and political relativism, including those deliberately elaborated as a defense against ideological domination by others, to enter into a dialogue that would transform the agonistic scene between "us" and "them" into the authentically intersubjective critical dialogue that, in my own comments, has been figured as the agora, the scene produced by an effort to move beyond the monologic discourse of the institution into a dialogic critical and cultural exchange. It is such an exchange, of course, that is the aim of this book.

Notes

1. See "It's Back to the Blackboard for Literary Criticism," in the *New York Times,* February 19, 1991, C11, 16.

2. Particularly important in this context are the two essays on Artaud found in Jacques Derrida, *Writing and Difference* (Chicago: 1978), 169–95, 232–51.

3. *Theater Journal,* March 1985, 13–30. I want to thank Una Chaudhuri for drawing my attention to this essay.

4. Constant, *Adolphe,* ed. F. Baldensperger (Geneva: 1950), 14, 16, 17, my translation. The page references for all further citations from *Adolphe* will be given in the text.

5. Although I will use the term *mise en scène* to describe Adolphe's activities, it is important to note that Constant would not have, since neither the term nor the practice

we currently associate with the work of the theatrical director were available at the time. I will have more to say about this fact and its relevance to our understanding of critical practices later in this essay.

6. "Aesthetic Formalization: Kleist's 'Über das Marionettentheater,'" in Paul de Man, *The Rhetoric of Romance* (New York: 1984), 263–90.

7. This fall, of course, is not, as far as de Man is concerned, a fall from some Edenic wholeness into critical "sin," but rather from naïveté into a false sense of self-conscious completion.

8. Bescherelle included the expression "mise en scène" in 1873, while Littré added it a few years later. In his *Art de la mise en scène* (Paris: 1884), Becq de Fouquières notes that mise en scène had only recently acquired some importance.

9. For a more detailed discussion of the notion of mise en scène in relation to the *metteur en scène* in France and Germany, see Michael Hays, "Theater and Mass Culture: The Case of the Director," in *New German Critique* vol. 29, 1983, 133–46, and *The Public and Performance: Essays in the History of French and German Theater 1871–1900* (Ann Arbor: 1981), 46–48. Adorno's discussion of the orchestral director is also relevant here. See his "Dirigent und Orchester," in *Einleitung in die Musiksoziologie* (Hamburg: 1968), 115–28.

10. The critical and historical perspectives derived from the theater by Adorno and Benjamin also enact this awareness, often as part of their efforts to understand the "modernist" and mass cultural contexts, and it is interesting to note that whereas their theoretical conclusions have been put to use by a number of contemporary critics, the functional importance of the relation between these conclusions and their concrete analyses of theatrical practices have not been retained. Equally forgotten by contemporary criticism is the fact that Gramsci began his writing career as a theater reviewer, and that the earliest suggestions for what later became his critique of ideology and the discourse of the intellectual appeared in these early comments on the theater and drama. I will return to this point later.

11. See my "Comedy as Being / Comedy as Idea" in *Studies in Romanticism* vol. 29, no. 2, 1987, 221–30, where I discuss the juridical grounding of this right, including the 1774 decision of the Court of the King's Bench, which affirmed the "undoubted right of the British audience founded on immemorial custom, to approve or disapprove of any actor or theatrical exhibition."

12. Matthew Arnold, *The Complete Prose Works*, vol. 3, ed. R. H. Super (Ann Arbor: 1955), 254. Italics in the original.

13. Decree of October 12, 1851, Articles 1 and 4.

14. A brief description of this transformation in Arnold's critical position can be found in Jonathan Arac, *Critical Genealogies: Historical situations for Postmodern Literary Studies* (New York: 1987).

15. *Deutsche Bühnen-Genossenschaft*, 1883, 379.

16. This is the expression used by Otto Brahm, one of Germany's early theorist / practitioners of the new mise en scène, to isolate an aesthetic "content" that was to be revealed by the director, the discoverer of its value and / or meaning. In the context of this turn to the aesthetic in the theater, it is worth pointing out in passing that one of the great weaknesses in Jacques Derrida's discussion of Artaud and mise en scène ("The Theatre of Cruelty and the Closure of Representation," *Writing and Difference*, 232–50) arises from his ignorance of the history and implications of the *metteur en scène* for his discussion of Artaud's theatrical project as a liberation from the mastery of the author and readerly interpretation.

17. See Paul Bové, *Intellectuals in Power: A Genealogy of Critical Humanism* (New York: 1986).

18. Useful contemporary contrasts to this situation can be found in a number of non-European theaters. See, for example, Onuora Osssie Enekwe, *Igbo Masks: The Oneness of Ritual and Theatre* (Lagos: 1987). See also Ngugi wa Thiongo, *Decolonizing the Mind: The Politics of Language in African Literature* (London: 1986), for a description of the popular theater in Kenya, a theater that can be open-ended in "meaning," entail public rehearsals, call on the local public for comments, and even bring them into the troupe—and that requires no director. His recognition of the political potential for popular opposition in these practices led to Ngugi's being jailed by a somewhat less open-minded central government. My thanks to Paul Bové for this latter reference.

19. This figure is precisely the opposite of that described by Gramsci and referred to in Paul Bové's essay in this volume (see Chapter 1, note 33). Although claiming to "work for the people, . . . the community," this institutionalized demiurge works *on* them.

20. *New York Times Magazine,* February 10, 1991, 58.

21. See Antonio Gramsci, *Selections from Cultural Writings* (Cambridge, Mass.: 1985), 79–80, 140–44, 267–69.

CHAPTER 1

Notes Toward a Politics of "American" Criticism

Paul A. Bové

> It is certain that they [American industrialists] are not concerned with the "humanity" or the "spirituality" of the worker, which are immediately smashed. This "humanity and spirituality" cannot be realised except in the world of production and work and in productive "creation." They exist most in the artisan, in the "demiurge," when the worker's personality was reflected whole in the object created and when the link between art and labour was still very strong. But it is precisely against this "humanism" that the new industrialism is fighting. "Puritanical" initiatives simply have the purpose of preserving, outside of work, a certain psycho-physical equilibrium which prevents the physiological collapse of the worker, exhausted by the new method of production. This equilibrium can only be something purely external and mechanical, but it can become internalised if it is proposed by a new form of society, with appropriate and original methods.
> . . . It is in their [American industrialists'] interests to have a stable, skilled labour force, a permanently well-adjusted complex, because the human complex (the collective worker) of an enterprise is also a machine which cannot, without considerable loss, be taken to pieces too often and renewed with single new parts.
>
> —Antonio Gramsci, *The Prison Notebooks*

One should never write in the abstract about the nature of "oppositional criticism." Criticism of any sort must always be concrete and specific no matter how theoretically informed. "Oppositional criticism," particularly, cannot be defined or theorized so much as it must be enacted. Only because academic criticism is carried out so often in a professionally and institutionally social space could one even imagine a "general theoretical discussion" of "oppositional criticism." Whenever oppositional critical work is done, it is always specifically placed (conjunctural) and so cannot be treated as a matter of "theory" rather than as the concrete form of practice it must be to be itself. Furthermore, if, as R. P. Blackmur always had it, criticism is a social gesture, highly contextualized, or "overde-termined," then it cannot be, as some naifs would have it, "defined" or

1

"debated"; it cannot be "represented" except by and as an enactment, a "dramatization"—in Blackmur's word—that engages specifically with the object of its critique.

There are several reasons why "oppositional criticism" must be enacted rather than abstractly theorized. Most important among them is the fact that the profession has an uncanny ability to adopt its seemingly most stringent critics by recycling their values and methods, transforming them into new fashions for replication and reward. That this could be the fate of "oppositional criticism"—if the notion is taken up in the abstract and made merely the subject of articles without consequence—no one should doubt. The genealogy of the "oppositional" makes it readily available for such recirculation.[1] "Oppositional criticism" should not be confused with an attitude of generalized dissatisfaction with the profession or the culture; it is not merely a weak effect of alienation and commodification. It should, I think, be differentiated from any proverbial articulation of attitudes toward values, institutions, and "life situations"; one thinks here of a tradition that extends from Kenneth Burke to Wayne Booth.[2] Nor does "oppositional criticism" train us to see literature as a way to deal better with the problems of modern life.

To catch something of the force of an oppositional critical act, one must first of all see it as an act and in action; one must see it engaging critically with some element of the empowered structure of the society and culture against which it takes up its stance. One must see it not as just a force for change and betterment but also as a relentless even if sometimes admiring but implacable agonism, as an indecorous enemy if you will. One cannot, therefore, speak merely generally to the topic of what "oppositional criticism" of American literature and culture would be; one must instantiate that criticism, for, in its "oppositional" position, it cannot exist as a series of generalities, of prescriptive statements laying out a program, method, or set of values. We cannot forget that Marx and Nietzsche teach intellectual warfare: critical instruments are weapons—even for those who argue so hard to deny the fact; especially so despite the ease with which many professionals so easily concede the fact. "Oppositional criticism" can be found only where these weapons are brought to bear on just the entrenched values, interests, and practices of professionals and institutions important to the academy and so to its effects upon and roles within the larger society.

It is with these thoughts in mind that I discuss in the following pages some of the work of Sacvan Bercovitch. His institutional distinction and his critical ambition bring him to attention as a figure to interrogate if one wants to mark some of the limits and possibilities of the criticism of "American literature."[3] Pointing to some of these limits and possibilities helps develop an image of "Americanist" criticism as emerging from a set of assumptions, values, practices, technologies, institutions, and languages—all relatively systematic, all interrelated—that suggest a link between a certain kind of rationality and certain more material, historical interests of a sort that need to be opposed for the political consequences of their link with that rationality. They need to be opposed if the possibility of a different order and organization of knowledge, self, and society is to be recalled and perhaps made possible.

II

Never before has so much of the study of "American" literature and culture been as critical of the classical forms of "American" writing and the dominant forms of "American" society as it is now. Bercovitch puts the matter succinctly when he says that the new generation of "Americanists" does not separate the "America of the spirit, represented by our classic writers, from the realities of American life, represented by ideologues and their victims."[4] Of course, in this day and age, the right wing does not want for followers who might challenge this "New Americanist" critical history.[5] The conservatives quite precisely bemoan the "New Americanists'" double ideological challenge: to the established disciplinary, discursive procedures that, in fact, depend upon the separation of the two forms of representation Bercovitch names; and to the liberal, pluralist ideology that that discipline's discourse reproduces and distributes in a normalizing relationship to the state and the constantly "new society" produced by "American" capitalism.

Everyone now knows the names of the books and critics that the profession feels have broken open the canon of "American" literature and reformed the ways in which that literature and its place in "American" cultural history are to be thought about.[6] Most agree that feminist revisions of history and feminist readings—including concerns with literacy— as well as objections to the "androcentric"[7] discourse of "American" studies itself have done most to reorganize the production of knowledge about our culture. Feminism has shown how women and their writing have been excluded from and by the valued realm of the "classic," and so extended the hermeneutics of suspicion to the term itself. In the process, an entire body of literary and cultural production has been recovered from the historical amnesia enforced even by such generously powerful texts as *American Renaissance*,[8] and these works have helped us to understand the power structures and determinative effects of the gender bias of "American studies" discourses themselves. In addition, of course, recovering the work of "scribbling women" has paradigmatically helped us understand how polymorphous, how differentiated, how filled with resistance and alternative forms of creation the once apparent monolith of "American literature and culture" has always been.

Feminism, of course, has not been alone in this remaking of "American studies." The new attention to minority—black, Hispanic, and Amerindian—writings has drawn our attention to the international nature of our history, to its founding involvements with other cultures of Africa and Latin America, as well as to our society's long history of extermination and imperial aggression. In black women's writing, many critics feel the questions of class, race, and gender can be uniquely studied to get a clear sense of the workings of powerful, authoritative, and complex structures of oppression and resistance.

It would seem, in other words, that in the very recent past, "Americanists" have come far toward meeting Edward W. Said's more than decade-old definition of real oppositional criticism: it must be "actively generated out of a genuine historical research," and it must be "ultimately fixed for its goals upon understanding, analyzing, and contending with the management of power and authority within the culture."[9] There is now enough energy being devoted to critiques of the origins of "American liberalism" in relation to the "self" in laissez-faire economics that we have no fear that the relations—sometimes oppositional, sometimes supportive—of our literary masters to the often awful forms of "American" political and social life will ever be forgotten.

Jonathan Arac has said that Sacvan Bercovitch's *American Jeremiad* should make it impossible for anyone to use easily the word *America*.[10] Indeed, obsolete as well as neoconservatives agree that the "New Americanists"—perhaps like the flag burners of whom we have recently heard so much—have no respect for the achievements of "American" culture and society. Often these conservatives disguise themselves as pluralists.[11] As "pluralists" they are often challenged, in turn, by ideology critique and by historicist recoveries of the "real differences" that exist within, but are often forgotten by, the recorders of "American" culture. For the most part, though, the future of "American" criticism of "American" literature and culture seems secure; we are, in a way, talking of generational change here, and the future, of course, belongs to the young.

III

Bercovitch suggests some of the problems and possibilities in the New Americanism: "America" has a habit of making it new, and although making it new—through ideology critique or historical recovery or whatever powerful critical device—cannot be trusted to provide us with any way out of the wilderness of the "American" ideology, it can move us toward "an alternative future" (A 439). Summarizing his sense of the value of the essays collected in *Ideology and Classic American Literature,* Bercovitch is unusually optimistic: "I would like to think . . . that among these ['the richness of the problems at issue, the methodolgical and practical challenges involved in these inquiries'] is the challenge of alternative ways of intellectual, moral, and political commitment" (A 439). Bercovitch clearly *would like to think . . .* But what are the problems that lead Bercovitch to express this relatively minimal (and desperate) desire in the face of his critical intellectual analysis—an analysis that suggests quite precisely the opposite outcome to this "New Americanism"?

Bercovitch remains interesting because—from the center of the profession, as it were—he so clearly and usefully lists what he takes to be the definitive problems molesting any "Americanist" critical project. As he puts the issues they do seem compelling; that he sees them molesting even the authoritative work of the brightest "New Americanists" gathered in his volume attests to the gravity of the issues in his vision and to the compulsive force of his final expression of desire. Yet the problems he imagines are not the final problems. Were we to mistake them for the most basic problems, we would lead ourselves to two unsatisfactory results: a persistent concern with the epiphenomenal that would always be preliminary to an "American" criticism; or, more dangerously, to institutionalizing a politically and aesthetically reductive model of critical practice. We would replicate the already established discipline by not querying its precise genealogical, discursive relations—even in its "oppositional" moments—to the state, to the dominant forms of rationality, and to the institutions of "American" culture. In other words, and to put the matter crudely, to take Bercovitch's problems as "radical" would allow us to avoid describing, theorizing, politicizing, and, where possible, resisting and reorganizing the forms and institutions that treat "American" literature and culture as a "subject" of knowledge. That is to say— and still too simply—Bercovitch's are problems of "content," of the "representations" "within" ideology, problems of "consciousness" that can be dealt with in "re-forming" modes, by adjustment and adjudication within the ongoing terms and institutions of "American studies," "American" culture, and the "American" state. His "problems" are not radical precisely because they do not and cannot lead to a new set of rationalities and practices or to a new politics. He can merely imagine the possibility that some truly new alternatives will emerge from the regular oscillation of old and new that makes up the jeremiad of "American" politics.

But how can one reasonably believe in this "possibility" or practice a discipline whose forms of rationality allow for such imaginings? I do not ask this question to object that Bercovitch seems to offer neither a plan for bringing it about nor a theory of agency that would account for the desire. I ask it, rather, to draw attention to the fact that one can believe in this possibility only if one accepts Bercovitch's theory of "consensus" and "dissensus" formation—in other words, his model of inner and outer, self and other, old and new—a model of rationality we should all recognize as problematic. In other words, one must first accept this possibility as such, even as utopian desire; and that acceptance depends, in turn, upon working within an institution and discourse that aligns a form of reason and forms of power in ways that allow individuals to speak of these matters, that determine what "American" literature and "American" critics can and might be. Michel Foucault's forceful phrase comes to mind: one must accept the "regime of truth"—in any or all of its variations—to be in a realm where what is thoughtful about Bercovitch's "Americanist" vision and project makes any sense. (The hidden questions, of course, are does one want to be in this regime, and if so why?)

Bercovitch, as always, puts the matter eloquently, reasonably, and lucidly:

> The option [for "American" critics] is not multiplicity or consensus. It is whether to make use of the categories of the culture or to be used by them. I do not claim that the essays here altogether avoid the peculiar cultural traps embedded in the quest for "America," in either its multiple or its unitary guises. Indeed, I am aware that what at the start of this Afterword I called a dialogue in the making has itself the makings, *in potentia,* of still another example of the special genius of the rhetoric of American consensus, which is to co-opt the energies of radicalism: to reabsorb the very terms of opposition into the promise of the New, that long-nurtured vision of Futurity that carries us forever back, through a procession of sacred landmarks . . . to the ideological premises of modern democratic liberalism. I am aware, too, that some of the central concerns . . . may be even more problematic than their treatments in this volume suggest. (A 438–39)

If Bercovitch seriously means that critics must either "make use of the categories of the culture or . . . be used by them," he repeats an authoritative blunder that restricts "criticism" to endless repetition. It would be interesting to ask how it came to be possible that Bercovitch could put the matter in terms of this unquestioned dualism. For a moment, let us rather think some of the consequences of what he has allowed himself to say: we have to imagine that critics—and all others, intellectuals in their own work, wherever that might be—are either always nothing more than the unquestioning agents of already inscribed categories; or, that somehow what privileges critics, indeed establishes their identity *as such*, is their ability to escape this determination and, by means of the knowledge of the categories, no doubt acquired through the practice of the "Americanist" discourse, not only rise above them but also put them to some use—a use that, in itself, transcends, is outside, the ideological realm made up and disseminated by those very categories. We have seen that Bercovitch's claims cannot be taken seriously without wondering what it is that allows him to propose such a simple opposition. Training as an "Americanist," as a "cultural critic" of his sort would not provide the grounds for choosing not to be a victim "of" the culture's categories. So what would be the source of the values and desires that would direct the operation of this critical use of the categories, and where would they originate if not also in and from the ideologies and powers of these "Americanist" discourses? And why should one assume that these discourses provide a set of possibilities to "use" rather than "be used" when the correlations between this discourse and its culture have not yet been made clear? Why assume these categories have any liberative possibilities at all when, as we see them at work in Bercovitch's "oppositional" practice, they allow him to deceive himself about the "freedom" he has to choose the model he proposes? To put it simply, what would be the source of this free critic's authority and whence such a critic?

So let us not quibble with Bercovitch's formulation; he certainly could not mean it if he thought more about it. Let us ask instead what it means that the thought was available to him; or, rather, that, in this context, he felt it desirable to enact such an emprisoning representation of critical possibility—in direct contradiction to his voiced desire.

One can find a partial explanation for the appearance of this representation in the logic that interweaves Bercovitch's own professional, institutional position and the discourse of "American studies." A detailed placing of that discourse is beyond the reach and purpose of this essay; but it is clear enough to say that it allowed Bercovitch to choose to study the "jeremiad" as a "cooptation" theory of "American" radicalism whereby all challenges to the "American" consensus shatter in the face of "America's" rhetorical, political uniqueness: "to reabsorb the very terms of opposition into the promise of the New." Donald Pease has laid out the consequences of this position.[12] Bercovitch's view of "America" as a "jeremiad," as a cultural machine for producing political "consensus," makes him suspicious of all critical claims to begin again, to stand outside the terms of debate. The logic of this suspicion, so the argument goes, is that one must postulate the possibility of being within that culture in order to knowingly use its very categories against itself. (The only other alternative—one Bercovitch does not examine—is to offer something "really new" that is itself, precisely, just the latest, empowered version or transformation of what has always come before.) The paradox is that we are to assume this is a potential of the very same device that manufactures consensus, but we know it cannot be so. In fact, the user of a culture's categories must emerge as the specular alternative to the dominant forms of "America," as its ghastly (spiritual) other somehow "in the world," as the church fathers would have it, but equally somehow not "of the world." In critical terms, we would say that not to be used by the culture means being beyond or outside it. This is what we sometimes call metaphysics, and it is a problem that theory has spent considerable time dealing with over the past twenty years.[13] It is also a problem that, cast in these terms, cannot be taken seriously in that no one can ever be "free" of the order of rationality of the time or of that order's relations—as technologies and practices, as intermediate rules of social combination—to the largest orders of power in a society.[14]

Bercovitch's institutional power and scholarly, critical decorum—the style of his writing and career—make him "representative" within "American studies." At this moment, one can best see much of what "American studies" traditionally allows one to choose to be as a critic by reading as closely as possible the work of precisely its most accomplished and thoroughly institutionalized figure. His "originality" lies, as it were, in his most fully extending the possibilities of his chosen discipline. One can read his text to say something about the empowered rationality of the very discourse he helps to extend and redefine; one can talk about how it exists, as he puts it, "in its theoretical fullness" (A 438). The process is doubly interesting in part because Bercovitch takes it as a central part of his task to reflect upon the ideological consequences of the workings and techniques of this discourse in its society. As he elaborates on it, this critical and scholarly discourse seeks the "American" dream in "American" literature; it continually realigns "classic literary" and ideological forms of representation; it involves the all too common occurrence of a radical criticism emerging in relation to professionalized "American" institutions. "America" has produced, according to Bercovitch's figure of the "jeremiad," no radical discourse—aimed at "renewing" this culture gone wrong—that has not, because of its very desires, lost its energies in the mainstream of "American" culture, business, and politics. Hence Bercovitch's own desire to see in the essays of the "New Americanists" the possibility of "alternative" forms of historical study and representation—alternatives that will not, as it were, always already be positioned to become part of the consensus of "America."

Bercovitch's vision of the peculiarly "American" nature of the problems facing any radical emergent culture helps identify the limits of actually existing "American" criticism:

> I think, for instance, of the problem of locating our radical tradition in a literature obsessed with an *American* dream; or of the problem of locating that dream, considered as our *radical* tradition, in the realm of literature; or again, of the problem of locating a radical discourse about American culture in what is after all a rather *traditional* exchange among professional *literary* critics. (A 439)

"Americanist" criticism has, in Bercovitch's view, made too much of the literary, taking it perhaps uncritically as the privileged site of cultural resistance to the oppression of society in the United States. In other words, this professionalized debate among academic literary scholars may, indeed, have invested the literary with a liberatory, critical possibility that there is no prima facie reason to believe it actually possesses. Or, to put the matter mildly, the literary—as represented by these academic "Americanists"—may not be the best evidence for the possibility that a radical alternative to the dominant order of "American" oppression, of the "ideologues and their victims," actually exists, has existed, or can ever exist in the life and economy of the United States (A 428). The critical error may lie in decoding or interpreting "American literature" as the expression of a dream for a better "America." This is not to say that this literature should be read as a collaborative enterprise, or even one in a mixed or dialectical relation to the oppressive and nonliterary. It is simply to say that the institutionalized discursive practice, the habits and procedures, of "Americanist" work has led to the consistent representation of "American literature" as an embodiment of utopian hopes, of aspirations for a fulfillment or recovery of lost dreams—or simply as a reservoir of unfulfilled potentialities.[15] "Americanist" discourse, in these simple terms, is part and parcel of the operations of "America." The discourse reestablishes "America" as the vision of the New; the discourse has legitimacy—no matter how critical it may be of actually existing U.S. society—only in an affirmative relation to "America" as the process of national self-affirmaton and international self-assertion.

We can imagine alternative ways to conceive the critic's relation to culture so that the binaries that emerge in Bercovitch's work do not define a dilemma—but not, I would argue, unless the very nature of "Americanist" discourse is overhauled so totally, or perhaps put aside so thoroughly, that it might not be recognized as "Americanist" at all. But is this a possibility? Operating within the boundary of "Americanist" discourse, trying, as they say, to "subvert" it from within—it is against the seemingly easy possibility of this tactic that Bercovitch warns us. Stepping "outside" this boundary? How does one do this when "American" literature and culture have come to be represented as they are by an "Americanist" discourse so aligned with the operations of its own "cooptation" that that literature cannot possibly be seen again "for the first time"? How can one use the categories of the culture against itself when these categories, these sets of representations and their systematic and asystematic organization are as powerful as they are, when they are so essential to making the critic who thinks he wants to be beyond them? What one would need to succeed at this transcendence would be a theory or myth of the self-originating critical mind. At least, one would need a theory of the critic as "master" of the discourse(s) that have made that critic expert and competent. What would be the grounds for imagining such a critic in this day and age? What would such a critic have to do?

That Bercovitch dedicates another of his edited volumes, *Reconstructing American Literary History,* "To the Memory of F. O. Matthiessen and Perry Miller" can be understood in several ways, any one of which might partially answer these questions.[16] In one sense, Bercovitch is the institutional successor to these luminous figures at Harvard, so the dedication is appropriate; in another sense, suspending consideration of their institutional position for a moment, these two men were the leading figures of their discipline, critics and historians whose founding and revisionary texts were authoritative and are, even today, the object of constant reconsideration. In any event, this dedication is a gesture of succession, of continuity with the master critics of the past.[17]

Is it true that "American studies" seems to have had greater need for these authoritative critical masters and their texts than most other subdisciplines of modern literary study? If so, the reasons would not be hard to understand: the literature needed a founding authority; the nation needed its identity and continuity; and in part all were provided by the professionalized, institutionalized success of the discipline in elite private, state, and state-related universities. This structure generates masters necessary to maintain discipline and to the power formations of training, rewards, and discursive regularity: leaders also align the discourse properly with the supporting state apparatuses. Not only in his own writing, but also in his massive and maieutic editorial enterprises, Bercovitch plays this role of the master in wonderful parts; I have focused so much on the afterword to *Ideology and Classic American Literature* precisely because the essay exemplifies the power operations I am suggesting. Summoning new essays, reprinting already published pieces, asking for "reconsiderations" from older "masters," this afterword positions not only a new generation in relation to an old—and mark how the inclusion of "old" masters means that generation here is a professional and not a chronological category—but also all the new in relation to his own sense of all relations between new and old and all these and his own sense of what, as midwife, he seems to want to aid in delivering: "alternatives."

Taking his position seriously—precisely as it is marked by his dedication to Miller and Matthiessen—means that his work can point beyond itself, to what needs to be, but, as I see it, cannot be done within that enabling discourse of "Americanist" criticism. It seems to me implicit, for example, throughout the resonant and sometimes knotty work of Jonathan Arac, perhaps the most brilliant young contributor to the new *Cambridge History of American Literature* that Bercovitch is editing, that the "Americanist" position on matters "American" cannot be sustained; from *Commissioned Spirits* through *Critical Genealogies* to "'A Romantic Book': *Moby Dick* and Novel Agency," Arac—perhaps like Matthiessen before him—has tried for an internationally comparative position on "American" literature of a sort that simultaneously accords the historical, geographic specificity of the conditions of cultural production their full weight while neglecting neither the "global" nor the theoretical view of the putative "American" subject at hand.[18] So the key, as it were, to Arac on Melville lies in Schlegel and Goethe! Arac's example can, of course, be compounded. Donald E. Pease is another instance of the limits of "Americanist" criticism. His work exemplifies another response to its crisis: Pease has so thoroughly made his own the work of Habermas and his predecessors that his vision of "America" is, we might say, as European as it is "Americanist." Bercovitch's writing points to this need in "Americanist" criticism and to his own hopes for a criticism beyond the "national." There is no doubt, I think, that the strictly "national" focus of "Americanist" criticism cannot be sustained; indeed, Richard Poirier made a point of criticizing the "parochialism" of this criticism in a recent essay in the *London Review of Books:*

> The result [of such nationally focused criticism] is a stifling parochialism exactly where there is most need for comparative studies involving other literatures of much longer duration. Principally, this has to mean literature in English. . . . Those who refuse . . . to inquire into "the Atlantic double cross". . . are not able in an effective way to speculate on a phenomenon of immense consequence.[19]

Arac, Pease, and the others engaged in similar projects suggest the sort of paradigm shift that Poirier obviously feels is essential to provide the "New Alternatives" Bercovitch requires.

If we recall our Foucault, if we recall the Gramsci with whose words I began this essay, we would understand that the radical change in the "regime of truth" necessary to shift us beyond the iterations of "American studies" cannot occur without both a genealogical critique of the emergence of that discipline and its discourses (or the discourses that generate it; the question of priority is open) and a political theorization of the relation not just of the ideology but of the discursive and institutional relations of "Americanist" criticism—even in its oppositional moments— to the larger systems of representation essential to state and other forms of power in our imperial and oppressive cultural, social order.[20] Of course, such a set of critical investigations would require borrowing critical tools from any number of places other than "American studies." It would also mean a willingness to theorize the discourse with no advance regard for its "accomplishments." This is not to say, however, that such theorization should have no interpretive sympathy for its objects: minus that sympathy, even the critical understanding necessary to struggle cannot be achieved.[21]

A critical genealogical awareness of "American studies" as a set of established and oppositional discourses and disciplines must be achieved if the criticism of United States literature and culture expects to distance itself enough from its determinant affiliations and its regulating rationalities to gain some control over the means of intellectual production inherited from the past and entangled with other practices and ideologies in the present. Of course, we must recognize the conundrum in what I am suggesting. The study of United States literature and culture cannot transpire without drawing on the textual, historical, and critical resources established in the disciplines of "American studies." More important, a critique of these disciplines and their cultural, political placement cannot occur without the enabling, authorizing, empowered devices and insights provided by a number of critical discourses often affiliated with "American studies" itself. As an example of the sort of problem that faces the intellectual self-consciously carrying out such a project, one thinks immediately of the similarities between "American studies'" involvements with myth, typology, and historicism and the historicist edge to genealogical critique. As I see it, however, these problems need to be taken not as limits, but as occasions and opportunities for reflecting upon the issues that arise in attempting to carry out a critique with instruments entangled in the very "regime of truth" under investigation. One wants to say that such problems are occasions for genealogical, theoretical reflection upon "American" literature and culture as constructs of U.S. society; upon the formation by that society of the established and oppositional "Americanist"; upon the position of any agent attempting to carry out such a reflection, a reflection—we must repeat—enabled, in part, by those discourses themselves; upon the needs of the present that encourage, make possible, require, or call forth such reflection.[22] Perhaps the demise of the cold war and the weakening of "American" imperialism in a time of different global relations of power, race, gender, economy, and technology so alter the position of any "critic" that a set of complexly polyvalent, perhaps kaleidoscopic reflections and discourses alone can provide the conditions of critical practice.

Following Erich Auerbach, Edward W. Said has made much of the fact that the critic must be distanced from a dominant culture, must be an "exile."[23] That "exile" is the appropriate emblem for critical distance reflects a complex understanding of the material workings of "culture":

> I shall use the word *culture* to suggest an environment, process, and hegemony in which individuals (in their private circumstances) and their works are embedded, as well as overseen at the top by a superstructure and at the base by a whole series of methodological attitudes. It is in culture that we can seek out the range of meanings and ideas conveyed by the phrases *belonging to* or *in* a place, being *at home in a place. . . .* Culture is used to designate not merely something to which one belongs but something that one possesses and, along with that proprietary process, culture also designates a boundary by which the concepts of what is extrinsic or intrinsic to the culture come into forceful play. . . . But . . . there is a more interesting dimension to this idea of culture as possessing possession. And that is the power of culture by virtue of its elevated or superior position to authorize, to dominate, to legitimate, demote, interdict, and validate: in short, the power of culture to be an agent of, and perhaps the main agency for, powerful differentiation within its domain and beyond it too. . . . What is more important in culture is that it is a system of values *saturating* downward almost everything within its purview; yet, paradoxically, culture dominates from above without at the same time being available to everything and everyone it dominates.[24]

One must understand not only national and regional "cultures" but also their interrelations and relations to "metropolitan" cultures in an imperial (whether colonial, postcolonial, neocolonial, or decolonizing) order to understand how differentiated the distantiation of critical exile has come to be.[25] Auerbach could write *Mimesis* in Turkey because his distance from libraries allowed the synthetic point of view on the topic of "realism" that defines his book. When culture becomes so clearly a set of processes and values that define and enable both that culture's defenders and its opponents, that is, like Satan's hell, always in our hearts—then the possibility of exile becomes harder. One must be in exile in relation not only to the national, but to the regional, local, and international effects of culture as well. Auerbach lets Said quote Hugo of St. Victor to the effect that exile and therefore critical perfection depend upon taking "the entire world as a foreign land." This remarkable asceticism in the face of the restrictive, but enabling, ravages of imperial nationalism—whether Roman, German, or American—makes it possible for the critic to occupy the paradoxical position of wordly transcendence, the old Christian position of being in the world, but not of it. To put it somewhat differently, "exile," as ascesis, is a demanding discipline of critical self-making.[26]

While honoring the values of distance and the experiences of exile that theorize it as a critical necessity, one must also wonder if the study of culture does not require an even more complex and difficult position: being in and of one's locale while understanding its needs and hence one's own projects in terms of a global or transnational set of interlocking perspectives. The best critical emblem for our time might be what Gayatri Spivak has taught us to call the "postcolonial subject," that is, the gendered intellectual engaged in agonistic analysis of global issues central to regional and national concerns and always motivated by an understanding of the complex position that any citizen of a postmodern cultural multiplicity must occupy.[27]

I want to suggest, rather crudely, that "American studies" taken as a field in its "theoretical fullness"—I realize this formulation occludes specific differences—has not yet reached the point of "exile" in relation to itself and its nationalist projects. This is an intolerable situation to be in because, like it or not, the citizens who carry out even "New Americanist" discourses do so precisely as persons whose own positionality, despite the appearance of their practice, is not solely determined or defined by their inscription within the professions that trained them (*pace* Stanley Fish!). This has, of course, always been true as any look at the monuments of the subdiscipline would show. It is intensely true now precisely because the historical multipositionality of the critic is a determining "fact" that has already been partly theorized within criticism in the work not only of Spivak, but also of Foucault, Gramsci, and others.

Jürgen Habermas makes an important point in his recent essays within the *Historikerstreit*. Commenting on his own authority to oppose Andreas Hillgruber's study of the German army on the Eastern Front— despite his nonexpert status—Habermas claims his right to intervene as a citizen affected by the public consequences of Hillgruber's and others' works: "I am thus making the self-observations of a patient who undergoes a revisionist operation on his historical consciousness."[28] In other words, Habermas implies that professional academic productions emerge into general culture along vectors constructed and kept open by the ideological and institutional operations of the dominant powers within our societies. The intellectual—both in the specialized sense and the Gramscian sense of "everyman"—has not only the right to intervene in the so-called "debates" that travel along these vectors and, in the process, make up some important parts of our political, ideological culture, but also the obligation to intervene given that the arrogant task assigned to the producers of institutionalized knowledge (especially of a historicist kind) is, as Habermas puts it, "to treat historical consciousness as a maneuverable mass in order to provide suitably positive pasts for the legitimation requirements of the present political system."[29] Of course, one sees in this remark some of the characteristic flaws in Habermas's own sense of the oppositional: not only the "contents" of the "representations" of the "past" should be our concern—although no doubt it makes a crucial human and political difference if World War II is seen as a common war against bolshevism or not—but also the structure of a persistent social system that needs a certain relationship between state, governments, and ideologies, for its hegemonic survival, that is, for its effort to master all possible forms of radical, nonstatist opposition.[30] We might say in this context that Bercovitch has mistaken "hegemonic" operations of the extended state for "America": an understandable error, perhaps, but one that should not be repeated.

"American studies" has always had admirable, important, and powerful oppositional figures and practices within and adjacent to it. In recent years, especially in its historicist, feminist version, revisionist critics have powerfully and crucially recovered the progressive energies of these figures and advanced the rights and identities of women and minorities within "American" society and its tradition. The work of Bercovitch and others, however, has reminded us of how "American" ideology and "American" discourses and institutions seem particularly well-suited to disarm these radical challenges by bringing them within the "pluralistic" economy of everyday political conflict and debate, the sort of struggle that always goes on within a "liberal" state system. Gramsci, however, has helped us further to understand that unless the "opposition" to a given "hegemony" attempts to build a counterhegemony, to resist encirclement by the hegemonic institutions, the fate awaiting that "opposition" can be anticipated in the strategy of "passive revolution": "the gradual but continuous absorption, achieved by methods which varied in their effectiveness, of the active elements produced by allied groups—and even of those which came from antagonistic groups and seemed irreconcilably hostile."[31] In other words, critical work must be directed at or against the present; let it emerge, if it must, from a historicist sense, but let it always be, as Foucault says, "a history of the present."[32] The issue must always be the placing of "Americanist" work in the contemporary national and world order—a placing that puts at risk not only those terms themselves, but also the disciplines and knowledges built up as the condition for the critical engagement with the present. To put the matter bluntly, one must say that merely historicist studies such as those of the "emergence of the bourgeois self in post-Civil War laissez-faire economics" matter hardly at all unless they are directed against both the present relation of the "regime of truth" to the structures of power and exploitation as well as all social, political elements that block the recovery of the "demiurge" of which Gramsci speaks so eloquently.[33]

I am suggesting that the critical preservation or reform of the discourses and institutions of "American studies" is analogous to capitalism's maintenance of a stable work force, a certain "equilibrium," the collapse of which would threaten both the workers, who fear the loss of the only order they know, and the capitalists, whose dominance depends upon the workers' internalization of that equilibrium. "Passive revolution" prevents the dismemberment of the discourse and its institutions; it encourages their "transformation," a notion that must be seen in the sense Foucault gives it in *Discipline and Punish,* where he refuses the rhetoric of metaphysical agency and causality to mark the anonymity of power's operations.[34] Gramsci speaks of "puritanism" as an ethic essential to control of the "American" worker; we need only recall the state-led assault on "drugs," the critical invocations of "ethics,"[35] and recent calls by high government officials for more Puritan values of hard work and saving to have a sense of certain alliances between cultural institutions and the state's capitalist roles.

Criticism of "American" culture must set out to have the present as its subject and cannot proceed to any high form of criticism of the institutions of culture and the state without considered and consciously politically motivated examinations—descriptive and theoretical—of the "regime of truth" to which such criticism has belonged and continues to belong. "American studies" cannot change its paradigm simply by thinking it is treating new topics or loosening up the canon. It must change its own relations to the present but must first attempt to know them and to know its own place within relations as these develop the technical empowerment of specialized "critical" intellectuals. Without such theorized, material forms of knowledge, politically directed at a remaking of the regime of truth, such criticism does not deserve the name. At most it remains "scholastic" or "academic" in the weakest and most perjorative senses of those words. Criticism cannot and should not attempt to prescribe or even imagine the future, but it can and must take aim at the unequal, imperial, antidemocratic present if its work is to be of use to anyone in our world. Critics should never be good company.

Notes

1. See Paul A. Bové, *Intellectuals in Power* (New York: 1986).

2. See, for example, Burke's "progressive" 1937 article, "Literature as Equipment for Living," reprinted in *Contemporary Literary Criticism*, 2nd ed., ed. Robert Con Davis and Ronald Schleiffer (New York: 1989), 76–81; see also Wayne Booth's *The Company We Keep: An Ethics of Fiction* (Berkeley, Calif.: 1988).

3. A detailed and extended study of Bercovitch's work taken as a "career" is beyond the scope of this essay. It would, however, allow one to see his writings as interventions within politically contested, culturally cathected structures of "truth-production."

4. Afterword, *Ideology and Classic American Literature*, ed. Sacvan Bercovitch and Myra Jehlen (Cambridge, England: 1986), 428; hereafter cited in my text as A. I am not treating Myra Jehlen's work in this essay not because it is unimportant. Quite the contrary. It embodies powerful feminist revisionist criticism and scholarship the relation of which to the image I am trying to summon from Bercovitch's work cannot be adequately dealt with here—since it is the dominant discourse I am trying to discuss. The already classical revision of Bercovitch's position can be found in "New Americanists," ed. Donald E. Pease, *boundary 2* 17, no. 1 (Spring 1990).

5. See Frederick Crews, "Whose American Renaissance?", *New York Review of Books*, 35, no. 16 (October 27, 1988): 68–69. See Donald E. Pease's irrefutable explanation of Crews's position, "New Americanists," *boundary 2* 17, no. 1 (Spring 1990): 1–37.

6. For a listing of many of the most important works, see the notes to Bercovitch, *Ideology*, 439–42.

7. Perhaps one can distinguish certain sorts of "American" feminism from some of the more theoretically inspired European versions by noting the difference between andro- and phallocentric. The latter term depends upon the Lacanian rereading of Freud in the light of semiotics; the former seems more empirically motivated, associated with anthropology. The difference is not universal, but see, in the context of Emily Dickinson and Adrienne Rich, Patrocinio Schweikart's prizewinning essay "Reading Ourselves: Toward a Feminist Theory of Reading," *Gender and Reading* (Baltimore: 1986), 31–62.

8. F. O. Matthiessen, *The American Renaissance* (New York: 1941).

9. "American 'Left' Literary Criticism," *The World, the Text, and the Critic* (Cambridge, Mass.: 1983), 175.

10. Arac offered this direct formulation in conversation; see also his *Critical Genealogies* (New York: 1987), 32, 169f.

11. For some discussion of the dangers of "pluralism" to criticism in the United States, see Bercovitch, *Ideology*, 438f.

12. For a powerful critique of and alternative view to Bercovitch's, one that is as extensive and as eloquent, see Donald Pease, *Visionary Compacts* (Madison, Wis.: 1987).

13. See Gilles Deleuze, *Foucault*, trans. Sean Hand (Minneapolis, Minn.: 1988).

14. See Michel Foucault, "The Political Technology of Individuals," *Technologies of the Self*, ed. Luther H. Martin et al. (Amherst, Mass.: 1988), 145–62.

15. That this is quite ordinary in national traditions can be seen from the work of Benedict Anderson, *Imagined Communities* (London: 1983).

16. Harvard English Studies 13 (Cambridge, Mass.: 1986).

17. For analysis of this figure of the masterful intellectual, see Bové, *Intellectuals in Power*.

18. Jonathan Arac, *Commissioned Spirits: The Shaping of Social Motion in Dickens, Carlyle, Melville, and Hawthorne* (New Brunswick, N.J.: 1979); *Critical Genealogies: Historical Situations for Postmodern Literary Studies* (New York: 1987); "'A Romantic Book': *Moby Dick* and Novel Agency," *boundary 2* 17, no. 2 (Winter 1990): 40–59.

19. "American Manscapes," *London Review of Books,* October 12, 1989, 18.

20. One should again see Arac's essay on Melville, which, in part, is a study of the possibility of agency, as an instance of this project.

21. See Daniel T. O'Hara, "The Poetics of Critical Reading," *Poetics Today* 11, no. 3 (1990): 661–72: "The productive power of critical reading must be balanced by an appreciation for the achievement being read" (671).

22. For the beginnings of critique of the value and function of "reflection," recall Kierkegaard's critique of reflection in Hegel. For a discussion of this issue, cf. Paul A. Bové, "The Penitentiary of Reflection: Søren Kierkegaard's Critical Activity," *boundary 2* 9, no. 1 (1980): 233–58; reprinted in *Kierkegaard and Literature,* ed. Ronald Schleifer (Norman, Okla: 1984), 3–35.

23. Edward W. Said, "Secular Criticism," in *The World, the Text, and the Critic,* 8ff. See also Bové, *Intellectuals in Power,* 271–75.

24. Said, "Secular Criticism," 8–9.

25. Think, for example, of how complex the differentiation must be when the term *exile* describes or points to enabling conditions in intellectuals as different as Auerbach and C. L. R. James. See James, *The Black Jacobins: Toussaint L'Ouverture and the San Domingo Revolution,* 2nd ed., revised (New York: 1963; originally published in 1939). See also Said, "Nationalism, Colonialism, and Literature," *A Field Day Pamphlet* no. 15 (Derry: 1988), esp. 6ff.

26. See Michel Foucault, "The Ethic of Care for the Self as a Practice of Freedom," trans. J. D. Gauthier, S.J., in *The Final Foucault,* ed. James Bernauer and David Rasmussen (Cambridge, Mass.: 1988), 13; the interview was conducted on January 20, 1984.

27. Spivak rightly catches the oppositional edge in laying out this sort of criticism in "Explanation and Culture," *In Other Worlds* (New York: 1987), 103–17; see esp. 109, where Spivak discusses the relation of critics to the culture as mediated through the university: "Individuals in the chosen profession of humanists can only be tolerated if they behave in a specific way. . . . (1) to reproduce explanations and models of explanation that will take so little notice of the politico-economico-technological determinant that the latter can continue to present itself as nothing but a support system for the propagation of civilization (itself a species of cultural explanation) . . . (2) to proliferate scientific analogies in so-called humanistic explanations . . . (3) at the abject extreme, the open capitulation at the universities by the humanities as agents of the minimization of their own expense of production."

28. "A Kind of Settlement of Damages," trans. Jeremy Leaman, *New German Critique,* 44 (Spring/Summer 1988): 25–39, esp. 29; see also in the same issue of *NGC,* Jürgen Habermas, "Concerning the Public Use of History," 40–50. To put these essays in context, see Charles S. Maier, *The Unmasterable Past: History, Holocaust, and German National Identity* (Cambridge, Mass.: 1988), esp. 9–33.

29. "Settlement of Damages," 28.

30. It was precisely Gramsci's intent to theorize this state of affairs in regard to the nineteenth century that led him to formulate the still crucial notion of the "passive revolution." See *Selections from the Prison Notebooks,* ed. and trans. Quintin Hoare and Geoffrey Nowell Smith (New York: 1971), 106–8.

31. *Selections from the Prison Notebooks,* 59. See also Partha Chatterjee's comments on "passive revolution" in *Nationalist Thought and the Colonial World* (London: 1983), esp. 50–52.

32. On some of the dangers in certain historicist projects see Donald E. Pease, "Greenblatt, Colonialism, and New Historicism," *Some Consequences of Theory,* ed. Jonathan Arac and Barbara Johnson, *English Institute Papers* (Baltimore: 1990), 108–53.

33. Gramsci, in Notebook 8, note 150, writes of the "demiurge" in its "original sense" as "one who works for the people, for the community (artisan)" and points out that this precedes and underlies the modern sense of the demiurge as the "creator." Here I translate from the French edition of the *Quaderni, Cahiers de Prison,* books 6–9, translated from the Italian by M. Aymard and P. Fulchignoni and edited, annotated, and introduced by Robert Paris (Paris: 1983), 343. My thanks to Joseph Buttigieg, who is preparing the English edition of the *Notebooks,* for pointing out this note.

34. *Discipline and Punish: The Birth of the Prison,* trans. Alan Sheridan (New York: 1977), esp. 80ff.

35. See, among many recent books, Wayne C. Booth, *The Company We Keep: An Ethics of Fiction,* x, where Booth tells us it is his aim "to restore the full intellectual legitimacy of our common-sense inclination to talk about stories in ethical terms." We need not note at any length that throughout this commonsensical book intended for specialist and "general reader" alike, the former president of the Modern Language Association thinks he carries out this restoration without even bothering to mention Gramsci, the most rigorous and important critic of the notion of "common-sense" in current discourse. Perhaps this is simply another example of the grace all "moderate pluralists" possess not to be complete in their scholarship. On this Gramsci has a good point: "Scholastic activities of a liberal or liberalising character have great significance for grasping the mechanism of the Moderates' hegemony over the intellectuals." It is one of the few avenues "open to the initiative of the petite bourgeoisie" (*Prison Notebooks,* 103).

CHAPTER 2

Theory, Criticism, Dissent
Toward a Sociology of Literary Knowledge

Donald Pease

When I was initially asked for a title for this essay, I chose one sufficiently broad to permit me to pick from among a variety of topics and so general that it needed the explanation that only a specific topic could provide. The title arose from my concern with academic disciplines and the larger social or political movements to which they are related. My concern can be stated as a series of questions: How is the process of discipline formation (its theoretical and self-rationalizing process) related to the formation of political movements? Can an academic discipline find itself developed in different but not necessarily incompatible directions when developed in the environment of the dissensus-in-formation of a political movement? Conversely, can a discipline simply invoke its relationship to an emancipatory social movement to claim greater authority as an academic discipline?

I want to explore the relationship between the political discourse a new academic discipline borrows to describe its formation within the academy and the different uses to which that discipline can be put in a political movement. The academic discipline I will be most interested in here is what Stephen Greenblatt calls the New Historicism.[1] And since the discourse of colonialism plays an important role in the formation of that discipline, I will frame a consideration of that discipline's formation in the different terms to which Frantz Fanon puts the discourse of colonialism.

With the publication of *Peau noire, masques blancs* (Paris: Editions du Seuil, 1952), translated into English as *Black Skin, White Masks,* Fanon proposed to begin an unprecedented cultural conversation.[2] This conversation, which should have taken place centuries earlier, included the colonized and the colonizer within a shared dialogue. In opening up this dialogue, Fanon did not speak in the primal voice of his native Antilles. That voice had been thoroughly distorted through cultural contact. But neither did he speak *with* any explicit dialogue partner separable from himself. Instead, he spoke from within a sophisticated and extremely articulate use of the French language. I say from within because, as the title of the book suggests, Fanon consistently splits himself into two speakers: the one who speaks the language as if it were an essential aspect of his identity and the one who experiences this linguistic identity as a form of colonization.

Fanon's terms for these two speakers are in the title. The speaker who says "I speak" and does not recognize any difference between himself and the language he uses Fanon calls a "white mask," while the speaker who experiences himself misrepresented by a language that speaks in his place Fanon designates "black skin."

By identifying the speaker who believes he speaks for himself as a theatrical effect, the production of a white mask rather than an authentic identity, Fanon violates ordinary usage of these terms. Although two figures from Western theater will play crucial roles in this conversation, Fanon does not violate ordinary usage merely for a theatrical effect. Instead he does so to insist on the difference between who speaks and what gets spoken whenever anyone (white or black) in French culture speaks. Fanon describes what gets spoken in the neocolonialist French culture of 1952 as a white mask, and he believes that everyone who speaks is compelled to wear this mask. He elaborates this belief in terms borrowed from the French psychoanalyst Jacques Lacan and by means of Caliban and Prospero, characters from Shakespeare's *The Tempest.*

The reason he chose Lacan's subdiscipline of psychoanalysis as a way of understanding these Shakespearean characters requires some explanation. Two years before Fanon wrote *Black Skin, White Masks,* another French psychoanalyst, Dominique O. Mannoni, had written a study of colonialism entitled *Prospero and Caliban: The Psychology of Colonization.*[3] In that work, Mannoni uses the Caliban/Prospero relationship as the basis for two interdependent psychological complexes that he found crucial to the colonial encounter. Caliban represented a "dependency complex" characteristic of primitive people whose lore included legends of the return of powerful white ancestors who would mark the recovery of a primordial inheritance. Such legends, Mannoni argued, indicated the "primitives'" psychological need for colonization. Caliban's identity depended on his submission to Prospero. Mannoni described Prospero's character, on the other hand, in terms of an authority complex. He needed to exercise the authority Caliban required. His authority consequently depended on his recognition of his authority through the signs of Caliban's submission to it.

Fanon, as you might imagine, found this account contemptible,[4] an ideological continuation of the psychology of colonialism rather than an explanation of it.[5] In proposing another, he turned to Jacques Lacan's project. Lacan explained the development of an infant's identity in terms of miming the coherent image of another. But while Lacan intended the description as an alternative to the oedipal model (which recently had been appropriated by American ego psychologists), Fanon found in it an alternative explanation of the psychology of colonialism. Like the infant, the colonized organized his official identity by miming the language, customs, and judiciary system (what Lacan calls "les noms du pères") of the colonizers.

In correlating Lacan's account of the white infant's process of identity formation with the colonialization of native peoples, Fanon proposed a social relationship they shared in common. This relationship, while founded on Caliban's with Prospero, dismantled Mannoni's account of it. Fanon found another of Lacan's notions, "the discourse of the Other," crucial to this dismantling.

"The discourse of the Other" is Lacan's haunting phrase for the difference Fanon cites between what does the speaking in ordinary conversation and what must of necessity remain speechless. What does the speaking Lacan describes as the perpetually reiterated motion of displacement that produces the symbolic. What gets displaced is the realm of the Imaginary, in which processes (either maternal or natural), in maintaining an undifferentiated state, make words (which depend on differentiation) unnecessary.[6] Lacan, in his various analyses of the difference between the Imaginary and the Symbolic, designates this difference as the discourse of the Other, and locates it in the speechless past of the human infant. But in the use to which he puts Lacan, Fanon relocates this discourse in the unarticulated space of the colonized other. Then he provides a different account of its origin in the French psyche.

In these native worlds, Fanon argues, European explorers encountered cultural realms quite different from their own; their discovery would ultimately result in the breakdown of a world that was presumed to be spoken by a divine Speaker, the Logos who, so they believed, spoke through every other enunciation. In order to deny legitimacy to any form of speech other than that spoken by the Logos, Europeans, in their role as colonizers rather than explorers, simply supplanted the natives' speech with their own, thereby leaving the traces of another discourse in the wake of this displacement. In a practice that Greenblatt tellingly refers to as "linguistic colonialism," the Europeans covered the new worlds with what they believed were their own enlightened discourses.

One effect of the Europeans' language lessons was the production of the "discourse of the Other," in themselves as well as the natives.[7] Definable as what gets displaced whenever the language of the fatherland takes the place of native speech, the discourse of the Other more usually remains unvocalized.[8] But this discourse becomes unusually audible in the conversation between Prospero and Caliban in which Caliban claims that the only lesson he learned from his European masters was "how to curse." Fanon takes this to mean that Caliban has learned the real lesson in the instruction, that is, if language teaching played a part in the grand strategy of colonization, then language learning, as an education in how to be properly colonized, taught the natives to curse both themselves and their former way of life. The lesson Caliban learned was not the one Prospero taught, but Caliban's lesson nevertheless instructed Prospero in a different way to understand the language lesson as well.

By experiencing the European language (and the cultural system it conveyed) as a way of cursing rather than a form of enlightenment, Caliban worked with the counterenlightenment forces that would lead to civil wars, Protestant reformation, and, at the time of Fanon's writing, anticolonialism. Learning the master's language only as a vivid lesson in what he was compelled *not* to speak led Caliban to experience another, as yet inarticulate, discourse. When it developed its emancipatory potential, this other discourse resulted in another Europe for Prospero, if not yet another new-found land for Caliban.[9]

For Fanon, then, the discourse of colonialism produced alternative discourses in both Caliban and Prospero. Positioned between these two different discourses, the one they spoke and the one they suppressed by speaking, the inflections in the language and the character of Caliban and Prospero depended upon their differing relations to these discourses. When they were constituted as identities within the discourse of colonialism they did not dissever their relation to this other discourse. Instead, their mutual experience of the discourse they spoke as a form of cursing resulted in the one recognition that the Lacanian symbolic exists to deny; that is, they experienced themselves as displaced from within the language that (as the Lacanian symbolic) should have positioned them as identities. In their relationship, Fanon maintains, Caliban and Prospero experienced the difference between the language that colonized them (a white mask) and a different language through which they could experience their freedom. This new language could be neither the discourse of colonialism nor Caliban's native speech. Instead, it is a discourse that arises out of the limitations in both those discourses. This discourse is inseparable from an emancipatory praxis, a joint effort that arises from the recognition on the part of both Caliban and Prospero of their shared linguistic colonialism. And it is inseparable from the shared resolve at the basis of their anticolonialism: to free themselves from the world that imprisons and to free the world from its status as a prison.

This resolve no more appears in Shakespeare's play than the praxis appears within Lacan's new psychoanalytic discipline (for Lacan the discourse of the Other designated the impossibility of such a collective praxis rather than an enabling instance).[10] But by putting Lacanian analysis to work within a worldwide political movement directed against colonialism, Fanon developed an environment other than the institutional one for this discipline. Here it led to the formation of a coherent account of collective praxis.[11]

Jean-Paul Sartre found in Fanon's Black Skin, White Masks a devastating critique of the Hegelian master/slave dialectic at work in his own account of the existential phenomenology of the authentic self. Fanon enabled Sartre to understand the origins of that work in his own experience of colonialization. Sartre had worked out the political implications of Being and Nothingness during the German occupation of France. In it, his account of freedom was dependent upon a reaction against colonial power: only by totalizing all aspects of the environment other than the free self could Sartre conceptualize a self that existed utterly for itself. In recovering freedom from that power, Sartrean subversion was indistinguishable from the recovery of the position of a colonial master (who is also utterly for himself). In ways too complex to do justice to here, Sartre recognized what Fanon had: that the discourse of colonialism was responsible for the Western conception of subjectivity.[12] And in the Critique of Dialectal Reason, Sartre offered an alternative to the dialectic of the self and the other confirming that subjectivity. That alternative includes a discussion of collective praxis, which Sartre calls a "group-in-fusion." In the years of France's occupation of Vietnam and Algeria, this group was composed of two constituencies: the French, who felt victimized by the discourse of colonialism, and the colonized people of Vietnam and Algeria. The praxis the group developed resulted from the give and take, the ongoing discussion engaged by these two constituencies. And that discussion resulted in an experience of personhood quite different from that of either master or slave.

Like Lacan's psychoanalysis, Sartre's *Critique* took on a life of its own within the movement of anticolonialism, where it continues to play a crucial strategic role today.[13] Whereas Sartre worked out the implications of *Black Skin, White Masks* in philosophical terms, Aimé Césaire, Fanon's mentor and author of *Discourse of Colonialism,* worked out these implications for Shakespeare's play. Altering the title slightly to *Une Tempête,* he characterized Caliban as a rebellious slave who not only recovers his island but persuades Prospero to remain and help him in the process of decolonization. In the use to which Sartre, Césaire, and others put Shakespeare in the development of an emancipatory discourse for a political movement we can see the alternative lives academic works can lead when they enter social movements.[14]

By concentrating on the emancipatory potential in Prospero's relationship with Caliban, Fanon further opened up the relationship between Shakespeare and anticolonialism. In "Learning to Curse: Aspects of Linguistic Colonialism," Stephen Greenblatt follows Fanon's line. The article—published in *First Images of America,*[15] edited by Fredi Chiapelli—was written in 1975 while Greenblatt was working out the argument that would become *Renaissance Self-Fashioning.*[16] Although it was not included in *Renaissance Self-Fashioning,* it is cited frequently by New Historicists. The article turns on an interpretation of a line from Prospero. In his reading of Prospero's "this thing of darkness I / Acknowledge mine," Greenblatt refuses to let the discourse of colonialism displace the line's ambiguity. "Like Caliban's earlier reply," Greenblatt contends, "Prospero's words are ambiguous." He offers two accounts of the lines that would "colonize" this ambiguity. The first would assimilate the lines to an affirmation of colonial mastery, the superiority of Prospero's to Alonso's colonialism: "They might be taken as a pure statement that the strange demi-devil is one of Prospero's party as opposed to Alonso's." The second account, that Caliban is Prospero's slave, "would only absorb the lines," Greenblatt says, back into slavery, the most peculiar and abominable institution of colonialism. But Greenblatt refuses both of these accounts as insufficient in their empathy. In his reading, the lines "acknowledge a deep if entirely unsentimental bond." And to underscore the ethical imperative in this bond, Greenblatt risks a moral lesson that almost turns into a curse: "Perhaps, too, the word 'acknowledge' implies some moral responsibility, as when the Lord, in the King James translation of Jeremiah, exhorts men to 'acknowledge thine iniquity, that thou hast transgressed against the Lord thy God' (3:13)."[17]

If Greenblatt concludes his discussion by drawing on prophetic wrath, he does so both because he never loses sight of the continued power of colonialism to repossess the relationship between Caliban and Prospero and because he feels himself bound to oppose this repossession. To foreclose this colonialist repossession, Greenblatt first finds it generalized (in the work of another Shakespeare scholar, Terence Hawkes) into the interpretive master plot for all of Shakespearean drama. The colonist, in Hawkes's reading, establishes a homology with the dramatist. "Like the dramatist, a colonist imposes the shape of his own culture, embodied in his speech, on the [new world]."[18] But the colonist cannot articulate the new world into one as recognizable as his own without the help of the dramatist, whose language, Hawkes says, "expands the boundaries of our culture and makes the new territory over in its own image."[19] To hear colonialism described in these terms is precisely *not* to acknowledge it as a dark thing. And it is this refusal on Hawkes's part to acknowledge the immorality of colonialism that leads Greenblatt to turn to Jeremiah for an appropriate curse on such a reading.[20]

But in a dramatic reversal of his cultural duties, in the essays following "Learning to Curse," Greenblatt restores this homology between the colonist and the dramatist. More precisely, he reinstitutes this homology with an essay that he first read at the 1978 English Institute. This essay, entitled "Improvisation and Power," constitutes a watershed moment in Greenblatt's career. It was collected in Edward Said's edition of selected 1977–78 papers for the English Institute. And, as the last chapter in *Renaissance Self-Fashioning: From More to Shakespeare,* it marked the conclusion of one interpretive schema and the inauguration of a new discipline. In different contexts and on different occasions, Greenblatt describes this new discipline either as "cultural poetics" or "the new historicism." The flexibility in naming just what it is you do when you follow the rules of this new discipline only enhances its applicability:[21] whatever one chooses to call it, the new discipline supports many disciples, most of whom are sufficiently revisionary (or improvisatory) in their handling of New Historicist matters to produce the internal differentiation constitutive of the discipline's rationality. Greenblatt himself founded a new journal, *Representations,* which often features the work of New Historicists; and the new discipline has become the subject of books as well as of issues of journals and academic conferences. In what may be the most reliable sign of its status as burgeoning critical enterprise, the New Historicism has become the target of critics who, in some cases, are defectors from the new discipline.[22]

I am neither a defector nor a practitioner, but I am an admirer of the New Historicism. Along with many others, I was present at the 1978 English Institute session when Greenblatt delivered "Improvisation and Power." I found his presentation as invigorating as his subject was liberating. On one level, what I have to say about Greenblatt's New Historicism is the result of what this new discipline has taught me. The

New Historicism, in Greenblatt's description of it, "erodes the firm ground of both criticism and literature. It tends to ask questions about its own assumptions and those of others." It might even "encourage us to examine the ideological situation not only of a play but of a critic on that play," as well as the relationship "between a critical reading and its occasion."[23]

In the remainder of this discussion I hope to follow this recipe for examining the "ideological situation" of the New Historicism. But I shall also add one more feature: the relationship between the New Historicism and linguistic colonialism. And I will add that feature by now risking an assertion: the ideological ground of Greenblatt's New Historicism corroborates in its discipline formation the enterprise of linguistic colonialism he earlier questioned.

For the purposes of this discussion, Greenblatt's continuation of the colonialist enterprise constitutes his definitive break from the anticolonialist praxis Fanon called for in *Black Skin, White Masks*. This break necessarily involves him in a reinterpretation of the relationship between Prospero and Caliban. Curiously, this reinterpretation does not appear in "Improvisation and Power" (at least not explicitly) but in the essay following it: "Invisible Bullets: Renaissance Authority and Its Subversion, Henry IV and Henry V."[24] The order of the essays is an important indication of the material Greenblatt excludes in order to found the New Historicism.

Greenblatt organizes "Improvisation and Power" by establishing a linkage between an obscure anecdote from the archives of colonialism and Shakespeare's *Othello*. The anecdote, which is Peter Martyr's account of the exploitation of Lucayan natives by Spanish conquistadors, might be described as the story of a Caliban who does not know how to curse. It seems the Lucayans believed that their dead would one day return to them in boats from across the sea. When the Spaniards learned of this belief they identified themselves with the Lucayan dead in order to persuade the living to work for them in the gold mines. According to Greenblatt's recounting of Martyr's narrative, "the entire population of the island . . . thus deceived . . . passed 'singing and dancing' . . . onto the ship and were taken to the gold mines of Hispaniola."[25]

What differentiates this account of cultural contact from the earlier ones in "Learning to Curse" is the reciprocity missing from the exchange. In what we might call the Fanonian moment in Greenblatt's treatment of colonialism, he did not eliminate accounts of duped natives. But he carefully balanced such accounts with contrary ones, which often assumed the form of reciprocal exchanges rather than colonial exploitation. In "Learning to Curse," for example, Greenblatt cites a report from a Spanish captain in which the Cenu Indians refute the Europeans' ideological claim to their land: "'When I said,' the captain began, 'that the Pope, being the Lord of the universe in the place of God, had given the land of the Indies to the King of Castille,' the Indians' chief responded, 'The Pope must have been drunk when he did it, for he gave what was not his.'"[26]

Whereas the anticolonialist in Greenblatt carefully included such accounts of reciprocity, the New Historicist in him is more interested in the relationship between the Spaniards' control and nonreciprocal exchanges. For it is in maintaining their control that they exemplified what Greenblatt means by an "improvisational self." Improvisation results from the ability Greenblatt calls empathy, the ability to identify, no matter how briefly, with the role of another, for the purpose of exploitation. The Spanish conquistadors displayed a gift for improvisation when, in order to exploit their labor, they identified themselves with the Lucayans' belief in the resurrection of the dead.

In the course of this improvisation, the Spaniards put into operation the two activities that Greenblatt believes essential for a felicitous improvisation: displacement and absorption. I used them earlier in presenting Greenblatt's interpretation of "The thing of darkness I / Acknowledge mine." In that earlier usage, displacement and absorption subverted a colonialist reading of the lines, and Greenblatt's empathy with Caliban was the result. But Greenblatt's *technical* definition of these terms assigns them different duties. By displacement he now means "the process whereby a prior symbolic structure [such as the Lucayans' belief in the resurrection of the dead] is compelled to coexist with other centers of attention [like the Catholic faith of the Spanish conquistadors] that do not necessarily conflict with the original structure but are not swept up in its gravitational pull."[27] This final qualification is the key to a successful improvisation, for without it the conquistadors could find their Catholicism susceptible to a counterdisplacement into the symbolic structure of the Lucayans, that is, they might recover their "empathy" in the nonimprovisational sense. Such a mutual displacement would restore reciprocity to this exchange, rendering it akin to Prospero's exchange with Caliban in Fanon. As if in acknowledgment of this danger, absorption, the second improvisational gesture, completes the defense against reciprocity. Greenblatt defines it as "the process whereby a symbolic structure is taken into the ego so completely that it ceases to exist as an external phenomenon."[28] In terms of the Lucayan episode, absorption refers to an assimilation of the Lucayan beliefs into the Roman Catholic faith so thorough that nothing remains of those beliefs other than the traces of their displacement into the Spaniards' state of mind.

The necessity of this activity becomes clearest when we consider the danger it defends against. This danger can be expressed as a question: If the Spaniards can treat the Lucayans' belief structure as an ideology vulnerable to exploitation, why don't they treat their own beliefs as an exploitable ideology? J. G. A. Pocock, for example, asks this question in *The Machiavellian Moment,* a different account of the same materials.[29] He concludes that the encounter with the Other led to the return home of Europeans other than the ones who left; their questioning of the Catholic faith would support the Protestant Reformation, and their opposition to monarchy would result in civil war. While Greenblatt never asks this question in "Improvisation and Power," it nevertheless influences the way he conducts his argument. I will return to that argument shortly, but now I have two reasons for turning to "Invisible Bullets: Renaissance Authority and Its Subversion," an essay in which Greenblatt considers this question explicitly but in a way quite different from the way Pocock does in *The Machiavellian Moment* and Greenblatt himself did in "Learning to Curse." In so doing he utterly revises his earlier interpretation of the lines "This thing of darkness I / Acknowledge mine." In ways I hope to make clear, Greenblatt's ability to reinterpret these lines carries with it the authority of the New Historicism.

This essay also depends upon a linkage between an anecdote from colonialist archives and Shakespeare's plays: not this time the story of the exploitation of Lucayan faith by the Spaniards (Greenblatt's use of that anecdote contained an implicit critique of colonialism, or, what is more to the point, he took the critique for granted), but the exploitation of the Algonquin Indians' faith by a British dissenter. The difference between these two anecdotes carries with it a change within the character of the improviser—from a Spanish believer to a British nonbeliever—that implies an equally important shift in the motive for the improvisation. The Spanish conquistadors had fairly obvious reasons for their exploitation of the Lucayans' beliefs: they needed cheap labor in the gold mines. But Thomas Herriot, in his "brief and true report" of an encounter with Algonquin Indians, expresses a more subtle need. He uses their religious beliefs as a way to displace his own religious doubts.

In manipulating the Algonquins' religious beliefs, Greenblatt contends, Herriot turns his doubts about religion into opportunities for control. In a brilliantly perverse reading of *Brief and True Report,* Greenblatt argues that Herriot displaces his religious doubts onto the belief structure of the Algonquins, after which he can treat the Algonquin nation rather than the British monarchy as an oppressive state. And his subversion of that state takes the form of governing a colony of Algonquin Indians.

As an explanation of Herriot's psychological solution to a difficult problem, I find this argument quite compelling. But Greenblatt does not read the *Report* in terms of Herriot's biography. Instead he generalizes its applicability:

> One may go still further and suggest that the power Herriot both serves and embodies not only produces its own subversion but is actively built upon it: in the Virginia colony, the radical undermining of Christian order is not the negative limit but the primitive condition for the establishment of the order. And this paradox extends to the production of Herriot's text. *Brief and True Report,* with its latent heterodoxy, is not a reflection upon the Virginia colony nor even a simple record of it—not, in other words, a privileged withdrawal into a critical zone set apart from power—but a continuation of the colonial enterprise."[30]

What is unique about this passage is its status as an unprecedented moment in Greenblatt's criticism. In it he doesn't depend on any agent other than himself for the display of improvisational power and in it he does not oppose but celebrates colonialism. The origin of this improvisation, the symbolic structure capable of initiating and absorbing these powerful displacements, has nothing to do with Thomas Herriot's doubt. Herriot consigned his doubts to a particular aspect of the Renaissance power structure, that is, religious belief. Herriot believed enough in the dominant religion to *need* to doubt it. That his doubts were turned into a form of colonial domination only indicates the presence of a power more pervasive than the displacement of his doubts.

This power finds its expression in what we might call Greenblatt's hymn to colonial power, his elevation of it into a religious power. This elevation serves a purpose: it provides a symbolic structure perdurative enough to outlast either religious faith or monarchy as a belief structure. When in these lines Greenblatt invokes a power that Herriot "both serves and embodies," he addresses a power that transcends the entire symbolic structure of organized religion. This transcedent power can displace and absorb the Christian belief structures as readily as Christianity absorbed the Algonquins'. We earlier heard Greenblatt voice his opposition to the entire colonialist enterprise, but "Invisible Bullets" does not continue that opposition. Instead it turns colonialism into so pervasive a structure that "Learning to Curse," his previous critique of colonialism, now seems more a colonial anecdote, an exemplification of a "privileged withdrawal into a critical zone set apart from power" and thereby discontinuous with everything else in the colonialist enterprise.

In examining why Greenblatt withdraws his previous criticism, we should recall that "Learning to Curse" was written before Greenblatt developed the two concepts crucial to his new discipline, that is, "Renaissance self-fashioning" and "improvisation." These two concepts produced a critical persona whose relationship with both literature and history was quite different from the Greenblatt of "Learning to Curse."

In order to be fashioned, such an interpretive persona requires a power or authority as absolute as is colonialism in the previously cited passage. As the absolute authority that replaced religion as a pervasive belief structure, colonialism in the essays following *Renaissance Self-Fashioning* became the basis for the improvisations of power needed to work the discipline. But the colonialism with which a self-improviser works is precisely not the colonialism that existed as an actual historical force.[31] The colonialism operating within the essays following "Improvisation and Power" is the necessary raw material for a theatricalization of society, the conversion of *everyone* into a self-fashioner. Following the demotion in power of the symbolic structure of religion, only colonialism, as the basis for a common understanding of freedom and bondage, could solicit the deepest beliefs about freedom and constraints needed for empowering improvisations.

This second version of colonialism is the one at work in what Greenblatt calls the New Historicism. In that discipline Greenblatt has maintained a rhetoric of anticolonialism but preserved colonialism's operations—or rather he has redistributed the location for the exercise of his anticolonialism. The object of the anticolonialism in New Historicism is not any colonial power, but the power of the historical narrative in old historicism to turn literature itself into one of its linguistic colonies. The reason why should be clear. The notion of history as a cultural dominant turned both literature (like *The Tempest*) and colonial anecdotes (like Martyr's account of the Lucayans and the Spaniards) into marginal texts, raw material for historical illustrations; though at the same time, *as historical evidence,* a narrative such as Martyr's would have priority over a play by Shakespeare. In this older historicism, colonialism existed in two different registers: it designated a specific conjuncture of events and forces historians wrote about, but it also referred to the relationship established between history and related disciplines.

As a movement within the humanistic disciplines, the New Historicism was emancipatory: it decolonized literature. To realize its emancipatory effect, we need only recall the prior relationship between history and literature in Renaissance studies. Tillyard's world-picture approach read complex literary texts in terms of a stable historical worldview that at once guaranteed the autonomy of these texts and their irrelevance to the way in which the world organized itself. Greenblatt emancipates literature

from its irrelevance by resituating it within a set of related social practices, then he carefully discriminates the interrelationship between the
practices literature produces and the literatures produced out of related
materials.

In Greenblatt, history becomes an aspect of literary studies, a colony
of literary history, or more precisely one of its theatrical productions.[32]
History no longer authoritatively represents past cultures. In Greenblatt's
essays, old historicism is produced as part of a vast cultural mise en
scène. His treatment of colonial anecdotes is a cogent example. In "Invisible Bullets," he lifted the anecdotes from their marginal status in the
old historism (where their very irrelevance to the larger social narrative
turned them into metaphors for literature) and treated them as episodes
in a much vaster historical drama whose means of production they
clarified. In producing the linkage between colonial anecdotes that would
otherwise remain marginal to history and the rest of what should now
be called the social text, Greenblatt simultaneously exposes and operates
the praxis (displacement and absorption) that he claims organizes the
entire social field.

But in socializing these colonial anecdotes by means of the New
Historicism, Greenblatt produces a new discipline that cannot be distinguished from colonial disciplines. In what I have called its inaugural
moment—Greenblatt's reading of "Improvisation and Power" at the English Institute—the New Historicism displaced the discourse of colonialism
from its site within historical discourse and turned it into the stage where
literary studies put on a successful revolt against the colonialism of
history. And the proof of the New Historicism's victory was its power
to include within its territory anecdotes that previously were situated in
colonialist archives. Hence in Greenblatt's writing the New Historicism
exists simultaneously in two conflicting registers. As a movement within
the humanistic disciplines, it functions as an anticolonialist emancipatory
movement, liberating literary studies from colonization by history. But
as a new discipline, it produces a set of disciplinary practices that cannot
be distinguished from colonialist policies. Neither the discipline formation
of New Historicism nor that of colonialism acknowledges any opposition
to its operations that cannot be subsumed into a continuation of its
enterprise. For all of its claim to infinite inclusiveness, however, the New
Historicism is founded on an internal contradiction. As a discipline
formation, it describes its operations in terms of anticolonialism even as
it denies anticolonialism as an effective emancipatory movement external
to the workings of the discipline.

One way to come to terms with this inner contradiction might be to
imagine Greenblatt attempting to bring his pre-New Historicist essay

"Learning to Curse" within the field of the New Historicism. As I have already suggested, "Learning to Curse" occupies an unusual place within Greenblatt's corpus. In a way it exists in two different historical realms at once. Written before Greenblatt "decolonized" literary studies in relation to history, the essay corroborates the domination of literature by history. Greenblatt himself proves this point when he invokes *The Tempest* primarily to illustrate historical points about colonialism that he derived from colonial anecdotes. Here Greenblatt in his own treatment of these materials acknowledges the literary critic's submission to the greater cultural authority of the historian. As an example of history's colonization of literary studies, "Learning to Curse" justifies the colonial revolt of the emancipatory movement called the New Historicism.

But the essay establishes another relation to the New Historicism. It is what Fanon understood as the "discourse of the Other" to the colonialist enterprise with which Greenblatt identifies the New Historicism. Hence the argument at work in this essay cannot be transformed into the discipline of the New Historicism. Neither can the Greenblatt who wrote it. Having written it before his "interpretive persona" was reconstituted by *Renaissance Self-Fashioning,* Greenblatt here believed in the possibility for an authentic collective praxis between the colonizer and the colonized. The Greenblatt in this essay was equally opposed both to colonialism and to Terence Hawkes's notion of drama that turned the dramatist and the colonist into homologies for one another. He found Hawkes's account an ideological justification for colonialism rather than an account of it. In subverting his earlier opposition to Hawkes's prefiguration of his own New Historicism, Greenblatt included a crucial revision of Hawkes's account. Thus, in order to accept Hawkes's equation of the colonist and the dramatist, after he wrote this essay Greenblatt had to *refashion* Hawkes's colonist. In revising Hawkes's colonist into an improvisational self, Greenblatt used his own profound reaction against colonialism as the raw material for this improvisation. He could not accept Hawkes's equation because in his mind the colonist grounded his personal authority on another's submission to it. Such authority, as well as the character it uses, Greenblatt found antithetical to human freedom, and to undo that authority he had to reinterpret the exchange as theatrical rather than critical. Unlike the colonist, the Renaissance self-fashioner identified his authority with another's belief structure. Following this reversal, the colonist derived his authority only from the belief of the colonized in it. But as the Renaissance self-fashioner made clear, the only actual authority at work in this exchange was the *need* to believe in any authority whatsoever. Once the belief was exposed as a theatrical prop, the duped figure would be free as well.

Unlike Hawkes's colonist, Greenblatt's Renaissance self-fashioner originated with a theatrical relationship to colonialism. For him, colonialism
was never anything but a repertory theater for the endless display of the
power of social roles. Greenblatt's redefinition of colonialism as theatricality contained its own critique of colonization. The theatrical, so he
believed, exposed the ideological mask, the transfer of power, at work
in both the colonizer and the colonized. In redefining it as self-subverting,
he exempted himself from the need to oppose colonialism. Instead he
identified himself with the power to continue—even celebrate—a colonialism that alone freed the self from the illusion of any identity other
than a mask.

But this powerful revision, as well as the remarkable collective enterprise resulting from it, depends upon an experience of colonialism as a
liberating theatrical experience rather than a form of coercion. And this
experience depends upon a modern societas organized as a circulation
of endlessly mobile energies in which any ideological identification—even
an identification with an autonomous self—would be considered a form
of specular captivity, a failure to be distanced from the procedures
through which mobility is engaged.

Such a societas is clearly different from the colonial one Greenblatt
describes in "Learning to Curse." There the colonial world is one in
which the colonizers need to identify their authority with the colonizeds'
submission to it. Before either the colonizers or the colonized can enter
the world of theatrical colonialism, they must first be able to experience
their relationship as theatrical rather than necessary. In Greenblatt's
description of theatrical colonialism, only the colonizers can experience
colonialism as a mask. And they can do that only after undergoing the
same modernization process Greenblatt has—that is, Renaissance self-
fashioning. But since that process depends upon the colonizing figures'
denial of a reciprocal relationship with the colonized, those who know
they are wearing masks can never let those who are not in on the show.
If the Other exists only as the basis for a display of the power to
manipulate, then the *Other* must always experience what the New Historicist in Greenblatt calls improvisation as what the old historicist in
Greenblatt would call plain old colonial subjection.

To enable the practitioners of the new discipline to experience colonialism as theatrical, Greenblatt provides a set of instructions on how
to understand subversion. "Subversion is for us" Greenblatt explains, "a
term used to designate those elements in Renaissance culture that contemporary authorities tried to contain or, when containment seemed
impossible, to destroy and that now conform to our own sense of truth
and reality. . . . That is, we locate in the past what is precisely *not*

subversive to ourselves. Conversely, we locate as the principle of authority in Renaissance texts things that we would, if we took them seriously, find subversive for ourselves"[33]—things such as religion and political totalitarianism, demonology, and so forth.

These instructions enable all of the agents of Greenblatt's new discipline to become improvisational selves who simply displace and absorb Renaissance texts onto their own value systems, which Greenblatt goes on to say are "sufficiently strong for us to contain almost effortlessly any alien forces." In interpreting a Renaissance play they can find themselves agents in a decolonization process, one in which they are liberated from the powers of church, political totalitarianism, and superstition.

But Greenblatt's own interpretation in "Improvisation and Power" complicates these instructions. In that essay, Greenblatt maintains that Iago *colonized* Othello by exaggerating Othello's anxiety over his excessive love for Desdemona. Othello became Iago's dupe, Greenblatt contends, because he had already been duped by the Catholic church. The church defined adultery as the openly impassioned love of a husband for his wife. So the real colonizer was the church, and what it colonized was sexuality. And we presently have a consensus about liberated sexuality that perserves us from colonization by the church—or so we would believe. But in the remainder of his interpretation, Greenblatt multiplies the positions of the colonizer: not just the church over sexuality, but a sexist male (not Iago this time but Othello) whose "brutish violence is bound up with his experience of sexual potency".[34]

As we witness Othello colonized by sexual repression and sexism, we decolonize these forces, but in the name of two modern consensuses (i.e., liberated sexuality and feminism) that have recently come into conflict. Moreover, the outcome of the decolonization we engage by means of Greenblatt's reading is a version of Othello as an oversexed black male from whose violence no white woman can believe herself safe. And this version is precisely the one that colonialism depends upon to justify itself. So by internalizing the operation of decolonization, Greenblatt has not disconfirmed the discourse of colonialism but has reproduced its fundamental figure, Caliban, though this time in the displaced form of Othello.

Despite the later Greenblatt's having passed colonialism through the defiles of self-fashioning, the earlier Greenblatt would be unable to recognize it as anything but the old colonialism dressed up in a white mask. For that Greenblatt, the unfinished conversation between Prospero and Caliban would have become all the more urgent for having been denied any possibility for reciprocity. If we can imagine a critique of the later by the earlier Greenblatt, it might appear as a refusal to enter the new discipline. To enter it, he would have to accept the liberation of his literary studies from the old historicism and in exchange give up his anticolonialism.

When we realize that the anticolonialist in Greenblatt would find himself misrepresented by the New Historicism, we locate the Fanonian moment in the New Historicism. Insofar as it is organized around the denial of the recognition of anticolonialism, the New Historicism also founds itself on the denial of any collective praxis like the one espoused by Fanon. To understand how deep that denial is, we need to be reminded of Greenblatt's New Historicist interpretation of "This thing of darkness I / acknowledge mine." In that reinterpretation he claims that Prospero has merely turned Caliban's attempted subversion into a sign of the colonial power Prospero exercises over him.[35]

Notes

1. Greenblatt first uses the term in his introduction to *The Forms of Power and the Power of Forms in the Renaissance.* "Diverse as they are, many of the present essays give voice, I think, to what we might call the New Historicism, set apart from both the dominant historical scholarship of the past and the formalist criticism that partially displaced this scholarship in the decade after World War II." ("Introduction," *Genre XV* [Spring 1982]: 5).

2. For the discussion of Mannoni's use of Caliban and Prospero, see Fanon, *Black Skin, White Masks,* trans. Charles Lam Markmann (New York: 1967), 83–108.

3. *Prospero and Caliban: The Psychology of Colonization,* trans. Pamela Powesland (New York: 1956).

4. For example, in response to the implication of Mannoni's psychological analysis of colonial exploitation, Fanon writes: "All forms of exploitation are identical because all of them are applied against the same 'object' and when one tries to examine the structure of this or that form of exploitation from an abstract point of view, one simply turns one's back on the major, basic problem, which is that of restoring man to his proper place." *Black Skin, White Masks,* 88.

5. Fanon also uses Lacan to explain the origins of racism: "It would be interesting on the basis of Lacan's theory of the *mirror period,* to investigate the extent to which the *image* of his fellow built up in the young white at the usual age would undergo an imaginary aggression with the appearance of the Negro." *Black Skin, White Masks,* 161.

6. For Lacan, the ego itself is born out of the misrecognitions of the pre-oedipal stage of development. He locates the origins of these misidentifications in the "mirror stage," a period lasting roughly from the age of six months to the age of eighteen months. During this period, the infant, utterly dependent and uncoordinated, misrecognizes the unity of its body by identifying it with the image of its mother. Antoine Vergote provides a concise discussion of this distinction in "From Freud's Other Scene to Lacan's Other," in *Interpreting Lacan,* ed. Joseph H. Smith and William Kerrigan (New Haven, Conn.: 1983), 193–222.

7. For a remarkably similar analysis of the origins of modern man in the "discourse of the Other," see Michel de Certeau, *Heterologies: Discourse in the Other,* trans. Brian Massumi (Minneapolis, Minn.: 1986), 3–34, 67–79, 225–36; Homi Bhabha, "Of Mimicry and Man: The Ambivalence of Colonial Discourse," *October* 28 (Spring 1984): 124–35.

8. In Lacan's understanding of the child's resolution of the Freudian oedipal conflict, the father's name (*le nom du père*) as a signifier substitutes for the desire for (and of) the mother.

9. For an exhaustive account of the ways in which Caribbean and African intellectuals put Shakespeare's *The Tempest* into the service of anticolonialist struggles, see Roberto Fernández Retemar, "Caliban: Notes toward a Discussion of Culture in Our America," trans. Lynn Garafola, David Arthur McMurray, and Robert Marquez, *Massachusetts Review* 15 (Winter/Spring 1974): 11–16.

10. For an analysis of the relationship between the visions of Lacan's theory and the infighting of competing schools of psychoanalysis, see Sherry Turkle, *Psychoanalytic Politics: Freud's French Revolution* (New York: 1978), 47–140.

11. For an interesting version of this different life, see "Caliban on the Couch" in O. Onoge, "Revolutionary Imperatives in African Sociology," in *African Social Studies: A Radical Reader*, ed. Peter C. W. Gutbind and Peter Waterman (New York: 1977), 32–43.

12. Sartre relates his previous works to the question of colonialism in his preface to Frantz Fanon's *The Wretched of the Earth*, trans. Constance Farrington (New York: 1966), 7–26. For an analysis of Western self-consciousness and the master/slave dialectic, see Mitchell Aboulafia, "Self-Consciousness and the Quasi-Epic of the Master," *Philosophical Forum* 18 (Summer 1987): 304–28.

13. For a useful reading of the transformations in Sartre's critique see Ronald Aronson's "Vicissitudes of the Dialectic," *Philosophical Forum* 18 (Summer 1987): 358–91.

14. Rob Nixon provides a fine critical account of these matters in "Caribbean and African Appropriations of *The Tempest*," *Politics and Poetic Value*, ed. Robert von Hallberg (Chicago: 1987), 185–206.

15. "Learning to Curse: Aspects of Linguistic Colonialism in the Sixteenth Century," *First Images of America: The Impact of the New World on the Old*, ed. Fredi Chiapelli (Berkeley and Los Angeles: 1976), 561–80.

16. *Renaissance Self-Fashioning: From More to Shakespeare* (Chicago: 1980).

17. Greenblatt, "Learning to Curse," 570.

18. Greenblatt, "Learning to Curse," 569.

19. Cited in Greenblatt, "Learning to Curse," 569.

20. Greenblatt, "Learning to Curse," 569.

21. For good accounts of the new practice see Jonathan Dollimore, "Introduction: Shakespeare, Cultural Materialism and the New Historicism," in *Political Shakespeare: New Essays in Cultural Materialism*, ed. Jonathan Dollimore and Alan Sinfield (Ithaca, N.Y.: 1985), 2–17; Louis Montrose, "Renaissance Literary Studies and the Subject of History," *English Literary Renaissance* 16 (Winter 1986): 5–12; Stephen Greenblatt, *Genre* 15 (Spring 1982): 3–6; and Howard Horwitz, "I Can't Remember: Skepticism, Synthetic Histories, Critical Action," *South Atlantic Quarterly* 87 (Fall 1988): 787–820.

22. The numbers of dissenters from the new practice are by now legion. Among the many fine critiques are Edward Pechter's "The New Historicism and Its Discontents: Politicizing Renaissance Drama," *PMLA* 102 (May 1987): 292–303; Jean E. Howard, "The New Historicism in Renaissance Studies," *English Literary Renaissance* 16 (Winter 1986): 13–43; Jonathan Goldberg, "The Politics of Renaissance Literature: A Review Essay," *ELH* 49 (Summer 1982): 514–42; Judith Newton, "History as Usual? Feminism and the 'New Historicism,'" *Cultural Critique* 9 (Spring 1988): 87–121; Walter Cohen, "Political Criticism of Shakespeare" in *Shakespeare Reproduced: The Text in History and Ideology*, ed. Jean Howard and Marion O'Conner (New York: 1987), 18–46; Carolyn Porter, "Are We Being Historical Yet?," *SAQ* 87 (Fall 1988): 743–86; and especially Frank Lentricchia in *Ariel and the Police: Michel Foucault, William James, Wallace Stevens,*

(Madison, Wis.: 1987), 86–102. As an example of its prominence, at the 1988 Modern Language Association convention I counted more than thirty papers in which the New Historicism figured in the title.

23. Greenblatt's original sentence includes a specific example: "In the present case, for example, it might encourage us to examine the ideological situation not only of *Richard II*, but of Dover Wilson on *Richard II*. The lecture from which I have quoted—'The Political Background of Shakespeare's *Richard II* and *Henry IV*,'—was delivered before the German Shakespeare Society at Weimar in 1939. We might, in a full discussion of the critical issues at stake here, look closely at the relation between Dover Wilson's reading of *Richard II* . . . and the eerie occasion of his lecture." *Genre* 15 (Spring 1982):5–6.

24. "Invisible Bullets" appears in *Political Shakespeare,* ed. Dollimore and Sinfield, 18–47.

25. "The Improvisation of Power," in Greenblatt's *Renaissance of Self-Fashioning,* 226.

26. Greenblatt, "Learning to Curse," 571. Greenblatt's point here is that the Europeans, in translating the native speech into their own diction, had altered it beyond recognition. He makes this point, however, as a plea for linguistic reciprocity as opposed to linguistic colonization.

27. Greenblatt, "Improvisation of Power," 230.

28. Greenblatt, "Improvisation of Power," 230.

29. See J. G. A. Pocock, *The Machiavellian Moment: Florentine Political Thought and the Atlantic Republican Tradition* (Princeton, N.J.: 1974).

30. Greenblatt, "Invisible Bullets," 24.

31. Only the colonial enterprise as a symbolic structure applicable both to Renaissance England and to the New World can establish an all-inclusive field for the New Historicism to explain. Once he has saturated the entire Renaissance field with the discourse of colonialism, Greenblatt can even read the great transformations in Europe's political arrangements as renegotiations of the colonial model. "Moreover," he writes of Pocock's argument, "the 'Atlantic Republican Tradition,' as Pocock argued, does grow out of the 'Machiavellian Moment' of the sixteenth century, and that tradition . . . does ultimately undermine, in the interests of a new power, the religious and secular authorities that had licensed the American enterprise in the first place." ("Invisible Bullets," 25.)

32. For a fine account of the struggle between literary history and the history professed in history departments, see Linda Orr, "The Revenge of Literature: A History of History," *New Literary History* 18 (Autumn 1986): 1–22.

33. Greenblatt, "Invisible Bullets," 29.

34. Greenblatt, "Improvisation of Power," 243.

35. I know that Greenblatt intends to keep his New Historicism separate from colonialism. He knows that a modern value system is opposed to colonialism. He nevertheless saw a homologous relationship between colonialism and New Historicism. The taut acknowledgment that colonialism is against our values allows him (as a New Historicist) to enact its operation but with the disclaimer that it is against our values.

CHAPTER 3

Critical Change and the Collective Archive

Daniel T. O'Hara

For a complex set of reasons, some of which I will explore in this essay, critics today have little good to say about their work or, at times, even about themselves. Listen to what one of America's leading literary critics recently has said on the subject:

> All of the current critical schools in the United States and Britain and France and Germany, I guess, almost without exception . . . could be linked together. Whether you call it deconstruction, Marxism or neo-Marxism, feminism, black and hispanic, New Historicism, it is exactly what Nietzsche called Resentment with a capital R. They really should be called the School of Resentment. The last critics with whom I can fully empathize would be Ruskin and Pater and Oscar Wilde. I mean, it strikes me that criticism and literature are either primarily aesthetic or they're something other than criticism and literature. But I sometimes wonder if there can be five people beneath the age of 40 now teaching literature in the better universities and colleges in the United States who have ever in all their days loved a poem for being a poem or a story or a novel for being a story or a novel. They are looking for social utility; they are looking for something. . . . The primary question always has to be, "is this a good poem, or is it just verse?"[1]

That it is Harold Bloom who is making this indictment of the School of Resentment is, of course, almost amusing. Bloom is the critic who, in attributing a fiercely competitive sense of anxious belatedness to the

Great Dead, made the public attribution of a resentful will-to-power
motive informing every text virtually respectable in contemporary criticism. If any one critic can be said to be responsible for a lowering of
the tone of criticism, for making criticism more the embodiment of what
Nietzsche, referring to *ressentiment,* calls "the spirit of revenge," rather
than of magnanimity, it is certainly Harold Bloom.

Bloom's remarks are important, however, not simply because they
expose the fundamental contradiction of his own prominent position.
Nor does their importance lie in their rearguard, elitist, and humanistic
recuperation of the purely aesthetic formulation of literature and literary
study. That Bloom sounds more like William Bennett—President Reagan's
secretary of education, President Bush's drug czar, and Matthew Arnold's
would-be heir—is telling, but not crucial to my argument. What is crucial
is that these remarks expose the representative anxiety of the profession
concerning the highly vulnerable sense of place any critic, including,
perhaps especially, a major critic, now feels. Although Bloom character-
istically casts this anxiety of place, of status, in generational and oedipal
terms, what his remarks really disclose is the revisionary conditions of
work in the profession of literary study. These are perceived to be conditions of perpetual change that promote the ideology of perpetual novelty. Historical changes envisioned and executed for particular institutional and political ends of liberation are subsumed by and in the formal
processes of revisionism as merely the latest examples of the profession
at work, or as in Bloom's psychologizing indictment, the profession's ven-
erable business of *ressentiment* as usual operating under the guise of
"making it new."

To discover the most effective analysis of the forms of change within
interpretive communities such as professions, however, we must turn to
the latest work of Stanley Fish. But before doing so, I must admit that
I am less interested here in all the details of his typically brilliant analyses
than I am in the demoralizing vision of the profession his neutrally stated
conclusions unintentionally promote. For the purpose of my present
argument, I am willing to stipulate that his analyses are generally persuasive, even as I plan to challenge the key unexamined belief in the
continuing power of instrumental reason underlying his representation
of the institutional mechanisms of change in the profession's ideological
practices.

Fish concludes a recent article entitled "Change" with characteristic
insouciance:

> Perhaps the most persistent charge against the notion of interpretive
> communities is that it seems to make disciplinary and professional activity
> its own end. But, since that end itself is continually changing, the charge

can be cheerfully embraced because it says only that the members of a community will always believe in the ends for which they work, and that therefore their work will never be ended even though it will be ceaselessly transformed. (444)[2]

Fish's conclusion captures in pure form the vision of the profession as profession, as an endlessly self-revising interpretive community with no definite final end in sight other than the perpetuation of its own cease-lessly transformed and transforming, revisionary or modernizing, pro-jects. Fish has already claimed that such a vision of the profession neither promotes nor inhibits any particular social agenda or course of political action or historical change. Whether partisans of the "right" or the "left" ultimately prevail in professional terms is made entirely the "determi-nation of empirical fact," according to the victorious community's estab-lished procedures, that will take place after the successful takeover oper-ation has occurred. In short, Fish's "theoretical" model of change would be entirely practical and pragmatic, and not predictive of specific changes, even as it does represent itself as the general intelligible form of all such changes of the professional guard imaginable: "In all of these cases, and in any others that can be imagined, a theory of change is inscribed in the self-description that at once directs and renders intelligible the char-acteristic labors of the workers in the community" (442).

I think Fish is basically correct here. History does emerge in criticism as the assumed theory of change implicit in any interpretive community's self-description of its labors. The key and worrisome point in this last quotation, however, is the innocuous-sounding phrase "renders intelli-gible." According to what standard is the process of rendering intelligible going to be carried out and judged, especially while the struggle for control of any aspect of the profession is still continuing? Or rather, according to whose standard of judgment is any of the mechanisms of professional change to be analyzed and evaluated? Clearly, it must be a community's—or at least some group's—standard, but which community or group? And is there a standard of judgment that all interpretive communities or critical groups in the profession share in common? And, finally, is this commonly shared standard of judgment, as Fish suggests, universally "true," that is, simply the state of affairs for any and all imaginable cases of critical change? From one set of representative remarks, Fish does appear to endorse a particular standard of judgment as the standard of judgment currently and continually operating in the profession:

Does an interpretive community encourage or license change by relieving its members of any responsibility to the world or to the text, or does it inhibit change by refusing to take into account anything that is contrary to its assumptions and interests? The bulk of this essay has been concerned to demonstrate that this question, in either its left or right versions, is misconceived: since an interpretive community is an engine of change, there is no status quo to protect, for its operations are inseparable from the transformation of both its assumptions and interests; and since the change that is inevitable is also orderly—constrained by evidentiary procedures and tacit understandings that at once enable change and are changed by what they enable—license and willful irresponsibility are never possibilities. (440)

The standard of judgment that Fish takes as operative in the profession now and throughout all the changes to come is one that recognizes endless modernization, constant change, as definitive for any profession as a profession and yet clearly enforces an orderly form of all such changes upon the community by means of the enabling constraints of certain "evidentiary procedures and tacit understandings," that is, by means of the post-Enlightenment mode of human rationality known as instrumental reason. Given this belief, Fish reassures his community, "license and willful irresponsibility are never possibilities."

For example, in his commentary on the essays collected in *The New Historicism* entitled "The Young and the Restless," Fish argues that virtually all of the contributors worry about the same problem or impasse, namely, how to do new historical research with valid truth claims while accepting the now established poststructuralist principle of the textuality of all facts. Fish's response to their dilemma is interesting and typical of his practice and position. He claims that the principle of the textuality of all facts is one that functions solely in the critical practice known as theory, whereas doing specific historical research, making specific historical claims and mounting specific arguments in their support are particular activities in the critical practice known as literary or cultural history writing. For him, there is no necessary connection between the practice of theory and the practice of history; that is, no necessary consequences for the practice of history follow from the principles of theory. New Historicism or any other form of poststructuralism is merely a theoretical superstructure, as it were, that rests upon and is governed finally by the same pragmatic base of rational argument and empirical criteria of judgment, that is, upon the strategies of rhetorical persuasion, as has always been the case. Styles of persuasion may change somewhat, what counts as a good argument or proof may fit the moment, but the general forms of persuasion, the appearance of rationality (or, shall we say, rationalization), the appeal to what the community knows conventionally to be the case, all these things constituting the schemes of critical reason remain fundamentally the same.

A conviction that all facts rest finally on shifting or provisional grounds will not produce shifting and provisional facts because the grounds on which facts rest are themselves particular, having to do with traditions of inquiry, divisions of labor among the disciplines, acknowledged and unacknowledged assumptions (about what's valuable, pertinent, weighty). Of course, these grounds are open to challenge and disestablishment but the challenge, in order to be effective, will have to be as particular as they are; the work of challenging the grounds will not be done by the demonstration (however persuasive) that they are generally challengeable.[3]

Theory, in short, has no practical consequences or effects at the level of everyday or "normal" criticism. Only the practical counts for Fish, and it counts in terms of long-established criteria of rational or rather rationalizing argument and appeals to empirical facts everyone in the community conventionally admits. Although Fish does acknowledge the principle that each interpretive community may decide again what counts as reasonable or factual, he also claims that in practice the intelligible forms of critical work continue, however much or little their theoretical and material contents change. Fish's pragmatism, in sum, is really the latest mode of formalism.

To displace any one historical claim by another thus requires, in Fish's view, that we play the current version of the long-established game of arguments and proofs, and so the conventional forms of debate go on, acting to inhibit if not to preclude from the conceivable space of critical debate new objects of analysis or newly recovered materials of the past. An analogy with the legal profession may be appropriate here. The basic structure and procedures of contestation in the profession remain generally the same despite new laws, new precedents outmoding older ones, new styles of lawgiving, and new theories of law. That is, the system of legal practice retains its basic shape and structure of authority. The law is Fish's model for how a profession works, and because it is he can claim that "license and willful irresponsibility are never possibilities" in literary study, because our formal "evidentiary procedures and tacit understandings" work to preclude the very emergence of all truly radical possibilities, which have always been dismissed "out of court," as it were, as merely "license and willful irresponsibility."

Fish's version of instrumental reason, these "evidentiary procedures and tacit understandings," is greatly revised and qualified for the contemporary scene. No individual autonomous faculty of rationality, as in Kant, Fish's "reason" is simply a community's agreed-upon set of "evidentiary procedures and tacit understandings," a historically specific form of human rationality, clearly masquerading as a universal standard of reason, whose successful deployment is the prerogative of certain classes of people within highly selective social and professional circumstances. Such selectivity, however, necessarily restricts considerably and often effectively proscribes the power of such reason to make a significant structural difference in the larger world or even within the confines of the profession or of any of its interpretive communities. The often intricate and sophisticated arguments of Fish himself are examples of the kind of reason his practice assumes and would necessarily replicate through all the changes to come. As his essay "Change" concludes, any other form of reason, or of "unreasonable" (read: historically revolutionary) change cannot even be recognized:

> The question of change is therefore one that cannot be posed
> independently of some such self-description [of a community's work and
> implicit theory of change] which gives a shape to the very facts and events
> to which the question [of change] is put. Does this mean, then, that we
> can never say "what really happened" because we can only say what
> happened under some description or account? Not at all. Every description
> and account—including the descriptions and accounts that make up this
> paper—is an attempt to say what really happened. If the claim to be
> saying that is contested (as it often is), it will not be contested by some
> view of the event independent of description but by a competing
> description, and the competition will be adjudicated with reference to the
> norms, standards, and procedures understood by the community to be
> appropriate to the determination of empirical fact. (442)

The problem with Fish's position here does not so much concern his competitive model of critical change, although I will challenge it shortly, as it does his vision of deciding between competing descriptions. Surely Stanley Fish knows how members of an interpretive community obtain the common understanding of "norms, standards, and procedures"—by the authoritative imposition of power upon people's minds and sometimes their bodies. Surely he knows, too, that the best argument within any interpretive community does not necessarily win widespread acceptance in either critical or political arenas. Besides, even if the best argument did usually win out in literary study, there is no reason to assume that the "norms, standards, and procedures" of instrumental reason are necessarily appropriate in other than current professional contexts. Why does Fish need to make such naive-sounding assumptions? Perhaps the use of the legal term *adjudicate* in the passage is a clue—to what, I will show, is the essentially irrational, broadly aesthetic basis of his position.

Fish is a professor of English and of law, and when he speaks about the legal profession in this essay, he admits that one of its founding beliefs is necessarily a convenient fiction, which for all its fictionality is indispensable and constraining on all its members, regardless of their legal philosophy or "theory":

> The enterprise of law, for example, is by definition committed to the historicity of its basic principles, and workers in the field have a stake in seeing the history of their own efforts as the application of those principles to circumstances that are only apparently new (i.e. changed). That is why a judge will do almost anything to avoid overturning a precedent, and why even those who hold to the doctrine of legal realism—the doctrine that the law is whatever the courts happen on that day to say it is—are uncomfortable with that doctrine and wish that they held to something else. In short, the very point of the legal enterprise requires that its practitioners see continuity where others, with less of a stake in the enterprise, might feel free to see change. (441)

And are we to draw the further conclusion that, now, a similarly ironic situation holds true for the profession of literary study: whereas we are committed to see change and to "making it new," others, outside the profession, "with less of a stake in the enterprise, might feel free to see" continuity? Whether or not Fish's conclusion does indeed entail this further conclusion of mine, his vision of the fictional foundations of the legal enterprise's necessary belief in an ideal continuity can provide a clue to why Fish assumes the standards, norms, evidentiary procedures, and tacit understandings of instrumental reason. In taking the law as his model of a profession (something Magali Larson's *The Rise of Professionalism* licenses him to do), Fish is both ignoring literary study's difference from the law, its unrationalized object of analysis, and tacitly admitting that his commitment to the current professional mode of instrumental reason is serving him and his interpretive community in the same way as the legal profession's rigid belief in the sanctity of precedent: as a useful fiction without which he could not imagine the familiar, self-revising, and aesthetically pleasing pattern of change he articulates in the essay. (The profession of literary study as a self-transforming, purely formal system is a seductive reincarnation of his idea of Renaissance texts as self-consuming artifacts.) The belief in rationalized, orderly, continuous change is necessary to the ever-modernizing professional establishment or ironic "status quo" of fasionable change to which he belongs. This "interpretive community" subscribes to what could be called—following Fish's own account—the doctrine of critical realism. This would be the belief in the Humpty-Dumpty principle of professional politics: that criticism is whatever the "community" of apparently like-minded leading critics and their disciples happen on that day to say it is.

Whether or not my last speculative barb hits the mark, I think we have seen enough of Fish's vision of change to draw certain conclusions.

First of all, although his practical "theory" of change depersonalized the modernizing procedures of the profession, making the endless displacement and strategic resentment Bloom worries about less a matter of individual or even obviously generational animus, it retains as the form of all change imaginable this very mode of endless displacement for its own sake. In fact, it conceives of a permanent structure of displacement as the fictional origin of critical judgment. Such revisionism is conceived in terms of interpretive communities committed to the apparently impersonal practices of instrumental reason. But this idea of human rationality is actually (in large part) no more than an updated, professionalized, 1980s-style version of the conventional understanding of the "taste" and "common sense" that distinguishes a cultural elite from the untutored masses.

Secondly, Fish's model of change authorizes no clear direction for change. Outcomes are no more than what the sum total of the individual professional projects of contestation happen at any one time to add up to within an interpretive community or within the sum total of interpretive communities in the profession. In this fashion, the free-market, utilitarian, postivistic, and pragmatic view of classical liberal capitalism has been displaced from individuals and attributed to interpretive communities, so that although Fish would never maintain that individuals are finally "free agents," however much different contexts might make them "feel free," his representation of the model of professional change does grant all the power for basically beneficial choice to the operations of the invisible hand of the interpretive community of the profession as a whole. Typically, a politically demoralizing idea is "cheerfully embraced" by Fish, the good professional. One could propose a democratic rationale for the modesty Fish appears to display in refusing to authorize a specific agenda for change. One could claim that Fish does not want to play the prophet and coercively predetermine the shape of changes to come. One must also remind oneself, however, that such a refusal to take the lead and play the speculative theorist or prophetic critic occurs in the context of promoting a vision of change dependent on the acceptance of professional elites continuing to operate their modernizing procedures according to a conception of instrumental reason appropriate for the standard of taste and value current in late-capitalist America. In short, such a refusal to play is playing at refusal and really accepting things as they are, as how things must be and even should always be.

The final conclusion to be drawn from Fish's latest work is that, despite its trappings of realism and worldly wise, even cynical reason, the vision of change presented there is truly a vision that should be

familiar to us from the romantics, and even more so from the deconstructive critique of the romantic practice of attempting to represent in
sublime or "romantic" images of natural objects and processes matters
that are entirely cultural and textual—indeed, often purely rhetorical.
Fish's representation of a continuously changing interpretive community
that is a self-regulating, self-perpetuating, self-transforming ensemble of
revisionary forms without specific content is, to my mind, as sublimely
aesthetic as anything in Harold Bloom's theories or in Emerson's visions
of nature. Fish's theoretical conception of critical change is really a figure
of speech projecting a spectral fiction that would impersonate all the
anonymous force of natural fact.

With this topic of the displaced romantic sublime we are indeed back
to Harold Bloom and an understanding of "community" based purely
and simply upon naked self-interest. Let me cite Jonathan Arac, one of
Bloom's recent critics, on the nature and sources of his critical vision:

> The classical source for literature as fragmentary and competitive is
> Longinus "On the Sublime." Longinus helped extricate the romantics from
> the dilemmas of eighteenth-century poetry and was crucial to Bloom's new
> romantic criticism. Longinus is extravagant and difficult, and since Bloom
> rarely cited him, many readers have not appreciated his place in Bloom's
> work. Longinus held that the sublime was disjunctive, a power that
> "scatters everything before it like a thunderbolt," in a moment. This power
> derived from the grandeur of the human mind, "the echo of a great soul,"
> and was freed from any natural mimesis. It offered a theory of inspiration
> that depended on no divinity. Men became gods to one other, as the
> "effluences" of past greatness filled the young writer. To achieve full power,
> however, one must leave such passive receptivity and emulatively combat
> one's predecessor, as Plato did Homer, "entering the lists like a young
> champion matched against the man whom all admire." Thus Bloom's
> agonistic metaphors joined a tradition of discourse. Likewise, another of
> Bloom's important, apparently idiosyncratic notions: the Scene of
> Instruction. To achieve the sublime, one may conjure up the great past
> writers as judges and exemplars: the "ordeal" of this ghostly "tribunal"
> will yield us the power to immortalize ourselves, or else it will quell us if
> our spirits are inadequate.[4]

Bloom's sublime vision of the fiercely competitive "ordeal" of facing the
"ghostly tribunal," his "scene of instruction," is the religious and individ-
ualized version of Fish's secularized, rationalized (hence seemingly more
"enlightened"), and depersonalized notion of the interpretive community
of change. Fish's model of "norms, standards, and procedures" that
decides which of the competing critical descriptions an interpretive community adopts as its own takes on in Bloom's criticism the form of the

Longinian "ghostly tribunal" and the ordeal or scene of judgment, which Bloom generally reads into the processes of poetic and critical canon formation. The models of change that Bloom and Fish propose are really interchangeable, equivalent parts of the profession's self-justifying ideology that attempts to ensure the replication of the profession's basic structure of power relations into the future without substantial change. Furthermore, the force of these competitive models of professional work and critical change, whether represented in explicitly "visionary" (Bloom) or more "instrumental" (Fish) terms, functions in the same fashion to constrain the production, distribution, and acceptance of all alternative views. The result is that the conditions of work in the profession are felt to be purely self-interested for the individual and the group to the point of being essentially destructive of any conceivable possibility of human community of shared beliefs, values, and general life experiences that transcend narrowly defined, often improvised professional strategies and goals.

At this point, several questions arise: How it is that anyone can perceive the limits of this pervasive model of professional work? To what can one compare it? Whence comes the alternative cooperative vision of the social character of work? Fredric Jameson in a recent essay provides the best answer I know when he introduces "some notions of Jean-Paul Sartre (in the *Critique of Dialectical Reason*) which seem to open up new avenues for exploration":

> For Sartre, social praxis—which always involves solving problems and confronting contradictions—also always tends to leave a kind of residue, what he calls the practico-inert. This residue, this dead mark or trace of a now extinct praxis, survives to form a part of the new situation, the new dilemma or contradiction, which people confront in their new historical present. Would it therefore not be plausible to suggest that what is called social character is to be seen as just such a residue, just such a form of the practico-inert, just such a scar left in the present by the outmoded and forgotten practices of the past?[5]

By "social character" Jameson means not simply the social dimensions of collective projects but also the kind of subject formation now all but totally outmoded in our late-capitalist epoch, a form of human subjectivity that still possesses a residual if now not entirely appropriate sense of that much-abused word *community*. (One can catch glimpses of this fading phenomenon in the relations between members of formerly subaltern groups—such as women, people of color, and postcolonial peoples—now making their way upon the world-historical stage. Jameson continues his analysis with a critical surmise:

We may conjecture, for example, that in a certain communal situation certain kinds of character traits prove necessary and effective in overcoming specific concrete social difficulties and dangers: forms of puritanism, for example, or authoritarian family structures organized around a patriarch. When the problems in question are surmounted, these specific collective stances—something like the muscular contraction of a body resisting a specific weight and pressure—do not go away put persist without function, in the forgetfulness of the purpose they once served (and I may add that this forgetfulness of the crucial role of forgetfulness in social reproduction is not the least problem with contemporary appeals to social memory). Social "character" would then be this persistence of traits which have lost their function and which now exist as givens or data, as elements of a new situation and as themselves problems which must be overcome (as in various efforts to alter collective habits which have become counterproductive). (553)

What I want to suggest, following Jameson's lead here, is that literature is the place in our culture where one can still discover the persistence of collective stances, those chronologically overdetermined but otherwise apparently outmoded forms of communal vision. In fact, I want to define the aesthetic dimension of literariness, of powerful imaginary effects, as "the collective archive," that is, as the cultural site for the conscious preservation of the history of humanity's collective projects, all its models of community, tradition, and change, both canonical and subversive. (This is, of course, especially but not exclusively true of the novel.) By turning to the literary tradition, even with all the institutional problems of canonization still in mind, we can recuperate the idea of a collective project yet to be realized, which can give shape and direction to the future of the profession and, more importantly, of society, and so provide a more viable basis of comparative judgment on the present state of things. Our work of critical change can then take on a larger meaning than merely the narrow self-interest of the resentful individual or the self-justifying group. In this way, too, our work can be related, via the mythological resonance of literary language, to the universalizing projects of liberation, which often use the language of myth and religion to express their purposes, both here in this country and around the world. In short, our work of critical change would have a coherent imaginative vision of what we want change to make possible.

Does this mean that just any model of the collective project drawn from the literary tradition is itself necessarily viable and appropriate? Well, obviously not. Then how does one determine what is an unfinished vision of human community that can still be realized, rather than only another exhibit in a museum of muscular poses? The beginning of an answer is, I think, that critics must look to the immediate contexts in which they do their work, not only the local work of teaching, of course, but also the work in which they are engaged within the specific field or subdiscipline of the profession. We must take our lead, as it were, from what we perceive as the needs of our areas of study. Ideally, we critics will not stop there, but at least we must begin definitely somewhere in a concretely historical oppostional manner. In this way, we can better avoid the fate of resurrecting from the past what would only be, in Jameson's formulation, a complex of "counterproductive" albeit "collective habits" (553) that would also have to be radically altered for the needs of our time.

I want to explain further why we need this corrective vision of the collective archive by looking at the latest work of Gerald Graff and Richard Poirier, both of whom propose to renovate literary study without such a vision. In a recent critical history of the institution of American literary study, Graff has argued that the profession as a whole has been plagued for the last century or so by an ideological split between those who accept in one form or another the scientific and professional model of specialization and those who, opposing such reductive professionalization, desire in some way to have a more pervasive influence on modern culture. Whether staged as a contest for professional power between scholars and generalists, critics and humanists, pragmatists (Fish) and theorists (Jameson), or deconstructionists and New Historicists, this ideological split has continually haunted literary studies, and it has been accompanied by a process of institutionalization that Graff calls "patterned isolation."[6] What Graff means is that as each new development in critical method or ideology appears, it is assimilated into its own separate compartment or niche in the profession, its own "interpretive community" in Fish's phrase. This enables everyone on the local level to evade facing directly the challenge posed to the first principles other approaches necessarily entail, especially in light of the many polemical theoretical and antitheoretical manifestos over the years. At the same time, this "liberal" or "pluralistic" mode of assimilation and institutionalization, while it makes for a minimum kind of peaceful coexistence, also ensures that the latest critical innovations will quickly become mere routine, even as the essential split between scientistic specialization and critical humanism continues to inspire a fiercely competitive situation made all the more fierce, since the institution, in the name of academic freedom, can never permit any "final solutions." In this viciously circular fashion, professional change occurs as the periodic displacement of routine by novelty and novelty by routine.

American literature studies proves to be no exception to the general rule. Its distinctive feature, Graff claims, is its origin in the promise it held out that, as a viable, interdisciplinary mode of cultural studies, it could successfully oppose the hegemony of New Critical formalism. In fact, according to Graff, the major works of American literature studies, from *Maule's Curse* (1938) and *American Renaissance* (1941) through *Symbolism and American Literature* (1953), *The American Adam* (1955), and *The American Novel and Its Tradition* (1957) to *The Machine in the Garden* (1965) and *A World Elsewhere* (1966), all tend to deploy in their analyses cultural archetypes, based upon "a very limited number of works" (221). And, ironically enough, these analyses continue to celebrate the very aesthetic and moral features of irony, paradox, ambiguity, symbolism, existential complexity, tragic vision, and so on that New Criticism assigned to all literary texts. The disillusioning result, Graff concludes, is that if during this period all "literature was New Critical," then "American literature was somehow a bit more so" (220). In the attempt to displace and assimilate its rival, therefore, American literature studies continues to preserve many of the major elements of the New Critical complex, even as it still adopts the radically opposing stance of cultural studies—an outcome that Jameson's comments on Sartre cited earlier would theoretically predict.

The Renewal of Literature: Emersonian Reflections (1987), Richard Poirier's latest contribution to American literature studies and indeed to contemporary criticism as a whole, clearly confirms Graff's general point about the cycle of novelty and routinization in the profession.[7] I think it also replicates some of the major features of the discipline to which it belongs, even though, while explicitly endorsing the method of close reading, it nonetheless also condemns the aristocratic ideology of New Critical modernism. The major disciplinary features of American literature studies that this study replicates are: the formulation of a culturally specific archetype, that of the transcendental American genius of revisionism, based on a very limited number of works—in this instance, texts by Emerson, William James, Stevens, and Frost that constitute a subtly pervasive Emersonian countertradition to Arnoldian humanism and Eliotic modernism. And this restrictive genius archetype, it is nevertheless claimed, defines the essentially American nature of all American literature. Here we see, in other words, one of the hoary "classics" of American literature, Emerson, that transcendental pragmatist of imaginary compensation for all ills, once again trotted out in a currently fashionable revival of ideal cultural types à la Max Weber and Karl Mannheim. Indeed, Poirier makes Emerson and his heirs more radically "new" and "deconstructive" (because so casually, nonchalantly so), than Foucault, Nietzsche, or any of their many followers can even pretend to be.

It is around the subject of "genius" that Poirier most clearly discloses at work the endless displacement ideology of the profession and the increasingly common desire to transcend the evident vicissitudes such critical practice produces. Poirier argues, based on Emerson, that literature "is supremely the place where . . . the reader and writer become indistinguishable" (77). Yet such identification is neither a sympathetic imaginative one nor something that makes us "better citizens or even wiser persons" (77). Instead, this identification of reader and writer enables us to "discover how to move, to act, to work in ways that are still and forever mysteriously creative" (77). "Genius," Poirier continues in this vein, "describes those moments when language and the person using it reach a point of incandescence. It marks the disappearance of individuality on the occasion of its triumph" (80). This self-destructive mode of individuality, in which language and subjectivity fuse together, defines "genius" (as Poirier presents it) as a compensatory dream, quite horrific and antisocial, in which good professionals of the type Fish's vision of change would promote can find momentary release from the vicissitudes of meaningless change despite the ever-present threat of their being made obsolete—has-beens. And yet, this dream of genius would go even further in the name of compensation by obliterating material "things" themselves, a project expressing a nihilistic state of mind:

> Why, under the Emersonian dispensation, should anything at all be preserved as an example to the future? Why not erase every sentence just as soon as it is written and read? Wouldn't that be the purest form of action as Emerson imagines it? (83)

Poirier's argument thus concludes in this vision of a self-destructive mode of individuality that in seeking to evade the endless repetition of professional displacements, change merely for the sake of change, would consign to the future only its own disintegrating gestures of *ressentiment*, as it exits the world of human practices altogether:

> Genius involves itself in processes which, when they arrive at practical expression, especially in any mode of writing, become immediately filled with the apprehension of dissipation and loss of energy. To overcome this apprehension we need to convince ourselves, as Emerson says in the essay "Art," that "the real value of the Iliad, or the Transfiguration, is as signs of power." (85)

In these passages, everything goes—and goes on: text, author, reader, things themselves. All is dissolved into the ceaseless process of rhetorical transition that defines the ideal type of the American genius, whose only enemy is the lapse into the habitual, the merely practical, the material:

that is, the socially reproducible. The resort to Emerson is evidently a last-ditch effort of a major representative of one entrenched interpretative community in the field of American literature studies once again to undergo in a distinctive fashion the modernization of himself and his corner of the discipline, in the face of the inevitable outmoding, the becoming a personal and collective has-been, that necessarily defines the profession and its various "areas of study" as being "professional" in the first place. Signs of power? I think not.

Where are we to discover a vision of human relationship not reducible to Bloom's, Fish's, and Poirier's world of resentful competition and strategic displacement? In the collective archive of literature that Jameson's remarks led me to there are many such visions. I choose Wallace Stevens's "Large Red Man Reading," a late poem of the 1940s, because it is appropriate to the previous discussions of vision, change, the sublime, and imaginative compensation and because it offers an alternative prospect. In fact, the poem supports both a resentfully competitive and a magnanimous vision, depending on the context, narrowly professional or broadly imaginative, in which we choose to read it.

> There were ghosts that returned to earth to hear his phrases,
> As he sat there reading, aloud, the great blue tabulae.
> They were those from the wilderness of stars that had expected
>   more.
>
> There were those that returned to hear him read from the poem of
>   life,
> Of the pans above the stove, the pots on the table, the tulips
>   among them.
> They were those that would have wept to step barefoot into reality,
> That would have wept and been happy, have shivered in the frost
> And cried out to feel it again, have run their fingers over leaves
> And against the most coiled thorn, have seized on what was ugly
>
> And laughed, as he sat there reading, from out the purple tabulae,
> The outline of being and its expressings, the syllables of its law:
> POESIS, POESIS, the literal characters, the vatic lines,
>
> Which in those ears and in those thin, those spended hearts,
> Took on color, took on shape and the size of things as they are
> And spoke the feeling for them, which was what they had lacked.[8]

Read in the specialized terms of contemporary criticism, the poem justifies Bloom's anxiety of influence theory of literary history. "Large Red Man Reading," in this light, expresses a latecomer's vision, in which the usually repressed desire to see oneself as the primal source for the greats to whom one feels anxiously indebted beautifully if self-deceivingly articulates itself. Consider how the "he" of the poem provides, through his acts of reading the changing colors of the heavens, all that the ghosts of his literary ancestors lacked. He creates "the poem of life" and speaks "the feeling for them." In this fashion, Stevens would become more powerfully original than any of his precursors, even Walt Whitman. The transcendental American genius for forgetting the past and delighting in the changes that destroy one strikes again here.

Or so it seems. But read in a less restrictive way, the poem sounds a radically different note. If we take the speaker and his ghosts not in their purely literary roles as the belated modern poet and his sublime predecessors but rather in their human roles as survivor and his dead, we get a very different poem. That Stevens composed the poem during the time when he lost a parent and two siblings to death reinforces such a reading. In this different light, "Large Red Man Reading" becomes a poignant expression of the pathos of desire that would triumph over death, a pathos made all the more piercing by the poem's repeated, self-conscious use of the subjunctive mood for its grand vision of the poem's "setting" solar protagonist reading the great blue and then purple tabulae of the twilight heavens for all his ghosts. The creative act, in this context, is not an anxious repression of precursors; it is instead the generous, even noble (if self-consciously doomed) vision of giving imaginative life back to the dead. For the collective archive, as Stevens performs it here, is the communal memory of exemplary acts read from the changing horizons of one's world and rearticulated, with feeling, thereby blooding the ghosts of the dead and making them real again. This poem is thus an allegory of the literary act as creative reading, a poetic outlining of a being, once lost, now reenvisioned and worthy of becoming an instructive model of future existence. Literary texts at their best are thus inhabited not only by the distorted traces of the political unconscious, but also by the spectral lineaments of noble magnanimity.

Consider, as another and final instance, the famous and much-disputed concluding vision of Joyce's "The Dead," a long coda to *Dubliners* intended to be a more sympathetic reappraisal of Ireland, which is otherwise viciously satirized in the collection.[9] Does Gabriel Conroy, the protagonist, as he contemplates the snow that is now general over Ireland, really suffer a surprising release from his paralyzing egotism in shedding "generous tears" (223) for his wife's sense of lost love? Or is this just

Joyce's last savage twist of the ironic knife, as we recognize Gabriel's defeat in love expand, self-absorbedly, into the snowy apocalypse of the very universe? This is the critical dispute. And the reason for it is the mistaken critical focus on Gabriel. At story's end, it should be on what Greta and Gabriel Conroy and Joyce are making of Michael Furey. This is the story's focus. For Furey is the figure of romantic Ireland dead and gone and now returning to haunt the dismal present with a vision of greater possibilities. Furey is now more actively alive in Greta's memory, her husband's imagination, and Joyce's own text than any of the other Dubliners. Joyce, through the Conroys' final bedroom drama, recovers and delivers for critical understanding a mode of passionate being that dissolves, by contrast, the diminished present of mean-spiritedness and hypocrisy into slushy fragments. An outmoded or superannuated style of existence—romantic self-sacrifice—reappears both to judge all the living and the dead in post-Parnell Ireland by its higher standard and to offer that standard of a nobler vision to another generation for possible heroic repetition.

Such magnanimous visions drawn from the collective archive of literature can counter the mindless competitiveness and reductive displacements of the critical institution both by reminding us of the larger horizons of earlier epochs when modernization was not yet all in all and by guiding our work to make the future more (not less) human.

Notes

1. Cited in Stephan Salisbury, "Harold Bloom: A Massive Literary Undertaking," *Philadelphia Inquirer* 317 (December 23, 1987): 4F.

2. Stanley Fish, "Change," *South Atlantic Quarterly* 86, no. 1 (Fall 1986): 423–44. Hereafter all references to this essay will be given in the text.

3. Stanley Fish, "Commentary: The Young and the Restless," in *The New Historicism*, ed. H. Aram Veeser (New York and London: 1989), 308.

4. Jonathan Arac, *Critical Genealogies: Historical Situations for Postmodern Literary Studies* (New York: 1987), 17–18.

5. Fredric Jameson, "On *Habits of the Heart*," *South Atlantic Quarterly* 86, no. 1 (Fall 1987): 553. Hereafter all references to this essay will be given in the text.

6. Gerald Graff, *Professing Literature: An Institutional History* (Chicago: 1987), 5. Hereafter all references to this book will be given in the text.

7. Richard Poirier, *The Renewal of Literature: Emersonian Reflections* (New York: 1987). All references to this book will be given in the text.

8. "Large Red Man Reading," *The Collected Poems of Wallace Stevens* (New York: 1954), 423–24.

9. James Joyce, *Dubliners: Text, Criticism, and Notes,* ed. Robert Scholes and A. Walton Litz (New York: 1969). All references to this book will be given in the text.

CHAPTER 4

Irreconcilable Differences
Kant, Hegel, and the "Idea" of Critical History

Suzanne Gearhart

I

After a period marked by concern for the problems of language, structure, and the self-reflexive, autonomous nature of linguistic and literary objects, few would disagree that within the field of theory a general "return to history" is now well under way. At such a time it is especially important to raise anew the question of the critical function of history. For surely an important part of the impetus for at least some of the work now being done in the name of such a return is a desire to escape from what is seen as the abstract, speculative nature of theory and to focus on more concrete, palpable, "real" issues. In its simplest form this desire involves closing one's eyes to the theoretical advances of recent years and the problems they raise for any return to history. And it proposes, as something new, a historicism largely indistinguishable from nineteenth-century historicism, for an important goal of the latter was also to preserve the individual, the concrete, the unique, the real, from systematic philosophies or theories, which were seen as reducing them to mere elements of an abstract totality.

It is thus possible to return to history in a way that is ahistorical—that is, in a way that ignores the historical and hence problematic nature of history itself and thus also its critical possibilities. If there is to be a return to history that is not merely regressive, then it should not ignore but rather come to terms with the theoretical developments that precede the present moment. I am speaking both of those of the recent past and of the particular historical moment that is my focus in this essay. To do this, it does not suffice—though it is an important first step—to remain aware of the limits of traditional history and open to alternative models of history. The project of a critical history should also entail an investigation of the theoretical and practical contradictions and limitations of *any* attempt to define and practice history. A critical history would have to be always ready to question its own basic assumptions, however empirical or self-evident, however deeply rooted in tradition, logic, or rhetoric, or even in the exigencies of the contemporary moment they may seem to be. It would also have to remain open to the future, to the different and the new, to unforeseen and unforeseeable alternatives and possibilities. This is clearly a lot to ask of history, and it may be too much. Indeed, the idea of (a critical) history is problematic precisely because it is not certain that *any* history can meet such an uncompromising demand for (self-)reflection.

Despite its problematic character, I would argue that what I am calling "critical history" is a central if not the central concern of several of the most prominent modern French theorists and that their work provides valuable insights into the nature and possibility of such a history. For all these theorists, the work of Hegel represents an especially powerful form and interpretation of history. As a result, their interpretations of history have often taken the form of a critique of Hegel and an attempt to elaborate a non-Hegelian concept of history, and even in some cases a non-Hegelian practice of history. Of course, very important differences exist between the figures I shall be mentioning—differences that I in no way wish to depreciate, though a discussion of their significance is not relevant to my analysis here. Nonetheless, in their various positions with respect to Hegel and history it is possible to discern common theoretical interests that help to delineate an area in which the possibility of a critical history is being elaborated.

In his inaugural lecture for the Collège de France ("The Discourse on Language"),[1] Michel Foucault speaks for many others when he writes: "I know . . . our age, whether through logic or epistemology, whether through Marx or through Nietzsche, is attempting to flee Hegel. . . . But to truly escape Hegel involves an exact appreciation of the price we have to pay to detach ourselves from him. It assumes that we are aware of the extent to which Hegel, insidiously perhaps, is close to us; it implies a knowledge, in that which permits us to think against Hegel, of that which remains Hegelian" (235). From the perspective Foucault sketches in this lecture, his own work can be seen as an attempt to define history against Hegel, though it is clearly an attempt that also is aware of the shortcomings of any purely anti-Hegelian strategy. Where Hegel stresses that reason and history are one, Foucault seeks to write a history of madness; where Hegel seeks to guarantee historical continuity through a dialectical process that links opposing or discontinuous terms, Foucault attempts to break with the various forms of historical continuity and in particular with historical narrative. Whereas Hegel writes the history of the subject, Foucault focuses his "histories" on themes that reveal the precarious—or in any case the derivative—status of the subject.

Jacques Derrida is another philosopher who, from a different position, also has sought to redefine history "against" Hegel. From the early essay that prefaces his translation of Husserl's "The Origin of Geometry" to his essays in *Writing and Difference* and *Margins of Philosophy* (and even including *Glas*),[2] Derrida has sought to define what I would call an alternative to Hegelian history. According to the model offered more or less explicitly by Derrida in these various essays, this alternative history would differ from a traditional or Hegelian history in several ways, three of which are perhaps of special importance for Derrida. First, it would recognize and affirm the determining role played by language in relation to historical intention and historical consciousness. Second, it would no longer presuppose the existence of a linear time, composed of successive presents, but would respond to those aspects of history that defy linearity, that delay "the event" (or anticipate it), and that, in doing so, not only complicate temporality but ultimately make it impossible to speak of time (or history) in the singular. Third, it would no longer accept as self-evident the notion of historical context. Instead, it would recognize both the relative autonomy of events from their context and, correlatively, the complexity of history, a complexity that prevents the historical process from ever being adequately treated in terms of *a* (single) context.

Louis Althusser's reinterpretation of Marxism is another significant attempt to redefine history in opposition to Hegel. The focus of Althusser's work on Marx has been to determine the precise point at which Marx breaks with Hegel. This is the criterion by which he distinguishes the younger and the older Marx, the Marx still imprisoned in idealism from the scientific Marx. Unlike Hegel's, Althusser argues, Marx's sense of history is an "open" one in which contradiction is no longer taken to be a secondary or derivative process in relation to the historical totality, and in which totality, in turn, is no longer thinkable or graspable "from the outside." Althusser thus defends Marx and history against critics who have seen both as totalitarian, but he does so by accepting this criticism as it relates to Hegel.

It is important to stress that for these thinkers, the various empiricisms and historicisms are all complicitous with the Hegelian model of history. For despite the empiricist/historicist's suspicion of or even hostility to a conception of history that emphasizes the "concreteness" of the concept as opposed to the isolated fact and the crucial importance of philosophy for history, the concept of history he or she presupposes—and no empiricism or historicism is without an implicit concept of history—is still comprehended within a general Hegelian context. The basic assumptions of journeyman historians concerning history—that is, the belief in the overriding unity of history, the implicit view that time and historical causation are natural phenomena, that historical narrative and language do not have fundamental, constructive roles in the writing of history—all link historians to rather than dissociate them from Hegel.

Jean-François Lyotard is another thinker whose name figures prominently among those French theorists working to define a non-Hegelian concept of history. For Lyotard, Hegel's philosophy and its many avatars represent a general theoretical context in which and against which critical thought must define itself. In this sense, two recent books, *Le Différend* and *L'Enthousiasme, la critique kantienne de l'histoire*, can be seen as the culmination of a critique of Hegel that runs throughout Lyotard's work.[3] Lyotard's critical reading of Hegel and the Hegelian tradition uncovers a complex of characteristics or ethico-theoretical decisions that determine Hegel's system: for example, the privilege given to reason as opposed to judgment or will, to representation as opposed to the "unpresentable," and to a narrative that unfolds in dialectical fashion as well as to the dialectic itself as opposed to antinomies and *différends*.

Because of the project Lyotard shares to some extent with the other figures I have mentioned, there are important points of overlap between his work and theirs. But there are also differences in Lyotard's position that make his work particularly revealing of certain aspects of the attempt to develop a critical history. First is the emphasis—even the privilege—Lyotard gives to the philosophy of Kant. While Derrida and Foucault have also written on Kant, Lyotard is alone in placing Kant at the center of his critique of history. Another related feature that distinguishes Lyotard's discussion of history from theirs is the "militancy" of his opposition to Hegel. Of all these thinkers, Lyotard is certainly the least interested in exploring what "remains Hegelian" in any attempt to rethink history. But precisely because of his militancy and the corresponding privilege he ascribes to Kant in relation to Hegel, Lyotard's version of the critique of Hegel is perhaps the most revealing of the dramatic nature of the theoretical tensions involved in the attempt to define history critically.

Kant's philosophy is important for Lyotard in large measure because it provides him with a critical perspective on the philosophy of Hegel, and *Le Différend* attempts to articulate a critique of Hegel implicit in certain aspects of Kant's philosophy. Hegel has left us with numerous passages in which he both acknowledges the importance of but also criticizes Kant's work. Lyotard's interpretation of Kant is intended to articulate a "Kantian" response to Hegel, or at any rate a (post)modern response to Hegel that takes its inspiration from the philosophy of Kant. Lyotard's critique of Hegel is a highly paradoxical one, to say the least, for it claims that Hegel's system excludes nothing less than history itself. As Lyotard argues in his essay on Fredric Jameson's *The Political Unconscious*, from a Kantian perspective "history . . . is neither a narration nor a representation, it is never presented as history *per se*. It is what presents without presenting itself. . . . It is the 'real,' what escapes symbolization, even methodological symbolization. History is totality, but this totality is only a horizon."[4] When history is defined in this way, it becomes what Kant calls an "Idea of reason, the antithesis of a concept" in the positivist and also in the Hegelian sense ("The Unconscious, History, and Phrases," 73). Because, Lyotard argues, for Hegel history is precisely a system of representation, a narrative, and a concrete totality, what is putatively the most historical of all philosophies is in reality the most hostile to history.

Whereas other modern thinkers might stress the "teleological" character of the Kantian idea and the unquestioned assumptions concerning unity and the human subject that underlie it, Lyotard, on the contrary, stresses its unpresentable character and its critical possibilities. The idea is for him the antithesis of the Hegelian concept or absolute, because it does not close off the historical process and define a totality in the sense the Hegelian concept does. Because the unity it provides is purely formal, the heterogeneity of history can be respected and even affirmed in terms of the idea. When interpreted in such a light, the transcendental character of the Kantian idea appears to have a "positive" value, one that resides precisely in its utter negativity, in its lack of any content that would predetermine the nature of history. If historians for whom history is unpresentable can no longer write a history in the traditional sense, still they can do something even more important: attempt to give voice to the claims of those mute subjects and forgotten objects not represented in (Hegelian) history. The privilege Lyotard gives Kant is so enormous, precisely because for Lyotard he is the philosophical representative of all that history has excluded—because his philosophy is virtually unique in providing a framework for redressing the grievances of those who have been robbed of or removed from history.

Lyotard's work on Kant, then, is concerned above all with the unpresentable—whether it is thought of in terms of specific historical events that seem to defy the historical categories of Hegelian history or as history itself in its (open-ended) "unity." The special value of his work, as I have already indicated, lies in the radical manner in which he presents the contrast between Kant and Hegel, between a potentially critical history and Hegelian history. In Lyotard's exigency that history "present" the unpresentable, there is a demand not just for another version or form of history, but also for something seemingly impossible: that history negate itself in order to become truly critical. In this sense, Lyotard's "Kantian" perspective on history seems hopelessly self-contradictory, what Hegel might have called a mere "ought-to-be" without any content. But the force of Lyotard's analysis is that it makes the alternative appear equally impossible. It indicates that the price of equating history with what is, is ultimately to equate what is with what ought to be and implicitly justify the exclusions and silences that are of necessity part of all positive histories.

The possibility of a critical history, then, is highly problematic, for it is suspended between these two radically contradictory alternatives, one "Kantian," the other "Hegelian," one that obeys a "transcendental" imperative, but at the price of a certain abstraction, and one that reconciles the suprasensible and the sensible, the rational and the real, at the potential price of silencing any voice not deemed to be rational or real. My own aim in reading Kant and Hegel with Lyotard is thus not to establish that Kant's philosophy can, by itself, provide us with a critical history. Instead, I would argue, the sense of what such a history might be only begins to emerge when the theoretical conflict between Kant and Hegel is understood not as the moment of a dialectic in which one in effect sublates the other, but rather as "tragic"—that is, as a conflict in which, to borrow Hegel's terms, the principals are opposed precisely because the claim of each to represent the ethical (or in this case the historical) is equally legitimate. And just as in *Antigone*, which serves as Hegel's model for tragedy, "there is immanent in both Antigone and Creon something that in their own way they attack,"[5] so the conflict or *différend* between Kant and Hegel is so deep precisely because it is located as much in the work of each as in the relation of the work of each to the other.

II

The central importance of the theme of history in relation to Kant's philosophy is already apparent from the standpoint of Hegel's work itself, for it contains one of the first interpretations—and certainly the most important early one—of Kant's philosophy to be oriented by a concern for history. Indeed, in reading Hegel, Lyotard must not only confront a powerful philosophical interpretation of history, he must also confront a powerful interpretation of Kant's philosophy. Even if history is not at all times the explicit theme of Hegel's interpretation of Kant, his condensation of history and philosophy is so pervasive that, at the very least, the problem of history must be considered central to his reading of Kant as it is to every other aspect of his work. But as one could easily show, those moments where Hegel deals with Kant have a particular decisiveness. For in confronting Kant, Hegel confronts a particularly serious challenge to his version of philosophy and history.

The thrust of Hegel's critique of Kant is already evident in the preface to the *Phenomenology*, where Hegel writes: "Of course, the *triadic form* must not be regarded as scientific when it is reduced to a lifeless schema, a mere shadow, and when scientific organization is degraded into a table of terms. Kant rediscovered this triadic form by instinct, but in his work it was still lifeless and uncomprehended."[6] The long passage on Kant in the introduction to the *Aesthetics* is essentially an elaboration of this basic argument—that Kant's philosophy is an aborted dialectic, or a Hegelian philosophy without life. Hegel's aim is to resuscitate this lifeless form, to give it the life it lacks in Kant's philosophy—that is, to make it historical.

The interpretation Hegel gives in his *Aesthetics* of Kant's *Critique of Judgment* pinpoints what are, in Hegel's view, the deficiencies of Kant's philosophy. It also in a sense enacts the overcoming of those deficiencies by Hegelian philosophy. By the end of his discussion, the Kantian system has become a "stage" for Hegel's; it has become the implicit form of what has only become explicit with Hegel himself. What Kant implicitly says or shows, according to Hegel, is the role art plays as the mediator of opposition:

> The beauty of art is one of the means which dissolve and reduce to unity
> the . . . opposition and contradiction between the abstractly self-concentrated
> spirit and nature—both the nature of external phenomena and that of inner
> subjective feeling and emotion. It is the *Kantian* philosophy which has not
> only felt the need for this point of union, but has also clearly recognized it
> and brought it before our minds. (*Aesthetics,* 56)

At the most profound level, Hegel argues, Kant's *Critique of Judgment* presents the aesthetic as the third term bridging the opposition between "concept and reality, universal and particular, understanding and sense" (*Aesthetics*, 57). The secret élan of Kant's work is a hidden dialectic that guides it toward the reconciliation of the oppositions that structure it.

In this reading of Kant, history is present both as an explicit theme of Hegel's interpretation and as a formal and methodological concern. For history is the realm in which "external reality and existence," on the one hand, and the "*absolute*" (*Aesthetics*, 53), on the other, are opposed and reconciled. At the same time history is also the very process of opposition and reconciliation—it is the dialectic. By recognizing the "point of union" between spirit and nature, the *absolute* and existence, Kant's philosophy presents us with history—the dialectic—itself. Hegel nonetheless signifies to the reader that Kant's philosophy is *only* an implicit form of his own when he concludes that Kant's attempt to reconcile these opposites ultimately fails. Though the conciliation of opposites in Kant's work is "in appearance complete," it is, Hegel argues, really "only subjective, . . . it does not correspond to truth and reality in themselves" (*Aesthetics*, 122).

The heart of Hegel's interpretation of Kant lies in these two *apparently* contradictory points of view. Implicitly, Kant is a historical thinker who reconciles opposites. Explicitly, he is a failed dialectical thinker who does not succeed in attaining the reconciliation secretly intended by his work. From Hegel's standpoint this means that the philosophy of Kant is implicitly a philosophy of/as history and explicitly an ahistorical philosophy. For if, in the last instance, reconciliation is absent from Kant's philosophy, then history itself is absent. According to Hegel, the source of Kant's ultimate failure as a historical thinker is the subjective nature of the reconciliation in his philosophy. Though Hegel's precise meaning and the broader significance of this judgment is not altogether clear in the passages quoted from the *Aesthetics*, it is important to keep the association Hegel makes between the subjective and the ahistorical in mind. By implication, if one begins to interpret or reinterpret the problem of history in terms of the Kantian subject, then one is engaged in overturning Hegel's notion of history.

In the texts Kant devotes to the problem of history, it is difficult not to be struck by the force and plausibility of Hegel's interpretation. Modest and almost circumstantial though it may seem, the "Idea for a Universal History," for example, proposes a reconciliation of the opposition between freedom and necessity, between the phenomenal and the noumenal realms. It is as if Kant were here looking for the bridge that, as Hegel would have it, the *Critique of Judgment* fails to provide. Elsewhere Kant asks, "How is a history a priori possible?" and he gives an ironic reply: "if the diviner [i.e., the historian of events that have not yet happened] himself creates and contrives the events which he announces in advance."[7] But in the "Idea for a Universal History" it seems that Kant is responding to the same question in a more straightforward though still humorous fashion. A universal history would be a history a priori, that is, a history guided by an idea for which there is a corresponding, albeit negative, intuition. The idea in the case of history would be none other than reason, and in order to "see" it in history, the historian does not have to be a diviner but has only to interpret the implicit sense of history, to recognize that the principle linking the events of history together is reason itself, in the guise of nature:

> By "antagonism" I mean the unsocial sociability of men. . . . This opposition it is which awakens all his [man's] powers, brings him to conquer his inclination to laziness and, propelled by vainglory, lust for power, and avarice, to achieve a rank among his fellows whom he cannot tolerate but from whom he cannot withdraw. Thus are taken the first true steps from barbarism to culture. . . . Thanks be to Nature, then, for the incompatibility, for heartless competitive vanity, for the insatiable desire to possess and to rule! Without them, all the excellent capacities of humanity would forever sleep, undeveloped.[8]

Thus the "folly, childish vanity, . . . childish malice and destructiveness" of "men's actions on the world-stage" do not simply hide a natural (rational) purpose. They in fact *fulfill* the purpose of reason, of a clever reason that employs means apparently incompatible with its nature yet nonetheless manages to make them serve its own ends. The difference between Kant's interpretation of history in this text and Hegel's interpretation in his *Lectures on the Philosophy of History* is so slight as to appear to be nonexistent. The term "ruse of reason" is not expressly employed by Kant, but it seems that only the term is missing.

One could say, then, that Hegelian philosophy is born out of Kant's failure to reconcile the contradictions of his own system; Hegelian philosophy is already implicitly "at work" in Kantian philosophy. Thus it seems that what Kant has to tell us about history is said even more directly and explicitly by Hegel. But one could also argue that Hegel's reading of Kant, which "opens" Kantian philosophy to Hegelian philosophy, also "opens" Hegel's philosophy to that of Kant. Once Hegel has decided to construct or interpret his own philosophy as the *Aufhebung* of Kant's, then Kantian philosophy becomes a constitutive moment of Hegelian philosophy. The philosophy of Kant ceases to be an exterior limit of Hegelian philosophy and becomes instead an interior limit dividing it as much from itself as from what is external to it. Similarly, Kant's failure to achieve reconciliation becomes a permanent risk *within* Hegel's system, a form of radical alterity that inhabits the dialectic itself and gives the dialectic its own contradictions and its own historicity.

III

I would argue that Lyotard's reading of Kant, despite the many passages in his work in which Lyotard explicitly contrasts his own or Kant's philosophy with that of Hegel, in many respects strongly resembles Hegel's, for Lyotard focuses on themes and strategies similar to those found in Hegel's texts. But at the same time Lyotard pushes those themes and strategies to a limit where their sense is radically transformed. The question is, just how radically? In other words, can Lyotard in the end sustain his more or less explicit claim to have found in Kant's philosophy terms that permit him to articulate the problem of history in a way radically different from Hegel? Can history as Lyotard redefines it be considered truly critical? Any return to history is obliged to "plunge into" the history of philosophy and history precisely because these questions are anything but rhetorical, that is, because the critical value of history is a *problem*.[9]

Lyotard's investigation of the problem of history from the perspective of Kant in a sense begins in the *concluding* chapter of *Le Différend*, entitled "The Sign of History," when he asks what the status of history might be from the perspective of the Kantian "critical judge." His initial answer is a restatement of Hegel's thesis that there is a gulf between Kant's philosophy and the problem of history, between Kant and the post-Kantian tradition. Insofar as history implies the constitution of series of events and insofar as there can be an intuition that corresponds to the event, history falls under the jurisdiction of the understanding. But Lyotard argues, following Kant, that an "abyss" exists between history and judgment, the same abyss that exists between understanding and judgment. What concerns the critical judge is whether or not history is progressing toward some end and, specifically, toward the full realization of human rational potential. But given the gulf that exists between reason and understanding, or between the transcendental and the empirical, it is obvious that there can be no empirical evidence of the kind of history (progress) that alone is of interest to the critical judge: "So much, in brief, for the cognitive phrase: it doesn't have much to say about history that could be validated by the critical judge" (*Le Différend*, 234).

Lyotard's reading thus begins where many others have ended, and, to an important extent, he respects their conclusions. His aim is not to close the abyss between understanding and judgment or between Kant and history. In his terms, it cannot be closed without succumbing to what Kant denounces in the "Dialectic of Pure Reason" as the transcendental illusion, according to which ideas of reason are thought to correspond to phenomena just as intuitions and concepts do, that is, without making Kant's notion of progress into a dialectic. In the brief passage on the critical judge and his perspective on history, a crucial aspect of Lyotard's reading of Kant has already begun to emerge. Throughout *Le Différend* an essential part of Lyotard's strategy is to confirm and affirm the value and necessity of the abyss, that is of irresolvable difference (in this case, among the Kantian faculties), which he designates with the term *le différend*: "a *différend* is a case of conflict between at least two parties that cannot be equitably resolved because of the lack of a rule of judgment applicable" to the arguments of each party (*Le Différend*, 9). His aim in reinterpreting Kant in terms of a notion of *différend* is to respect and treat contradiction *as such*, rather than taking it as a moment of a dialectical process that leads in all instances toward reconciliation. As Lyotard puts it, the critical judge "makes his ruling without there being any rule to authorize him, except perhaps the principle that heterogeneity must be respected affirmatively" (*L'Enthousiasme*, 42–43).

Still, like Kant himself, Lyotard conceives of the *Critique of Judgment* (and particularly of the "Critique of Aesthetic Judgment") as a "bridge" spanning the abyss—though not closing it. As a consequence, he sees the Third *Critique* as occupying the place of or indicating the way toward an implicit political philosophy and a certain critical perspective on history. True, the aesthetic and the historical are quite different: he even cautions that the aesthetic and, in particular, the enthusiasm that accompanies certain forms of aesthetic judgment are "pathological" from an ethico-political standpoint (*Le Différend*, 240). Nonetheless, Lyotard typically argues that the aesthetic in general can provide a valuable analogy for the historico-political.

The analogical principle is a key to Lyotard's rereading of Kant. In fact the analogy can be considered one of the principal figures of *le différend* in the sense that, in formal terms, it maintains difference even as it makes possible a certain degree of reconciliation. But there is an important instance in which Lyotard himself comes very close to contravening the spirit of analogy. Like Hannah Arendt, Lyotard places special emphasis on the passage from "An Old Question Raised Again: Is the Human Race Constantly Progressing?" in which Kant declares the enthusiasm felt by the spectators of the French Revolution to be a proof of moral progress, the sign of a history that conforms to a priori principles. And also like Arendt, Lyotard underscores the affinity between this enthusiasm and Kant's notion of the sublime (*Le Différend*, 238).[10] Lyotard's reading of this passage must be considered a cornerstone of his reading of Kant, for, Lyotard argues, in it one finds "in a succinct and even condensed form the thought, perhaps all the thought, of Kant concerning the historico-political" (*L'Enthousiasme*, 58). The passage on the spectators of the French Revolution is so important because in it, Lyotard argues, we can see that aesthetic judgment and especially the enthusiasm that accompanies estimates of the sublime are *more* than an analogy.

What makes the enthusiasm felt by the spectators of the French Revolution more than an analogy is that, in this instance, the "sublime feeling" occurs "in experience," that is, "within" the realm of history:

> Given if not *by* experience at least *within* experience, "made available," the *Begebenheit* must be the decisive index of the Idea of free causality. With it the rims of the abyss to be surmounted between mechanism and freedom or finality, between the domain of the sensible world and the suprasensible field, almost close without, nonetheless, doing away with it, and this infinitesimal gap suffices for establishing the inconsistent, perhaps indeterminate, but sayable and even "decisive" status of the historico-political. (237)

In the philosophical-historical event described by Kant, experience and idea almost meet, without suppressing or bridging the abyss between them. But here perhaps more clearly than anywhere else, an "impasse" serves as a "passage" (239).

The gap between the realm of experience and the realm of freedom calls for a bridge, and it is in *not* being bridged that the two realms make contact. The logic of Kant's philosophy as a whole and his critique of aesthetic judgment in particular tend toward a reconciliation of the difference between the realm of experience and the realm of freedom, but at the same time the nature of the distinction between the two spheres is such that they remain what they are only in their separation. A "dialectic" is thus at work here, but it works against itself as well as against opposition. According to the logic of *le différend,* the need for opposition and difference is exactly equal to the need for reconciliation. This conflict produces an impasse, but the impasse is not an obstacle to history or to understanding the critical possibilities of history. Those possibilities rest with the impasse itself, understood as a form of passage.

The historico-political is not, then, so much a hidden object of Kant's philosophical discourse as a gap in his philosophical system—an abyss that the *Begebenheit* itself does not completely obliterate, but to which it in some sense testifies. But it is not a gap in the sense that the historical is omitted or elided by Kant. This gap is *significant*, and its meaning lies in its emptiness. The contours of the gap define the space of the historical even though what they contain is not revealed in itself, even though the historical as defined by this gap has no positive content or concept.

"The Sign of History" is written as though the imperative for maintaining and articulating le différend as such came from, to use Hegel's term, the absolute or, to use Kant and Lyotard's term, the idea and as though the great danger to the sense of the historical implied by Kant's aesthetics comes from the realm of experience. Indeed, according to Lyotard, this is often the case. That is to say, when the Kantian idea is reduced to or equated with an empirical object, when the idea of a republican community is linked to an existing society as form to content, then Kant's political philosophy as Lyotard interprets it is betrayed and becomes indistinguishable from the political philosophies traceable to Hegel and his conflation of knowledge and will. In such instances the republican ideal becomes a totalitarian reality, and history, by implication, ceases to be a matter of judgment, becoming instead a (pseudo)science.

Le Différend as a whole, however, hints at the existence of another danger whose source lies "within" Kant's philosophy itself. It would be putting words into Lyotard's mouth to say that this second danger comes from the idea itself, or even that this second danger is that posed by the idea to the realm of experience. But something like this does appear to be the case for Lyotard. In its remoteness from experience, the idea is guilty of a kind of hubris for which Lyotard seeks a corrective. This, I feel, is why Lyotard constantly stresses perhaps more than Kant the need for a point of contact between the empirical and the transcendental as well as the separation of the two. It is in this sense, I would argue, that despite the opposition to Hegelian thought professed by Lyotard, his concern is as much with Hegel as with Kant—that is, if Kant can be said to provide Lyotard with a critical perspective on history and on Hegel, Hegel can be said to provide him with a critical perspective on Kant.

The search for a corrective leads Lyotard to a reinterpretation of the Kantian theory of intuition. If history from a Kantian perspective is to be understood in terms of a relationship (a différend) between idea and experience, then Kant's theory of intuition is crucial, for it is here that he provides a model for experience that has been reduced to its barest elements. If the idea can be seen to be if not immanent then at least in some sense "at work" in the most basic forms of experience, then the "impasse" can truly be said to provide a "passage" and Kant can truly be said to have a perspective on history that is both critical and affirmative.

The heart of Lyotard's interpretation of Kantian intuition lies in the distinction he makes between the way intuition has been theorized by the "philosophy of the subject" and the way it is presented by Kant; here, as at other key moments of Le Différend, Kant is being contrasted with Hegel. There is clearly something provocative about this contrast, because for most readers the philosophical notion of the subject evokes Kant's name as readily as and perhaps even more readily than any other. In the conclusion to L'Enthousiasme, Lyotard himself acknowledges that in certain respects Kant's philosophy is a philosophy of the subject and that, in this sense, a tension exists between Kant's notion of the subject and the notions of heterogeneity or of le différend in terms of which Lyotard reinterprets Kant. The Kantian notion of the subject does play a role in limiting dispersion and difference, and Kant can rightfully be seen as taking steps to protect the unity of the subject and assure that it does not "fly to pieces." Lyotard continues: "We today, and that is part of the Begebenheit of our time, sense that the fission that is given in [our Begebenheit] touches the subject as well" (L'Enthousiasme, 113).

Nonetheless, Lyotard's reading of Kant indicates that there is something in Kant's notion of the subject that authorizes us to betray the unifying principle it also represents in the context of his thought and to make the Kantian subject the point of departure for a rethinking of difference and the articulation of a radical sense of history. In very general terms, the theme of judgment, which Lyotard places at the center of his reinterpretation of Kant, is indissociable from the notion of the subject— to make history a matter of judgment is implicitly to attempt to understand it from the perspective of the Kantian subject. For the critical judge who judges history has no concept (and no corresponding intuition) to which to refer. He must judge with reference to an idea of reason whose source can only be the critical judge—the subject—himself. As Lyotard puts it, "What Kant persists (but it is perhaps the problematic of the subject that persists in his place) in calling the faculty of judgment, is the determination of the mode of presentation of the object appropriate for each family [of phrases]" (L'Enthousiasme, 33). The problem of judgment and the problem of the subject are perhaps at bottom one and the same.

In ways that are both explicit and implicit, the subject has an important role to play in Lyotard's interpretation of the Kantian theory of intuition. Though Kant's subject may bear a resemblance to that of Hegel, according to Lyotard they are not the same.[11] The philosophy of the subject, Lyotard argues, understands intuition by distinguishing receptivity from activity and by subordinating one to the other in the various aspects of intuition. This permits the philosophy of the subject to represent intuition as a line in which the "given" is first made available to the subject, then received by the subject, and finally processed by the subject, that is, given a sense. But, Lyotard argues: "In fact . . . the constitution of the given by sensibility" cannot be represented by a single line/sequence (or "phrase"). It takes two lines to represent intuition. The subject is already "active" *in* the given, impressing sensation with the forms of space and time: "The 'immediacy' of the given, as one can see, is not immediate. The constitution of the given requires on the contrary an exchange of roles between the . . . subject and object" (*Le Différend*, 97). Thus, while one must say that the subject is (also) receptive in intuition, this receptivity is never pure. Instead, it is paralleled by activity at every stage of intuition ("The subject is therefore neither active nor passive" [*Le Différend*, 100]).

But it is precisely because the subject is neither active nor passive, because the object is never simply given, that it is still present in the phenomenon ultimately intuited by the subject. The given is not a referent until it is given form by space and time, but what one could call the trace of the given is still clearly discernible in the referential function of the phenomenon. Lyotard argues that by superposing form, whose existence implies an active subject, and matter, which must "address" itself to the subject for there to be intuition, "transcendental idealism comes to blanket ["recouvrir"] empirical realism. It does not erase it. There is a first 'phrase,' and it does not come from the subject" (*Le Différend*, 99).

Whereas in the philosophy of the subject it takes only one line to map intuition, in Kant's *Critique of Pure Reason* there are two lines, one emanating from matter, the other from the subject. These lines never cross each other in a "now" of intuition, but it is for precisely this reason that they can be said to be constantly in touch. Once again, we find ourselves confronted with an analogy and a difference—between transcendental idealism and empirical realism, or between the "in itself" and intuition. And once again, difference is treated affirmatively by Kant.

According to the logic of Lyotard's reading, the value of Kant's theory of intuition is that it provides us with a model of a subject that is fundamentally open to experience. By implication, Hegel's subject is not open in the same way, for it always finds itself in its object. As Lyotard puts it, the Hegelian subject occupies not only its own position but that of the referent in the Hegelian model of the "phrase" (*Le Différend*, 138). Reconciliation is always possible in Hegel's system because it is always a matter of reconciling the subject with itself. Reconciliation is the basis of the dialectic, and the dialectic is in turn what defines history for Hegel. And yet the dialectic is precisely what, in Lyotard's terms, obliterates the possibility of genuine experience or history, that is, of an experience that "happens to" the subject rather than being the mere exteriorization of that subject. For Hegel, the movement in which the subject alienates itself in experience is always merely a moment in a process that leads back to the subject. But for Kant, the "alienation" is in a sense structural, because the subject will never find itself in (the object of) experience. Experience will always have to be given to an intuition that cannot provide itself with its own object. The boundary between the subject and object or between the subject and experience is not just an obstacle to be overcome but a difference to be respected. Though in general terms Lyotard's reading of Kant places special emphasis on the Second and Third *Critiques*, his analysis of the theory of intuition elaborated by the First *Critique* shows that the *différend* he affirms is as evident in the latter as in the former. It is as much the abyss between subject and object as between understanding and judgment or will.

In the minimal model of history provided by Kant's theory of intuition, history becomes "what happens" to a subject. (Lyotard uses the expression "il arrive"—it happens.) But *what* exactly happens? The terms of Lyotard's description of the historical event are as minimal when he discusses the object or event that impinges on consciousness when something happens as they are when he defines history as what happens. What happens is quite simply a *what* (a "quoi" [114]). Because the subject is active in intuition and not just passive, intuition does not yield the thing-in-itself. One could say that we have no knowledge of the event as a content. What we do know and experience is the event as an event— as something that "happens." This, if you will, is its reality.

The situation of the perceiving subject is thus fundamentally analogous to that of the subject who judges in matters of taste, for whom the object provides an occasion with which the subject does not provide itself. What is given in history and experience is quite simply history and experience themselves, the reality principle, if you will. What is not given is everything else that one might associate with the notion of history. This means that history is as much a matter of judgment as of "science"—and perhaps much more so—or that the scientist himself is in the position of the critical judge. For even the *series*, the determination that one event comes after another, which constitutes the basis of all history (and all science insofar as it is dependent upon notions of cause and effect) is in no way given: "The series is not given, it is the object of an Idea" (*L'Enthousiasme*, 45–46). The most rudimentary history imaginable, then, because it would necessitate the determination of a "before" and an "after," would still be a matter of judgment.[12]

This does not mean that historical events have no "objective reality" from Kant's perspective. The reality of the event is a corollary of intuition itself as the faculty to which something must be given. But the nature of intuition, which makes it necessary that something be given in order for there to be experience, also dictates that what is experienced is the phenomenon and not the thing-in-itself, that experience is always the experience of a (or the) subject. One could say that it is precisely because the Kantian subject is situated by and open to experience that for it history is of necessity a matter of judgment.

What this means for Lyotard is that history from a Kantian perspective is a matter of sentiment or even of enthusiasm, for the critical judge judges not with reference to the object, which in this case is an occasion for judgment, but rather with reference to the subject itself insofar as it is affected by experience. Since the subject cannot be known, feeling (or self-affection) is the only possible mode of relationship the subject can entertain with itself. As Kant puts it:

> We must also admit, with regard to the internal sense, that by it we only are, or perceive ourselves, as we are internally affected by ourselves, in other words, that with regard to internal intuition we know our own self as a phenomenon only, and not as it is by itself.[13]

Lyotard reminds us that Kant's conception of self-affection or feeling can only be properly understood if one remembers his harsh criticism of *Schwärmerei*, that is, of the "tumult of exaltation" (*L'Enthousiasme*, 63). The feeling at the basis of judgment borders on but is nonetheless distinct from emotion in the sense in which it is understood by the psychologist. It is, if you will, a feeling without emotional content, for it refers only to the subject itself understood as an "I think" (or an "I feel"). In this sense it is perhaps less misleading to say that history—whether it is the collective historical memory of a people or the historical text of an individual historian—is always autobiographical. Because it is a matter of judgment, history always engages what is most profound, most essential, in the subject.

But the subject too is "minimal" in Lyotard's interpretation of Kant's theory of intuition, for it has become merely the horizon within which something occurs. In this respect the Kantian subject is analogous to the idea (perhaps it *is* the idea). For like the idea, the subject is not a concept—that is to say, neither can be referred back to an intuition. Thus it is somewhat misleading to say that history is what happens to a subject. Strictly speaking, the subject, like the object, merges with the "what happens." This is why Lyotard uses the expression "il arrive" to describe the occurrence. Something happens, but neither the something (object) nor the subject is any longer indicated in this expression, only the occurrence that at the same time unites and separates them.

In Lyotard's attempt to rethink the Kantian notion of the subject in contrast to the Hegelian notion of the subject, his reading of Kant can be said to converge in many respects with that of Heidegger in *Kant and the Problem of Metaphysics*.[14] When Heidegger criticizes the traditional view of Kant's philosophy as a vindication of logic and reason divorced from experience, he redefines the subject as essentially a horizon for intuition and experience. Heidegger's reinterpretation of the problem of the Kantian subject focuses more particularly on the relationship between the subject and time. Lyotard himself also stresses the importance of the problem of time in his "Notice on Aristotle" in *Le Différend*, though he does not explicitly treat it in terms of Kant. Nonetheless, he does briefly allude to Heidegger and to "*Zeit und Sein* and the works of this period" (which would include *Kant and the Problem of Metaphysics*) and acknowledges the parallels between Heidegger's concept of the *Ereignis* and his own notion of the occurrence (*Le Différend*, 115).

In light of these very brief allusions and, more importantly, of the many similarities between Heidegger's and Lyotard's readings of Kant, it seems reasonable to conclude that *Kant and the Problem of Metaphysics* is a key part of the philosophical background of *Le Différend*. Even more, one could argue that Heidegger's text carries out a reading of an aspect of Kant's philosophy—his treatment of the problem of time—that is implicitly central to *Le Différend*, even though it is not explicitly treated. According to Heidegger's reading of Kant, the critical potential of the notions of history and temporality can be realized only if they are no longer conceived as mere attributes of the subject, substance, or Being but rather as its very "essence." Thus Heidegger's analysis of the relationship between temporality and subjectivity starts out from the premise that in previous interpretations of Kant has been accepted as self-evident—that for Kant time is subjective (*Kant*, 193). Heidegger's aim is not to disprove this thesis but rather, he implies, to understand its fullest and deepest implications. Whereas in the philosophy of Hegel, Spirit "falls into time," the implication is that in the (first version of the) *Critique of Pure Reason* the subject "*exists as* the primordial temporalizing of temporality."[15] Time is thus not something extraneous or secondary with respect to the subject; the subject *is* (pure) temporality and in this sense pure historicity. In the *Critique of Pure Reason*, Heidegger argues,

> Time and the "I think" are no longer opposed to one another as unlike and incompatible; they are the same. Thanks to the radicalism with which, in the laying of the foundation of metaphysics, Kant for the first time subjected time and the "I think," each taken separately, to a transcendental interpretation, he succeeded in bringing them together in their primordial identity. (*Kant*, 197)

This view of temporality relates directly to what both Heidegger and Lyotard have to say about intuition, in the sense that the "subjective" character of time is identical to the "subjective" character of intuition understood as active (Lyotard) or as "thinking intuition" (Heidegger). It is because time provides a horizon in which the essent (or phenomenon) offers itself to intuition that intuition "already" has the character of thought. In other words, it is precisely because of the "subjective" nature of the "reconciliation" between the subject and object in Kant's philosophy that it can be said to be truly open to temporality and history.

It is at this point in an analysis that is to an important extent common to both Lyotard and Heidegger that Kant's divergence from Hegel appears the most extreme. For as we have seen, Hegel argues that insofar as the reconciliation of opposition in Kant's philosophy is subjective in nature, history in the end must be argued to be absent from his work. But for Heidegger, it is precisely because of the "subjective character" Kant ascribes to time that Kant must be viewed as the philosopher who implicitly gives priority to the questions of history and temporality, who makes them no longer two questions among others confronted by philosophy but the very essence of a thought that in Heidegger's terms can no longer be considered to be strictly philosophical.

As much as Lyotard's analysis converges with Heidegger, Lyotard notes an important point of difference between them. In Heidegger's arguments concerning time, he always in the last instance insists on the importance of a distinction between an "essence of time" and a "vulgar"—that is, an at once empirical and metaphysical—notion of time as exemplified in the philosophy of Hegel. But Lyotard, referring to Derrida's analysis of Heidegger in the essay "Ousia et gramme,"[16] writes that "there is no 'vulgar' time, Derrida is right" (Le Différend, 115). In defining a Kantian perspective on history, Lyotard does not seek to establish a comparable distinction with respect to time. The Kantian subject in his reading is by implication as much one with a "vulgar" time as with a "pure temporality." Thus though Lyotard does not write about time in connection with Kant, he does consistently return to a problem intimately related to that of time understood in the most ordinary sense—the problem of the series.

Clearly the notion of a series presupposes time: there can be no sequence of any kind without temporality. The series, in turn, is of necessity presupposed by history: there is no history in the present or of the present, but only when there is a before and after. For Lyotard, as we have already seen, the series is subjective, that is to say "the series is not given, it is the object of an Idea" (L'Enthousiasme, 45–46). But just as for Heidegger the subjective nature of time must be understood in the strongest possible sense (subject and time must be understood as one), so one can argue that for Lyotard the subjective nature of the series must be understood in a strong sense (subject and series are one). The subject does not arrange moments or events in a series, the subject *is* the series understood as the serialization or "enchaînement" of occurrences. This is another sense in which one could say that events are not what happen to the subject; the subject is the event as it forms an element of a series.

For Lyotard too, then, the subject *is* history understood as the link between moments or events. But because of the minimal character of the subject, because the subject is a horizon for experience rather than, in Heidegger's terms, a "concrete self" (*Kant*, 194), the "law of history" does not permit us to predict events. It only dictates that there be history:

> If there is a necessity in history, it is a necessity that something happen. It is not possible for something not to happen. The necessity is not that this or that happens; on the contrary, *what* actually does happen is contingent, and that is why it is an event. . . . But *that* something happen (including what we call "nothing," as when we say "nothing's happening"), that is not contingent. The idea of necessity which is the humblest one possible, excludes the capitalization of history, for example, under the form of a totalizing dialectic. ("The Unconscious, History, and Phrases," 74)

The Kantian perspective on history can be considered critical precisely because it offers us so little. Despite what Kant argues in "An Old Question," one could say the most radical implication of his philosophy is that "one cannot extract an end" from history, "be it progress, regression, or eternal return" (*L'Enthousiasme*, 46). It is precisely for this reason that history does not constitute a totality and cannot be understood from a totalizing perspective—that is, that it cannot be given a specific interpretation or meaning within a given philosophical-historical system.

Thus while Lyotard takes up the theme of the subject and uses it as a starting point for the rethinking of history, it is important to see that *Le Différend* is not a call for a "return to the subject." In Lyotard's interpretation history never constitutes a totality, and by the same token the Kantian subject never succeeds in grasping itself reflexively. Instead, it is structurally alienated from itself, thanks to its dependence on intuition and the conflict among its faculties. As a result, the unity of the subject, like the unity of history, is always problematical. The subject can provide a starting point for the rethinking of history only because the contradictions constituting it threaten to undermine the limits encircling it, that is, only because the *différend* affects the subject itself.

IV

We have seen how a contrast between Kant and Hegel and between the perspectives offered by their respective philosophies on the subject, as well as on the problems of intuition and experience, provides Lyotard with a point of departure for the rethinking of the problem of history. And yet, I would argue, Lyotard's reading of Kant does not relate only negatively to Hegel. For, as I have shown, in its emphasis on the necessity of bringing the idea into contact with experience without obliterating the difference between them, Lyotard's reading of Kant obeys an imperative that owes something to Hegel as well as to Kant. Equally important, Lyotard's reading of Kant also provides an agenda for rereading Hegel in terms of the "Kantian" perspective on history. When read in the light of the themes and problems of Lyotard's interpretation of Kant, Hegel's own philosophy can be argued to be constituted by tensions as great as those Lyotard identifies between Hegel and Kant. Although a thorough investigation of Hegel's philosophy from such a standpoint would be long and difficult, it is nonetheless possible to briefly give some indications of the direction such an investigation might take.

The overriding issue in Lyotard's reading of Kant is perhaps the affirmative treatment of *différends* and heterogeneity. Hegel's philosophy is of course also one in which difference and otherness play a central role. The problem is to determine just how central. Lyotard's critique of Hegel places a heavy emphasis on the character of the Hegelian dialectic because in his view it is what effectively erases difference or, what is the same thing, subordinates it to identity, thereby making of it a mere negative moment of identity. But one could also argue that there is a genuine tension within Hegel's system between, roughly speaking, two aspects of the dialectic—the "labor of the negative" on the one hand and mediation or reconciliation on the other. As Hegel puts it in the preface to the *Phenomenology*:

> The life of Spirit is not the life that shrinks from death and keeps itself untouched by devastation, but rather the life that endures it and maintains itself in it. It wins its truth only when, in utter dismemberment, it finds itself. It is this power, not as something positive, which closes its eyes to the negative, as when we say of something that it is nothing or is false, and then, having done with it, turn away and pass on to something else; on the contrary, Spirit is this power only by looking the negative in the face, and tarrying with it. (19)

This passage clearly exemplifies the logic of the dialectic in Lyotard's sense, for in it the negative and the heterogeneous (in the form of "dismemberment") are affirmed only in order that spirit itself may be truly affirmed. And yet it also argues that spirit can truly be affirmed only when the negative is truly affirmed, when spirit does not "close its eyes" to the negative. How, then, can we be sure that spirit has truly affirmed the negative, that it has not merely closed its eyes to the negative after a brief glimpse? How can we be sure that spirit has not "maintained" itself simply because for it the negative is not "a serious business?" (*Phenomenology*, 41). Clearly, as long as spirit does in the end "find itself" or "maintain itself" we cannot be sure. We can only be sure if difference and negativity are themselves maintained and affirmed to the utmost. When read in these terms, the moment of sublation or *Aufhebung* becomes very difficult to distinguish from an "impasse" that also serves as a "passage."[17]

One could make an analogous argument in terms of the relationship between the Hegelian theory of perception and Lyotard's interpretation of the Kantian conception of intuition.[18] In the case of perception, as in the case of every stage of the *Phenomenology,* the "ground . . . of science or knowledge" is "pure self-recognition in absolute otherness" (*Phenomenology*, 14). In the section on perception, Hegel deals with it in a negative form. The errors of perception are exposed so that the truth of perception and of the sensuous—which will become fully apparent with the revelation of absolute spirit itself—is indicated only indirectly. The error of perception is precisely, one could say, that it does not affirm difference but seeks instead to negate it: "The percipient is aware of the possibility of deception; for in the universality which is the principle, *otherness* itself is immediately present for him, though present as what is *null* and superseded. His criterion of truth is therefore *self-identity*" (*Phenomenology*, 70). The irony here is that absolute spirit also supersedes otherness. But clearly it can do so only if it does not make the mistake of naive perception, only if it "tarries" with the object, only if it experiences it as devastation and dismemberment of the self. The self must thus arrive at absolute self-knowledge by way of the absolutely other object; with the risk that this detour by way of the object will turn out to be infinite.

The subject that tarries with the object and looks its otherness in the face will in the end grasp its (own) pure concept (*Phenomenology*, 487) and complete the circle that begins and ends with the subject (*Phenomenology*, 488). As such, the subject is for Hegel a figure of totality, a "gallery of images" (*Phenomenology*, 492) subsuming under itself all the various determinations or "*shapes of consciousness*" that constitute the experience of spirit in all its richness (*Phenomenology*, 491). But this point in the process can only be reached thanks to an impoverishment of the subject, which reduces it to the minimal form of a horizon for (sensuous) experience. Absolute, self-knowing spirit "is the immediate identity with itself which, in its difference, is the *certainty of immediacy*, or *sense-consciousness* . . . the beginning from which we started" (*Phenomenology*, 491). In this reduction of the subject to almost nothing, thought and knowledge become fundamentally dependent on sense-consciousness and experience: "It must be said that nothing is *known* that is not in *experience*" (*Phenomenology*, 487). Once again the dialectic can be seen to work against itself. For only the subject that tarries indefinitely with experience and sense-consciousness can be said with certainty to have overcome them.

The name Hegel gives to this process of tarrying with the absolutely other and the negative is of course history: "The movement of carrying forward the form of its self-knowledge [the self-knowledge of Science] is the labour which it accomplishes as actual History" (*Phenomenology*, 488). And as experience, that is, as the negative, difference, and otherness, history will be negated in absolute self-knowledge. For according to Hegel, spirit necessarily appears in history, and it appears in history just so long as it has not *grasped* its pure notion, that is, has not annulled history (*Phenomenology*, 487). History, according to Hegel's well-known expression, is a ruse of reason. But the ruse itself also ruses with reason, which cannot do without the ruse. Reason may only seek itself in history, but it cannot find itself without losing itself in history—at least if it is not content to be what Hegel calls "lifeless." This means that reason can never seize itself as history without at the same time being put into question.

The interpretation of Hegel, then, stands to gain as much as the interpretation of Kant from Lyotard's rethinking of the problem of history. Lyotard's work demonstrates the value of reading Kant "against Hegel." But when one brings the questions that emerge from his critical reading of Kant to a critical reading of Hegel, it becomes clear that Hegel can and to an important extent clearly should also be read "against Hegel."[19] Just as Hegel finds his own dialectical philosophy implicit in Kant, so one can see Kant's philosophy implicit in Hegel's, but not just as an earlier and inferior version of it. When interpreted in this way, Hegelian philosophy appears as an unceasing but never wholly successful attempt to "heal" what one philosopher has called the *schize* opened by Kantian philosophy,[20] a *schize* that Kant himself was the first to try to heal.

The philosophy of Kant, when read in terms of its relationship to Hegel, constitutes a crucial event in the history of history and philosophy. For in relation to Kantian philosophy, Hegel's conception of history as totality can be placed in a certain perspective—it can be seen that if the

Kantian *différend* is always a potential dialectic, if Kant is *already* Hegel, then the reverse must also be true: the Hegelian dialectic is always threatened from within by the irreconcilable differences of the *différend*, and Hegel, in this sense, becomes a philosopher of the *différend*. The "Kantian" oppositions (but do they belong to Hegel or Kant?) cannot be wholly overcome by the "Hegelian" dialectic (but is it the dialectic of Kant or Hegel?), and the ultimate implication of this fact is that history in and of itself remains not only what *is* but also an idea in Lyotard's sense.

The ethical and political implications of this point are the special concerns of Lyotard, but its theoretical implications are equally important. They are that history has its own intrinsic "ethicity," which is expressed in a continual examination and reexamination of its foundations, its presuppositions, and its "subject." A critical history is one that obeys this "theoretical imperative," that constantly engages in this reflective or self-reflexive search for a historical law that is not and cannot be pre-given. It is possible to have a version of history—a historicism or even a new historicism—without such a theoretical imperative, but not a critical history. A critical history, in other words, is one that maintains the tension between the "infinite task" of thinking history and the need to practice it and locates that tension not between history and some remote, transcendental term but *within* history itself.

Notes

1. Michel Foucault, *The Archeology of Knowledge* (New York: 1972).

2. Jacques Derrida, *Writing and Difference* (Chicago: 1978); *Margins of Philosophy,* trans. Alan Bass (Chicago: 1982); *Glas* (Paris: 1974).

3. Jean-François Lyotard, *Le Différend* (Paris: 1983); *L'Enthousiasme, la critique kantienne de l'histoire* (Paris: 1986). In *Just Gaming,* translated by Wlad Godzich (Minneapolis, Minn.: 1985), Lyotard discusses his previous work in terms of his critical relationship to the philosophy of Hegel and the theories of his modern heirs: "It was a matter of ridding political reflection of its Hegelianism, of purging it of this modern version of Hegelianism that is constituted, for me, by Lacanism, of the finally determinant use of concepts that is called 'semiotics,' and of a Marxism of the Althusserian type, let us say; well, not only, of Marx's Marxism as well, so as to relieve philosophy of the tremendous weight of the various political philosophies of reason and of the philosophies of reason" (89; translation slightly modified).

4. "The Unconscious, History, and Phrases: Notes on *The Political Unconscious,*" in *New Orleans Review* 11, no. 1 (Spring 1984), 73. Lyotard makes these remarks on history in the context of an analysis of Fredric Jameson's *The Political Unconscious* (Ithaca, N.Y.: 1981). In the introductory paragraphs of his essay, he states that what interests him in Jameson's interpretation of Marxist interpretation is not "its totalizing or capitalizing dogmatism but rather . . . its uneasiness: the critical task is not only endless; it might even be without fixed criteria. . . . I would like to expand on this aspect of Jameson's argument here, at the risk of betraying it" (73). In this passage, Lyotard is already doing what he

does throughout the article: (re)interpreting Jameson's concept of history in Kantian terms, making Jameson's Marxism Kantian.

5. G. W. F. Hegel, *Aesthetics: Lectures on Fine Art*, trans. T. M. Knox (Oxford: 1975), 1217.

6. G. W. F. Hegel, *Phenomenology of Spirit*, trans. A. V. Miller (Oxford: 1977), 29.

7. "An Old Question Raised Again: Is the Human Race Constantly Progressing?" in *On History*, trans. Lewis Beck White, Robert E. Anchor, and Emil L. Fackenheim (Indianapolis: 1963), 137.

8. "Idea for a Universal History from a Cosmopolitan Point of View," *On History*, 15–16.

9. "Whoever believes that philosophical thought can dispense with its history by means of a simple proclamation will, without his knowing it, be dispensed with by history. . . . He will think he is being original when he is merely rehashing what has been transmitted and mixing together traditional interpretations into something ostensibly new. The greater a revolution is to be, the more profoundly must it plunge into its history" (Martin Heidegger, *Nietzsche*, vol. 1 [San Francisco: 1961], 203).

10. The passage on the spectators of the French Revolution is quoted by Hannah Arendt in her *Lectures on Kant's Political Philosophy* (Chicago: 1982), 45, and discussed in the pages that follow. To investigate the many interesting parallels between the work of Hannah Arendt and Lyotard, especially their interpretations of Kant, would require a separate article discussing their shared sense of the need to reinaugurate political philosophy, the central importance both ascribe to Kant's work in permitting such a reinauguration to be envisaged, and the importance both attach to the *Critique of Judgment* in their reinterpretations of Kant. On the question of history they also share a common perspective, at least up to a point. Arendt uses Kant's work to provide a critical perspective on the modern concept of history in "The Concept of History," *Between Past and Future* (New York: 1980), 83. In the "*Postscriptum* to *Thinking*," which introduces her Kant lectures, she also makes the question of history central (5). Nonetheless, one perceives a difference in emphasis between Arendt and Lyotard. The *Lectures*—perhaps because of their unfinished form—do not, in the end, attempt to rethink history from a Kantian perspective. Arendt's most clearly articulated position on Kant and history thus remains the one she expresses in "The Concept of History," where she describes Kant as "reluctantly" introducing a concept of history into his political philosophy (83). This passage from Arendt's work as well as the significance of Kant's notion of the sublime with respect to history are discussed by Hayden White in an article entitled "The Politics of Historical Interpretation: Discipline and De-Sublimation" in *Critical Inquiry* 9, no. 1 (September 1982).

11. Lyotard discusses "the change in the 'subject' from Kant to Hegel" in detail in *Le Différend* in the Notice on Hegel, 137–45.

12. The interpretation I am giving here, though faithful to Lyotard's reading of Kant, also betrays it insofar as it contains a fundamental ambiguity that relates specifically to the problem of the series. The sentence quoted above on the series is reaffirmed and amplified later in the text, when Lyotard writes: "The exigency of presentation presses sensation to the utmost, it is necessary to document everything, and yet the series is only an Idea" (*L'Enthousiasme*, 50). Yet elsewhere Lyotard writes as though the series itself were given by experience alone. The critical judge, he argues, "cannot say when such objects [signs of progress] will present themselves, because historical sequences forming series provide the historian with givens (at best statistically regular), but never signs" (*L'Enthousiasme*, 77). Thus though there is a tendency in Lyotard's work to make history a question of judgment, there is a countervailing tendency to defend the "science of history" as well.

13. Immanuel Kant, *Critique of Pure Reason*, trans. F. Max Müller (New York: 1966), 91.

14. Martin Heidegger, *Kant and the Problem of Metaphysics*, trans. James S. Churchill (Bloomington, Ind.: 1962).

15. Martin Heidegger, *Being and Time*, trans. John Macquarrie and Edward Robinson (New York: 1962), 486.

16. Jacques Derrida, "Ousia et gramme," in *Margins of Philosophy.*

17. The fundamental and radical ambiguity I am arguing for here in the interpretation of Hegelian philosophy is a major theme of Jacques Derrida's readings of Hegel and in particular of *Glas.* As Derrida puts it there: "The logic of the *Aufhebung* at each moment turns itself back into its absolute other. Absolute appropriation is absolute expropriation. Onto-logic can always be reread or rewritten as a logic of unreserved loss or unreserved expenditure" (188).

18. I have chosen to compare Kantian intuition to Hegelian perception rather than sense-certainty because the overriding importance Hegel gives language in analyzing the latter makes a comparison with Kant's theory of intuition—which has nothing to say about language—difficult. Difficult though it might be, an important aspect of Lyotard's interpretation of Kant, which I have thrust into the background, would make it easier, for Lyotard in a sense condenses the philosophies of Kant and Wittgenstein and thereby introduces the problem of language into every aspect of Kant's philosophy. It could be argued that the effect of this strategy is to bring Kant and Hegel even closer together, by indicating that for Kant, as for Hegel, language is already at work in "sense-certainty." See in particular the section of *Le Différend* entitled "Le Référent, le nom."

19. In *La Remarque spéculative* (Paris: 1973), Jean-Luc Nancy adopts such a strategy of reading in his analysis of the function of the word *aufheben* in Hegel's text: "One perceives very quickly that something in Hegel's grammar resists what he wants to look for in it—the *aufheben.* Or rather, if one prefers, that something in [his own] grammar resists Hegel" (115).

20. Philippe Lacoue-Labarthe, "Hölderlin et les grecs," in *L'Imitation des modernes* (Paris: 1986), 72. This essay and a second essay on Hölderlin—"La Césure du spéculatif"— included in the same volume both treat Hölderlin from the standpoint of his paradoxical relationship to speculative philosophy. They ask how it is that what emerges from his texts is both a "rigorously dialectical structure" and at the same time an "interpretation of the truth that can no longer be reduced either to the Platonic-Cartesian interpretation of truth (as theoretical and enunciative adequation), nor to its speculative and dialectical reelaboration" (42). The implication is that Hölderlin's text can be both of these things because of the radically ambiguous nature of the dialectic itself.

CHAPTER 5

Hamlet, *Little Dorrit,* and the History of Character

Jonathan Arac

I

The most urgent agenda for contemporary literary theory involves all that it will take to forge a "new literary history." From Fredric Jameson's slogan, "always historicize," to Michel Foucault's "genealogies," to the critiques of traditional (teleological, periodizing, objectifying) historiography by Jacques Derrida, Paul de Man, and Hayden White, to British "historical materialism" and American New Historicism, this is the message.[1] The conjunction of Shakespeare and Dickens is propitious for taking another step into this project, for Shakespeare has been the object of intense recent attention by contemporary theorists concerned with history.[2] In the United States, the Berkeley journal *Representations,* widely acknowledged as most brilliantly instantiating the New Historicism, counted among its editorial group two powerfully learned and innovative Shakespeareans, Stephen Jay Greenblatt and, until his untimely death, Joel Fineman.

In order to reach my topic, I will ungratefully emphasize one respect in which even the most recently published work of Fineman and Greenblatt is still tied to an "old historicism." Both continue a massive nineteenth-century line of belief, broadly epitomized by Jakob Burckhardt on Renaissance individualism, in holding that Shakespeare inaugurated what Fineman calls "a recognizably modern literature of individuated, motivated character"; or as Greenblatt puts it, "Shakespearean theater virtually defines in our literary tradition the representation of individuals."[3] This is true enough in one sense, but my claim (not uniquely mine) is that the sense of character, and of literature, that they find in Shakespeare became available only in the nineteenth century. Recall that Samuel Johnson in the 1765 preface to his edition praised Shakespeare precisely because his works gave us the typical and general, not the individual or particular. This nineteenth-century sense is still considerably ours, but it is also no longer ours, at least enough so that it becomes possible to put that sense of character and literature to historical examination, and to find that it is part of our romantic and Victorian rather than our Elizabethan heritage.

I shall be using Dickens as a focus for thinking about the process by which the "modern sense of character" was brought into existence through—not by—Shakespeare. If Shakespeare is our contemporary, it is only because of a continual process of reworking that has continued to produce him in successive cultural formations. My exploration thus furthers the current theoretical concern with "new literary history" by opening up the New Historicism, by paying attention to the reception-history of works after their time of initial production, by concern with their cultural afterlives.[4] It also involves two other areas crucial for current work: the historical study of the "production of the subject" and the process of "intertextuality."[5] In the terms developed in a fascinating book by Ned Lukacher, who studies Shakespeare in Hegel and Dickens in Freud, I will be constructing a "primal scene."[6]

My procedure will involve first some characterization of *Little Dorrit* that moves to establish a precise philological connection between *Hamlet* and *Little Dorrit,* with a focus on Arthur Clennam. Such possible relations of "source" are not much concern in current theory, and my point is primarily rhetorical, to establish the plausibility of the larger set of "intertextual" claims and connections that I then wish to develop. With the leading string of *Hamlet,* I will relate the construction of Arthur Clennam as a character—in the larger sense of one who is conceived of as a character, not just characterization but also metacharacterization—to three distinct discursive strands that come together: one line from the inward-turned practices of *Bildung* fiction, one line from the highly externalized theatrical practices that feed into the projective and expressionistic atmospheric effects of Gothic fiction, and an intellectual line from the new literary criticism of Shakespeare that began in the romantic period.

The work of my own that brings me to this conjunction is the attempt to elaborate a full historical poetics of the novel in the nineteenth century.

Although obviously crucial in any such attempt, character has not been an effective concern of current criticism. Indeed, "character" in our times may be a critical concept useful only for thinking about popular fiction and biography. Its current obsolescence marks the historical specificity of a now receding cultural period. In reading the nineteenth-century novel (as for some other purposes), the notion of "character" has two major valences, predictive and interpretive. These correspond roughly to what E. M. Forster designated flat and round (better might be "deep") characters.[7] Of flat characters one feels safe in predicting what they will do in a situation. Round characters are more appropriately subject to interpretation after the fact: that is just what they *would* do. The sense of individual complexity and development associated with round character is my present concern.

To locate the "emergence" of the "individual" in life, or in literature, is impossible. Persuasive arguments have been made for "the discovery of the individual" in the twelfth century, at the time of the Reformation, by Shakespeare, by Descartes, at the time of the Seven Years' War, by Fichte—and so on.[8] Only to the extent, however, that these arguments are all the retrospective artifacts of historical interpretation as practiced in a given time and place (or culture) does it make sense to say of them that they all refer to the "same" individual. The sense of character I am studying here can be delimited politically between the French Revolution and the First World War, and economically between the full beginning of the industrial revolution and the height of imperialism. Culturally, this character is correlated with the rise of the science of psychology and its transformation by psychoanalysis, and it closely coincides with the emergence of the institution of "literature" in the sense that we still lingeringly know it:[9] a moment that we might begin with Goethe's *Wilhelm Meister* and end with Joyce's *Ulysses*. That concept of literature is now obsolescent, "residual"—just as Kantian aesthetics survives despite Heidegger.

In the nineteenth century, there was a close correlation between literary characterization and the scientific study of human personality. For psychology and literature alike in this period, *Hamlet* is crucial. This confluence may be signaled by Coleridge's dual role as the inaugurator in English of the romantic interpretation of Hamlet that will preoccupy us. He helped to found the criticism of character as an effective, gradually dominant critical mode, and he was one of the first to use such terms as *psychological* and *psychologist* (*OED*). Melville's *Pierre* and Dickens's *Little Dorrit* come in the middle of this period, and each—in returning to the model of Hamlet that had been crucial to Goethe and Coleridge and would be again for Freud and Joyce—significantly inflects both the literary genre of the novel of development and the larger cultural sense of how to understand a character. The culmination of character criticism in English comes in Bradley's lectures on Shakespeare, which are contemporary with the earlier work of Freud—who himself formulated the interpretation of Hamlet's character that would much later be elaborated in Ernest Jones's famous book.[10] By the 1930s, the New Critics had turned against character criticism, teaching us no longer to care how many children had Lady Macbeth, but to attend instead to patterns of language. (This has had consequences for criticism of the novel as well.) The renewed understanding of Freud begun in France through Lacan's work taught us to see in Freud a more fundamental linguistic emphasis—and genius—than we perhaps had before. It now becomes possible to return to the study of character, bearing in mind that "character" may be understood as one possible effect of language under certain historical and social conditions. Derrida began his essay "Freud and the Scene of Writing" by asking, "What must a psyche be if it can be represented by a text?"[11]

II

Little Dorrit has won strong admiration since the 1950s for its comprehensively critical sense of society and for its richness of character analysis, deepened by autobiographical reflections to which Dickens was impelled at this crucial turn in his life and career. The literary means by which this psychological deepening was mediated have been less remarked. Dickens overlaid the 1850s onto the 1820s and thus narratively combined the genesis of the Victorian age with its fully developed problematic complexity, including financial and administrative scandals contemporary with the time of writing. Thus the plot spans several years but feels as if it stretches several decades: Arthur Clennam's difficulties enact the problem of the Hamlet-like over-self-consciousness that for Carlyle vitiated the England of around 1830, while the cure of his will that Arthur finds by the novel's end marks a fully Victorian rectification of that problem. At the same time, the discovery of Arthur's parentage offers a wishful new genealogy for the Victorian age, from the love and art of Arthur's true mother rather than from the iron will of Mrs. Clennam's Protestant ethic.[12] Yet through the disastrous failure of Merdle and the Circumlocution Office, Dickens keeps always in sight the pathology of the high Victorian moment, not allowing the imaginary new foundation to obscure continuing urgencies. Moreover, the new lineage and new birth do not wholly work, for Clennam differs from his prototype in Goethe's founding novel of development. Wilhelm Meister passed through a phase of involvement with Hamlet before discovering his true vocation in the sphere of active life rather than that of the arts. Unlike Wilhelm Meister, who produces both the play and an interpretation of it, Clennam remains enveloped by Hamlet, for Dickens produces Arthur through Hamlet.

The kind of matter I have in mind is suggested by a reflection from Georg Lukács (citing Marx): "In imagination the individuals under the rule of the bourgeoisie are freer than before, because their conditions of life are more accidental for them; in reality they are naturally less free, because much more subsumed under material powers."[13] I am not persuaded that "the" individual under substantially different social orders is the "same" individual. Extending the work of Michel Foucault through study of nineteenth-century statistical inquiry, Ian Hacking has concluded that through the new power of a "particular medico-forensic-political language of individual and social control," the "sheer proliferation of labels" may have "engendered more kinds of people than the world had ever known before."[14] That is to say, the increased "material powers"— and cultural powers—of the fully developed bourgeois age made possible the specific type of individuality characterized by Lukács, an individuality possessing an interior space of problematic freedom that cannot be separated from a strictly limited set of exterior, worldly probabilities. Arthur Clennam is set firmly within the social world Dickens represents: the Protestant ethic of his "mother"; the power of British trade that placed him with his father in China for twenty years; the new bureaucracy satirized for its incompetence while acknowledged in its crucial omnipresence; the entrepreneurial and engineering values of Doyce's industrial activity; and the "allonging" and "marshonging" of the democratic revolution (in the 1820s the Napoleonic Wars were still a vividly recent memory; in the 1850s the example of France's return to revolution in 1848 was constantly present to politically concerned Britons).

I want to argue in addition, however, that Arthur has been textually produced by a web of interpretive reading and writing that, despite vigorous effort, escapes him, while he by no means escapes it. *Little Dorrit* is, as Shklovsky and others have observed, a "mystery novel," and what Roland Barthes called the "hermeneutic code" of the novel is crucially triggered by the repeated appearances of the watch that Arthur sent back from his father's deathbed to Mrs. Clennam.[15] The watch contains a watch-paper (75) on which are cunningly "worked" in beads the letters "D. N. F." (405). They are woman's "work," but they are caught up in the play of a man's testamentary supplement, for the secret to which they point is the codicil to Arthur's great-uncle's will. Arthur sees the watch-paper, suspects that it signals some "wrong to set right"

(87, running head), but he never succeeds in learning the facts. He never even learns of the codicil's existence as such, although as a "folded paper" (893) it is placed into his hands by Little Dorrit with the request that he burn it, which he does. Yet the codicil established the connection between the Clennams and the Dorrits responsible for Little Dorrit's being present for Arthur to notice when he returns home, and the watch-paper has provoked the state of anxiety that makes him especially susceptible to interest in her.

As read by Blandois in the middle of the book, the watch-paper contains "cyphers," which "might be almost anything." He deciphers them as "D. N. F." and proposes that they might be the initials of "some tender, lovely, fascinating fair-creature," but Mrs. Clennam corrects him: they are the initials "of a sentence." That sentence is "Do not forget" (405–6). We are already tangled in ambiguity, for the three words form a "sentence" of at least three types: grammatically they specify a complete relationship of subject and predicate; they also compose a wise saying, a sententious observation; and they have seemed to many readers the judgment passed upon Mrs. Clennam that sentences her to a paralytic preservation of the past. Blandois was, moreover, partially correct in his initial suggestion, for while the signified of these letters is no person (but a sentence), their initial referent was the love relation between Arthur's father and (real) mother, which Mrs. Clennam has hidden from Arthur while pretending to be his mother.

After Arthur's great-uncle tried by the codicil to make amends for this initial suppression, however, the letters took on a different meaning for Arthur's father, who intended by them to remind Mrs. Clennam to put into effect the long-hidden document. Or at least Jeremiah Flintwinch believes that they "could only mean" (851) this. Mrs. Clennam, however, insists that she is right and declares, "I do not read it as he did" (846). By this time for the reader too meanings have changed. When we first learned of the watch, Arthur explained to Mrs. Clennam that "it was not until the last, that [his father] expressed the wish; when he could only put his hand upon it, and very indistinctly say to me 'your mother.' A moment before, I thought him wandering in his mind, as he had been for many hours" (74). This could just as well mean that Mr. Clennam wanted Arthur to have this only token of his mother, to whose love and fate his mind has wandered, as that he wished Arthur to bring it to Mrs. Clennam: it may have been intended to mean only love, and it has inadvertently brought justice too—but not knowledge.

Wholly unknown to Arthur, despite his suspicions, this network of conflicting interpretations has crucially, although not totally, determined his life. This model of textual efficacy complicates our understanding of what Northrop Frye has taught us to call the "archetype" of Hamlet, that is, an element of literary experience that recurs often enough to be recognized, and brings it closer to what Nietzsche called a "sign-chain," the point of which is the differing interpretations to which it has been subjected over a history defined through those reinterpretations.[16] It took some two hundred years for the romantic reading of *Hamlet* to occur, and that reading has now largely passed, but it is crucial to understanding *Little Dorrit* and its place in the shaping of what is still our culturally unreflective sense of the self (that is, what we think of as the self when we don't think about it too hard).

For the "sentence" of the watch-paper alludes to the play that by the time Dickens wrote had come to signify within English and German culture the mystery of character, with equal emphasis on both terms. In the closet scene, the ghost of his father says to Hamlet,

> Do not forget. This visitation
> Is but to whet thy almost blunted purpose.
> But look, amazement on thy mother sits.
> O, step between her and her fighting soul.
> (3.4.110–13)

Thus the situation from which the "sentence" is drawn bears immediately upon Arthur's own situation, that of a man caught between his dead father and his morally compromised mother. More fully interpreted, the ghost's words continue to be relevant to Arthur, for the ghost is urging Hamlet to get on with things—paradoxically, by remembering he should whet his purpose for future action rather than remaining tied to the past.

This problem strikes the keynote of the romantic interpretation of Hamlet, which finds him inhibited, overscrupulous, lacking will. In *Little Dorrit,* within ten lines after Arthur Clennam is named for the first time, he declares, "I have no will," or at least "next to none that I can put in action now" (59). For he has been "always grinding in a mill I always hated" as a result of his upbringing. The notion of "will" is Janus-faced, pointing back to inheritance and forward to volition.[17] *Little Dorrit* sets both these dimensions to play in Arthur's backward-looking explanation of his problem in facing forward. Not only psychologically, however, as he recognizes, but also legally (and as we have observed, without his knowledge), Arthur is enmeshed in a problem of inheritance that is resolved only when the codicil is burned—that is, he has a problem about a will in quite another sense. Driven by guilt over a wrong of which he is unconscious, Arthur seeks to find a secret wrong to rectify. At the same time, however, he falls prey to an impotent self-denial, figured in the trope of "nobody" that the book develops around him (Book 1, chapters 16, 17, 26, 28). Hamlet's romantic problem in Arthur exemplifies imaginative freedom ("king of infinite space") cripplingly subsumed under material power ("bounded in a nutshell"—2.2.254–55).

This double problem of Arthur's inheritance that mars his volition may be posed this way: he inherits both secrets and dreams ("It had been the uniform tendency of this man's life . . . to make him a dreamer after all" [80]), and his volition is marred both by a drivenness, related to the secrets, and by a paralysis, related to the dreams. The paralysis paradoxically carries a positive value to the extent that it preserves Arthur from the fate of Pancks, who is always busy at work for Casby "like a little labouring steam-engine" (190). Yet Arthur's inhibitions and Pancks's compulsions are equally removed from the normative definition of character John Stuart Mill offered in *On Liberty*: "A person whose desires and impulses are his own—are the expression of his own nature, as it has been developed and modified by his own culture—is said to have character. One whose desires and impulses are not his own, has no character, no more than a steam-engine has character.[18] For in the problematic of the book, Arthur's desires and impulses are not his own but "nobody's."

In the literary development of character in the nineteenth century the depths, recesses, and intricacy made possible by such self-alienation, rather than Mill's integrity, became the model for what it was to *be* a character (whereas Mill was concerned with the ethical sense of *having* character). And Hamlet offered the model for character whose identity, emblematized in the problem of his "madness," was marked precisely by his deviation from the ethical norm, as in his apology to Laertes (5.2.222–40). Like Arthur he was at once an impotent "John-a-dreams" (2.2.563) and compulsively driven into activity by his sense that "the time is out of joint" (1.5.196). Hamlet as the exemplary character of romantic criticism also exemplifies the new mode of the "post-Christian soul" produced by the new social technologies of the nineteenth century, defined as an individual exactly by means of a pattern of deviations from the norm. Foucault's model helps us understand why so special a case as Hamlet could also be understood to have such representative significance.

III

But the production of Arthur Clennam as character owes more to the aftermath of *Hamlet* than can be accounted for by this inward-turned psychological line I have been pursuing. *Little Dorrit*, we all know, is not only a novel in the realistic mode; it also draws heavily on Gothic elements. *Hamlet,* as well as serving Goethe for the bildungsroman, was the primary earlier literary point of reference (along with *Paradise Lost*) for Horace Walpole and Anne Radcliffe as they founded the mode of Gothic prose fiction, paralleled by a line of similar dramas, from Walpole's oedipal *The Mysterious Mother* (1768).

In contrast to romantic, bookish inwardness, a "projective" tradition is associated with the popular stage history of *Hamlet* and helps to determine the Gothic fictional mode so important in *Little Dorrit.* The key figure is the ghost in armor walking the battlements of the castle his brother has usurped from him.[19] In the remarkable unity of place in Shakespeare's play, the castle of Elsinore offered the model for later Gothic materializations of the tragic "houses" of legend into the concrete architectural spaces that so concern the novelistic genre. We could speak of a shared claustral imagination. Such charged spaces helped the novel develop means of concentration, against the earlier fictional model of picaresque wanderings.

Hamlet is the great model in earlier English literature for the haunting ancestral presences, the ghosts, that define the Gothic ambience, even when they are displaced from a fully spectral figure into the discomforting vivacity of a portrait. In *Hamlet,* the ghost's appearance in the closet scene comes directly after Hamlet's comparison between the portraits of his father and Claudius. In Gothic fiction, the portrait of the ancestor becomes in *Little Dorrit* the portrait of Mr. Clennam, associated with Arthur's sense of his mother's hidden wrong: "His picture, dark and gloomy, earnestly speechless on the wall, with the eyes intently looking at the son, as they had looked when life departed from them, seemed to urge him awfully to the task he had attempted" (95). Later Blandois tauntingly suggests that the portrait seems to utter the ghostly admonition "Do Not Forget" (411).

Along with the castle, the ghost, and the portrait, the other crucial element *Hamlet* offered to Gothic fiction that finds its way emphatically into *Little Dorrit* is the motif of usurpation. Recall the false "patriarch" Casby who is father to Arthur Clennam's first love; the paternal inadequacies of old Dorrit, "father of the Marshalsea"; and the false motherhood of Mrs. Clennam. *Little Dorrit* is full of false father figures through whom are questioned the privileges of patriarchy, patronage, and gentility, but part of its importance springs from its shift to the false mother, Mrs. Clennam, as the hidden key. Dickens is one of the first to reorient the situation of *Hamlet* toward the mother, as did T. S. Eliot and Ernest Jones in their interpretations of *Hamlet* and Joyce in *Ulysses,* where Stephen is haunted by his mother.

To remind ourselves concretely of the Gothic in *Little Dorrit*, we might consider this passage: as Arthur approaches "that grim home of his youth"

> it always affected his imagination as wrathful, mysterious, and sad; and his imagination was sufficiently impressible for him to see the whole neighborhood under some tinge of its dark [Gothic word] shadow. As he went along, upon a dreary night, the dim streets by which he went, seemed all depositories of oppressive secrets [Gothic word]. . . . The shadow still darkening as he drew near the house, the melancholy room which his father once had occupied, haunted by the appealing face he had himself seen fade away with him when there was no other watcher beside the bed, arose before his mind. Its close air was secret. The gloom, and must, and dust of the whole tenement, were secret. At the heart of it, his mother presided . . . in firmly holding all the secrets of her own and his father's life, and austerely opposing herself, front to front, to the great final secret of all life. (Penguin ed., 596–97)

This passage, which could bear much more elaborate commentary than I can offer now, demonstrates one of the generic transformations that Georg Lukács specified in the shift from historical drama to historical novel around this period. Citing Hegel, he noted that the drama has as its unity a totality of action, while epic (which in this case includes novel) has a totality of objects.[20] The London world of countinghouses, books, papers, chests, safes, keys, church vaults, iron coffers—all of which I passed over in abridging the above passage—gives us the world of "things" that etymologically is what "realism" is about.[21] Lukács notes too that from *King Lear* to Balzac's *Père Goriot*, interest shifts to Rastignac, the figure corresponding to Edgar.[22] That is, the novel differs from both epic and tragedy in focusing on the *un*heroic, the younger generation. (Thus even at its most serious the novel has alliances with traditional comic emphases.)

Goethe's interpretation through Wilhelm Meister of the contrast between novel and drama as that between retardation and rapidity already begins to find *Hamlet* novelistic in its "expansiveness," and Wilhelm's distinction between the activity of the dramatic hero and the passivity of the unheroic novelistic protagonist also already aligns *Hamlet* with the novel.[23] But *Hamlet* differs from all of Shakespeare's other major tragedies precisely in that the identity of its protagonist remains to be forged. Unlike Othello, Antony, King Lear, Coriolanus, and Macbeth, Hamlet has no heroic preexistence. It was his father who "smote the sledded Polacks on the ice." If in this sense he is more oriented to the future than they are, he is at the same time more bound to the past. He lives in the aftermath of someone else's dreadful action, the crime of his mother and stepfather—with which he must come to terms that are not his own to set.

IV

Through the Gothic, we have now returned to ground more familiar to modern readers for thinking about *Hamlet*. This "inner" tradition of understanding Hamlet is intimately related to the romantic project of self-production. For the castle of *Hamlet* becomes not only the Gothic house of the Clennams, but also the prison so crucial for the plot and decor of *Little Dorrit*. Recall that Hamlet's imagination is not just claustral but also carceral: "Denmark's a prison" (2.2.243). Yet contained within that enclosure is the possibility of an inner richness. Hamlet could be "bounded in a nutshell" yet still consider himself "king of infinite space." We return to Foucault's argument in *Discipline and Punish* for the role of prisons and comparable institutions in producing what he called the "post-Christian soul"—what we may take as character. *Hamlet* stands on both sides of a cultural debate crucial for the formation of English romanticism: *Hamlet* fostered the "gross and violent stimulants" that Wordsworth rejected in Gothicism, but another *Hamlet* was involved in the delicacy by which the romantics constructed their alternatives to the Gothic.

Culturally, I am calling the romantic production of the self the work shared by Wordsworth's poetry and Coleridge's criticism and metaphysics and then by their interpreters through the nineteenth century. The distinctions I have drawn from Lukács seem to me especially valuable not because I believe in the genre categories of German idealism, but because Lukács is one of the few to have reflected in any terms on the tremendous change in medium that Shakespeare underwent in this period. The romantic Hamlet leaves drama and the stage to enter narrative and critical writing.

These were the decades that Shakespeare's "own" text was restored to its full authority on the stage, denying the opportunity to make Shakespeare "our contemporary" that the Restoration and eighteenth century had exercised. In the same vein of responsibility to Shakespeare—however different and mistaken it seems to us now—the "authenticity" of settings was insisted on, making for stifling antiquarian baggage and a radically reified mise en scène.[24] Just at the time of this double monumentalization, verbal and visual, the energies of Shakespeare seemed to pass over from the stage into prose narrative. I mean above all the novel, but it is worth recalling how much else there was. Charles and Mary Lamb in their *Tales from Shakespeare* (1806–7) turned the plays into popular narratives for children. Anna Jameson (1832) and Mary Cowden Clarke (1852), wife of Keats's friend Charles Cowden Clarke, published books on Shakespeare's heroines that explored their lives off stage.[25]

Charles Lamb's essay on the suitability of Shakespeare's plays for stage representation (1811) enunciated the fullest version of a position that he shared with Coleridge and Hazlitt.[26] He shows that you cannot interpret Shakespeare merely by repeating his words, which is what actors do; he must be interpreted by more, different words. Shakespearean exegesis can only be critical and textual, not dramatic—soulwork, not bodily gesture. This antitheatrical understanding of Shakespeare strongly determines also such Victorian works as Carlyle's treatment of Shakespeare in "The Hero as Poet" and Melville's interpretation of Shakespeare in "Hawthorne and his Mosses," in which he laid out the premises that were being put into practice in *Moby-Dick* (itself a narrativization of a certain understanding of *King Lear*).

A beginning for this romantic shift from the expressively theatricalized to the meditatively interiorized may be registered in Wordsworth's early drama *The Borderers,* which was never staged and remained unpublished from its completion in 1797 until 1842. It is notable that Wordsworth prefaced the play with the earliest piece I know of romantic character criticism, analyzing the villain Oswald (Rivers). The lines I am about to quote became famous long before they were published. However much critics might argue that they are unrepresentative of the play's overall message, spoken as they are by the villain, and as part of a temptation, they were quoted by Hazlitt, by Evert Duyckinck in his review of Hawthorne's *Mosses from an Old Manse,* and, most notably, by Coleridge in his lecture on *Hamlet*:[27]

> Action is transitory—a step, a blow,
> The motion of a muscle—this way or that—
> 'Tis done, and in the after-vacancy
> We wonder at ourselves like men betrayed.
> Suffering is permanent, obscure and dark,
> And shares the nature of infinity. (lines 1539–44)

Trapped in the sublime recesses of interiority, the richness of character is formed at the expense of action.

My argument holds that between *Hamlet* and *Little Dorrit* there intervened a series of cultural shifts, mediated by the romantic critics of Shakespeare, who staged him in writing. The corpus of this criticism provides a third intertextual strand for Dickens's work. Dickens was saturated in the Shakespearean milieu of the 1830s and 1840s. By 1824 Carlyle, whom Dickens admired beyond all other contemporaries, had translated *Wilhelm Meister,* but in fact the discussion of *Hamlet* had been separately translated almost immediately. A. W. Schlegel's *Lectures on Dramatic Literature* were translated (1815) by John Black, with whom Dickens was associated in the 1830s on the *Morning Chronicle.* Also associated with that paper was Dickens's friend Thomas Noon Talfourd, who put together an edition of Lamb in 1840.[28] No idiosyncratic "influences" are required to account for the traces of *Hamlet* in *Little Dorrit,* however much interest may follow from close comparative reading of the two.

But my emphasis now is on the broader cultural process at work. In seeing himself in Hamlet, Coleridge helped renew the figure for its further cultural life in the nineteenth century, but Coleridge was hardly a less special character than Hamlet himself. It was Hazlitt who performed the necessary generalization by which Hamlet was turned from a Renaissance prince into a petty bourgeois of the nineteenth century, and that allowed him to proclaim, "It is *we* who are Hamlet." Hazlitt transforms the figure of the play—both verbal and theatrical—into his own typification, elements of which are reprocessed in Dickens's narrative reindividualization:

> Whoever has become thoughtful and melancholy through his own mishaps or those of others; whoever has borne about him the clouded brow of reflection, and thought himself "too much i' th' sun"; whoever has known "the pangs of despised love, the insolence of office, or the spurns which patient merit oft of the unworthy takes"; he who has felt his mind sink within him, and sadness cling to his heart like a malady; who has had his hopes blighted and his youth staggered by the apparition of strange things; who cannot be well at ease, while he sees evil hovering near him like a spectre; whose powers of action have been eaten up by thought. . . . This is the true Hamlet.[29]

The "grave dark" (55) face of Clennam—literally "clouded" and like Hamlet too much the "son" in other senses also—his alienated love for Pet, the insolence of the Circumlocution Office to a man who "wants to know," the Gothic apparitions, all these combine to give us an Arthur Clennam-Hamlet. Hamlet's mysteriousness, his unheroism, his alienation as what Goethe called a "stranger in the scene which from his youth he had looked upon as his inheritance," all these for the romantics had become his universality—he was no longer an individual so much as the paradigm for all individuality.

From what he considered Hamlet's universal popularity, Coleridge surmised that "this character must have some connection with the laws of our nature."[30] From here the path lies open to Freud's analysis of Hamlet along with Oedipus in discovering what he came to call the Oedipus complex. Freud's theoretical matrix finally provided a justification for the interpretive method to which Wilhelm Meister had felt driven. Wilhelm was unable to make any sense of *Hamlet* as a whole until after "investigating every trace of Hamlet's character, as it had shown itself *before* his father's death." This genetic method was the key to the romantic Hamlet, as well as to the novelistic procedure that combined with the new techniques of social discipline to produce the kind of character that Freud could then analyze. I have begun to locate *Little Dorrit* in this history.

Notes

1. Fredric Jameson, *The Political Unconscious* (Ithaca, N.Y.: 1981), 9; Michel Foucault, *Power/Knowledge* (New York: 1980), 83–85; Frank Lentricchia, "Derrida, History, and Intellectuals," *Salmagundi,* nos. 50–51 (1980–81): 284–301; Paul de Man, *The Rhetoric of Romanticism* (New York: 1984), ix; Hayden White, *Metahistory* (Baltimore: 1973).

2. For example, Jonathan Dollimore and Alan Sinfield, eds., *Political Shakespeare: New Essays in Cultural Materialism* (Manchester: 1985); and John Drakakis, ed., *Alternative Shakespeares* (London: 1985).

3. Joel Fineman, "The Turn of the Shrew," in Patricia Parker and Geoffrey Hartman, eds., *Shakespeare and the Question of Theory* (New York: 1985), 157; Stephen Jay Greenblatt, "Fiction and Friction," in Thomas C. Heller, Morton Sosna, and David E. Wellbery, eds., *Reconstructing Individualism: Autonomy, Individuality, and the Self in Western Thought* (Stanford, Calif.: 1986), 46.

4. See, for example, Walter Benjamin, "N [Theoretics of Knowledge; Theory of Progress]," trans. Leigh Hafrey and Richard Sieburth, in *Philosophical Forum* 15 (1985): 5; and Hans Robert Jauss, *Toward an Aesthetic of Reception* (Minneapolis, Minn.: 1982).

5. See, for example, Catherine Belsey, "The Romantic Construction of the Unconscious," in Francis Barker et al., eds., *1789: Reading Writing Revolution* (Essex: 1982), 67–80; and Jonathan Culler, "Presupposition and Intertextuality," in *The Pursuit of Signs* (Ithaca, N.Y.: 1981), 100–118.

6. Ned Lukacher, *Primal Scenes: Literature, Philosophy, Psychoanalysis* (Ithaca, N.Y.: 1986).

7. E. M. Forster, *Aspects of the Novel* (1927; Harmondsworth: 1962), 75–85.

8. See, for example, Colin Morris, *The Discovery of the Individual 1050–1200* (New York: 1973); and Marcel Mauss, "A Category of the Human Mind: The Notion of Person; the Notion of Self" (1938), in Michael Carrithers, Steven Collins, and Steven Lukes, eds., *The Category of the Person* (Cambridge: 1985), 1–25.

9. On "literature," see Michel Foucault, *The Order of Things* (1966; New York: 1973), 299–300; and Raymond Williams, *Keywords* (revised and expanded, New York: 1985), 183–88.

10. A. C. Bradley, *Shakespearean Tragedy* (London: 1904); Ernest Jones, *Hamlet and Oedipus* (London: 1948).

11. Jacques Derrida, *Writing and Difference* (1966), trans. Alan Bass (Chicago: 1978), 199.

12. See the classic essay by Lionel Trilling, "Little Dorrit" (1953) in *The Opposing Self* (New York: 1978), 53.

13. Georg Lukács, *The Historical Novel* (1937), trans. Hannah and Stanley Mitchell (Boston: 1963), 141.

14. Ian Hacking, "Making up People," in Heller, Sosna, and Wellbery, *Reconstructing Individualism,* 226.

15. Charles Dickens, *Little Dorrit* (1855–57; Harmondsworth: 1967). The watch first appears on p. 74.

16. Friedrich Nietzsche, *On the Genealogy of Morals,* second essay, section 12, trans. Walter Kaufmann in *Basic Writings of Nietzsche* (New York: 1968), 513.

17. Edward W. Said, *Beginnings* (New York: 1975), 144.

18. John Stuart Mill, *On Liberty* (1859), ed. David Spitz (New York: 1975), 57.

19. Paul S. Conklin, *A History of "Hamlet" Criticism, 1601–1821* (1957; reprinted New York: 1968), 2.

20. Lukács, *Historical Novel,* 92.

21. On relations between the Gothic and realism in the nineteenth century, see Jonathan Arac, *Commissioned Spirits* (New Brunswick, N.J.: 1979), chs. 5 and 6; and John Frow, *Marxism and Literary History* (Cambridge, Mass.: 1986), 163–69.

22. Lukács, *Historical Novel,* 128.

23. Goethe, *Wilhelm Meister,* trans. by Thomas Carlyle (1824; London: n.d.), book 5, ch. 7.

24. See George C. D. Odell, *Shakespeare from Betterton to Irving* (New York: 1920), throughout vol. 2; and the essays in Richard Foulkes, ed., *Shakespeare on the Victorian Stage* (Cambridge: 1986).

25. See Nina Auerbach, *Woman and the Demon* (Cambridge, Mass.: 1982), ch. 6; and Elaine Showalter, "Representing Ophelia," in Parker and Hartman, *Shakespeare,* 87–89.

26. See Jonathan Arac, "The Media of Sublimity: Johnson and Lamb on *King Lear,*" in *Studies in Romanticism* 26 (1987): 209–20.

27. Coleridge quoted lines 1539–44 of *The Borderers* in his 1813 lectures; see *Lectures 1808–1819 on Literature,* ed. R. A. Foakes (1987), 1:539 (volume 5 in *The Collected Works of Samuel Taylor Coleridge,* ed. Kathleen Coburn [Princeton, N.J.: 1969—]).

28. Alfred Harbage, "Shakespeare and the Early Dickens," in G. B. Evans, ed., *Shakespeare: Aspects of Influence* (Cambridge, Mass.: 1976), 113.

29. William Hazlitt, *Characters of Shakespeare's Plays* (1817), in P. P. Howe, ed., *The Complete Works of William Hazlitt* (London: 1930), 4:232–33.

30. Coleridge, *Lectures,* 1:543.

CHAPTER 6

Hobbesian Fear
Richardson, de Man, Rousseau, and Burke

Carol Kay

The first part of this essay was presented in slightly different form in 1984, after the death of Paul de Man but before the discovery of his wartime journalism.[1] In that paper I sought to join recent deconstructive readings of Richardson's *Clarissa* to my reading of Hobbes, and by this means to demonstrate the place of skeptical arguments about language and interpretation in modern political theory. My hope then was to deflect the naive charge of "naive empiricism" leveled against British philosophy by critics in the theory movement. By showing that de Man's reading of Rousseau inadvertently reinvented Hobbes, I tried to turn inside out his incorporation of political theory into the problematic of the literary. The discovery of de Man's wartime writings subjected this argument to new pressures, to which I respond in the second part of this essay. In the final section I reflect on the historical contexts of my instances, the places in the eighteenth and twentieth centuries that are illuminated by Hobbesian thought, episodes in the history of nation-states.

Clarissa can be read as a fear-haunted narrative, not just because it contains a terrible act of violence, a victim, and a victimizer, but because power is not located just in one place or one party. That is why so much critical interest in choosing sides has been generated from the beginning. Lovelace complains of Clarissa, "Her terror is too great for the occasion."[2] The occasion of this complaint is not the immediate prelude to rape, nor is it the seminude fire scene of nocturnal terror that frightens Clarissa into running away from Lovelace. It is an episode in the long, quarrelsome courtship that precedes the fire scene and that stretches back all the way to Clarissa's unintended elopement from her father's house with the manipulative Lovelace.

At the point of this complaint, the couple have proceeded to explicit negotiation over the marriage settlements, a strange context for "terror." It is very hard to recover this "occasion" for fear, so much does this novel seem to lack discrete stages or single motivating causes. The critics who stress the scenic quality of Richardson's artistry ignore the streaming effect of the letters, which take no single scene as climactic. The problem is not the unselective tendency of representational art or the endlessness of interpretation, but what propels interpretation, the endlessness of fear and power. Why has Clarissa felt terror on this occasion? Because Lovelace has wrapped his arms about her knees, as she sat: "She tried to rise at the moment, but my clasping round her thus ardently, drew her down again; and never was woman more frightened. But free as my clasping emotion might appear to her apprehensive heart, I had not, at that instant, any thought but what reverence inspired." At second glance, the passage seems like many in which Lovelace has touched Clarissa and she has withdrawn. This could be her much-debated "punctilio." Was this nicety a necessary precaution, appropriate to the occasion as Richardson's notes remind us, or was it the provoking cause of Lovelace's violence?

Lovelace's assertion of his pure reverence might incline us to imagine a story of tragic misunderstanding, one in which she would have had no reason to be afraid. But looking harder, we find the scene is not one in which Lovelace tries to compel sexual signs of Clarissa's love. He has been trying to keep her from going out alone: he has told her she must not go, he has seized her hand, placed himself between her and the door, cast himself at her feet and then flung his arms around her knees, all the while charging her with scorn and complaining about the bad influence of the letters written by Clarissa's best friend, Anna Howe. On this occasion Clarissa surely fears Lovelace's violent willfulness, not his violent lust. Is this fear too great for the occasion? This argument is the continuation of one that began the day before, a Sunday that should have been happy because it followed a happy Saturday night at the theater. But Lovelace quarreled with Clarissa's decision to go to church, demanded her company in the evening, and, when he got it, complained of her neglect in a way that made Clarissa say, "Pray be not violent— *I have done you no hurt*—pray be not violent." As in the later scene, he took hold of her, she pleaded to withdraw, and he released her with a fervent kiss on her hand, "as if I would have left my lips upon it" (2:376).

Lovelace's "savageness," as Clarissa calls it, makes her think he wants her to provoke him: "But he certainly must have views in quarreling with me thus, which he dare not own! Yet what can they be? I am terrified but to think of what they may be!" (2:378). She urges Anna to perfect the scheme for helping her leave Lovelace. But the reason Lovelace was so angry, so eager to be provoked to violence, is that he has been reading about this scheme in the copies of Anna's letters to Clarissa that have been secretly made for Lovelace by the women of the house. Perhaps Anna, after all, has occasioned the violence. But Anna had decided on a scheme of escape because she had read Clarissa's account of Lovelace's "clenched hand offered in wrath to his forehead" when Clarissa refused him a kiss, the "innocent freedom" (as he saw it) to reward an offer of marriage, a proposal that was, however, offensive to her in its teasing combination of hesitancy and haste (2:312). Writing to his friend Belford about the copies of Anna's letters, Lovelace quotes Anna's words (first occurring in her letter, 2:317) about the fist raised to his forehead, "*I wish it had been a pole-axe, and in the hands of his worst enemy*" (2:371). After all, Anna Howe had cautioned in an earlier letter that if Lovelace should succeed in obtaining her correspondence with Clarissa, her "freedoms" in writing about him would so enrage him that "she should be afraid to stir out without a guard" (2:279). This passage joins a list of numerous infuriating quotations culled by Lovelace from the copied letters and sent to Belford. To this one Lovelace appends the commentary, "I would advise the vixen to get her guard ready" (2:367).

But then again, it is possible that the incitement to violence should instead be traced to the "abandoned" women, the prostitutes disguised by Lovelace, who by providing Lovelace with copies of Anna's letters create a reading they were never intended to have. The women try to persuade Lovelace that Clarissa's plan to spend Sunday without him is "tyranny," worse treatment than if he had been "guilty of the last offense" (2:374–75). They stir him to anger so that when he joins Clarissa, he "soon made fear her predominant passion."

Or perhaps the duel and the continuous mutual threat of violence between Lovelace and Clarissa's brother is the source of all of the other violent threats, or at least the source of Clarissa's vulnerability and defensiveness. After she leaves her family home in the company of Lovelace, her father, constantly incited by her brother and sister, pronounces a curse on her that reverberates throughout the narrative: "that you may meet your punishment both *here* and *hereafter*, by means of the very wretch in whom you have chosen to place your wicked confidence" (2:170). Before considering Lovelace's marriage proposals, Clarissa makes one more attempt at reconciliation with her family, only to read the report of her uncle's words: "they are all resolved not to stir an inch in your favour; no, not to save your life" (2:293).

How threatening are these threats, how terrifying the fears of the strategists, can be debated by the critics; they are persistently debated by the characters. But the debates of the characters only fuel the mutually inciting competition in power. The attempt to assert powerfully that there is no occasion for fear multiplies the occasions for fear by motivating the strategic search for power. This aspect of the novel makes it look like Hobbes's picture of the fearful passions that motivate a "restless seeking of power after power that ceaseth only in death." I have compared Richardson with Hume in his typical optimism about the social taming of the passions by a consolidating, pervasive moral discourse.[3] In *Clarissa* the moral discourse Richardson endorses is fissured strangely by the political revelations of Hobbesian competition in power. So, I suggest, are all accounts of society oriented only to social processes and social feeling, but that neglect or underestimate institutions of government. Richardson's fiction allows this insight partly because Richardson puts forward with such intensity the social ambitions of his own epistolary form.

The letters that structure Richardson's novel are the medium of and model for the social importance of his art. They reform the rakish Mr. B. in *Pamela* by drawing him into closer sympathy with the letter-writing heroine and by demonstrating the worthiness of their love to their whole society. But the circulation of letters is part of the problem of fear in *Clarissa*. Their use as a medium of moral discourse only raises the ante in disputes and makes the reader wonder what is taught by the whole huge collection of letters that makes up the novel. The fictional narrative of transmission presents this archive as Clarissa's alternative to the prosecution of Lovelace for rape, a legal procedure she resists as adamantly as she does the suit against her father that would have been required to obtain the income from the estate bequeathed her by her grandfather. Clarissa refuses both the possibility of economic independence and the possibility of moral vindication when it is to be obtained through the compulsory powers of the state, trusting always to the authority of discourse alone. But an implicit reliance on legal-political institutions, a kind of return of the repressed, appears in her final determination to frame a last address to her family in a legally binding will.

Richardson's narrative shows that the places of fear and the places of power are not stable geographical realms (such as the public sphere as opposed to the private sphere). Fear and power may be anywhere. But that is why Hobbes makes his sovereign government absolute, so that it has the acknowledged right to pronounce final judgment on any conflict it deems dangerous. Though we do not accept the institutional features of Hobbes's political solution, we may be inspired by his political analysis. Since descriptions and definitions of the place of power and the place of fear will be among the places where power is exerted, feared, and met by contending power, writing of all sorts, including the fiction, philosophy, and literary criticism I consider here, cannot be solid entities fixed in positions securely remote from political struggle and political history, and political struggle and political history cannot be entirely separated from the history of the state. Of course, among our fearful acts of power may be efforts to isolate some kinds of writing from some kinds of power. The new literary history I envision, the Hobbesian history of the eighteenth century, you could say, will join with others who question the definition of the "literary" and write the history of that term. For the purposes of this essay, it might be helpful to think of the attempted segregation of the literary as the history of an effort to put a boundary around fear, a history motivated by the fear of fear.

One episode in the history of the fear of fear was staged as a competition among deconstructive studies of *Clarissa* in the early 1980s. In *Diacritics*, William Warner, the author of the first deconstructive book on *Clarissa*, reviewed rival poststructuralist books on *Clarissa* by Terry Castle and Terry Eagleton. Warner saw these books as symptoms of a critical trend toward capturing for political criticism radical, deconstructive insights into the indeterminacy of texts. I also had reviewed these books, and in doing so I had praised Warner's book for its ingenious attack on the humanism that it finds in Clarissa's letters and in pro-Clarissa critics, that is, "humanism" as a discourse on human nature that hides its own power as discourse.[4] Outrageous as it was, Warner's attack on Clarissa showed something I see too—that moral discourse is one of the locations of power. But all the same, Warner's defense of his book was marred by the fear of fear. Castle and Eagleton included Warner in their feminist polemic, which Warner understood to rely on raising and extending the fear of rape. This sort of feminist critique condemns many social structures that make rape possible, that excuse violence against women, and that blame the victim. So Eagleton and Castle included Warner and other pro-Lovelace critics as participants in the violence against Clarissa.

It is easy to see why Warner should have wished to vindicate himself by establishing a particularly firm line between art and life. But there is no particular reason why a theory of indeterminacy should not provide a strategy of reading that questions this boundary rather than one that establishes indeterminacy in the realm of the literary alone. Warner's essay contains interesting revelations in the following passage:

> Of course there is nothing abstract or funny about the crime of rape. If the letters contained in *Clarissa* were documents held in evidence by the London Police Department, reading these letters could draw me into joining Castle and Eagleton in repudiation of the senseless suffering caused by this crime, and urging a swift conviction of the perpetrator. In looking through these records I might also find Gloucester's gruesome blinding by his bastard son, Tess' murder of Alex D'Urberville for his rape/seduction of her, and perhaps in the misdemeanor section, even the "rape" of a lock.[5]

The passage takes back its initial gesture of admitting that there is a place for fear and a place for powerful condemnation. In trying to keep fear in its place, Warner has been led to deny any place for fear.[6] The list of literary crimes that might be brought to trial is revealing. "Gloucester's gruesome blinding by his bastard son" is of course not the way it happens in *King Lear*. This is not a deconstructive misreading, it's a mistake, because the reading implied is a humanist one. Warner implicitly recognizes a connection between Edmund's witty malice and the terrible violence enacted on Gloucester by others. This is the sort of connection he wants to deny in the case of his praise for Lovelace's libertine wit and the culture of violence against women.

The phrase "Tess's rape/seduction" is interesting because in Warner's book "rape/seduction" is his term for what Lovelace does to Clarissa. The term is better applied to Tess's story than to Clarissa's, but it is in any case revealing. We now talk about this sort of rape as "acquaintance rape," or "friendship rape," or "date rape," and some say it is the most common kind. So the indeterminate case, the hard-to-decide case that has drawn the artist's imagination in such a way as to solicit the anti-mimetic, deconstructive reader, this kind of case turns out to be the usual form of the crime. Indeed, if "crime" were an intuitively obvious category instead of a debatable judgment, we would not need laws and courts to render decisions. The distinction between art and life cannot be maintained by an argument about indeterminacy, and that is why indeterminacy can be captured for political criticism and historical study.

For providing a link from my Hobbesian history of the literary to de Man's fear of fear, I am indebted to Suzanne Gearhart, who has called attention to passages in which de Man treats the passion of fear.[7] In "The Rhetoric of Blindness," an essay in *Blindness and Insight*, de Man praised Rousseau's assertion that the origin of language is in figural

language motivated by passion. De Man wanted to harness this observation to his own argument about the nonreferential status of language
and literature. Metaphor, de Man explains, refers to an absence, and it
is engendered by passion, which also refers to absence: "All passion is
to some degree 'passion inutile' made gratuitous by the non-existence of
an object or cause."[8] De Man relies on Rousseau's own distinction
between needs and passions for his explanation that the passions are
impractical. But then de Man halts at Rousseau's remarkable example
of the passional origin of a figural word, because the passion he chose
was "fear": "A primitive man on meeting other men will first have
experienced fright. His fear will make him see these men as larger and
stronger than himself; he will give them the name giants."[9] De Man
explains that the choice of fear was a mistake (not a blind spot, since
he argues that literature has insight into its own blindness): "In Rousseau's
vocabulary, language is the product of a passion and not the expression
of a need; fear, the reverse side of violence and aggression, is distinctly
utilitarian and belongs to the world of 'besoins' rather than 'passions'. . . .
Fear is . . . much too practical to be called a passion."[10]

In a later essay entitled "Metaphor," to be found in *Allegories of
Reading*, de Man no longer condemns Rousseau's choice of fear as a
passion, because he now accepts it as a nonreferential term. Perhaps he
felt it was even more effectively nonreferential because the language
provoked by fear "refers to a condition of permanent suspense between
a literal world in which appearance and nature coincide and a figurative
world in which this correspondence is no longer *a priori* posited."[11] De
Man comes to terms with his fear of fear when he recognizes that fear
is hypothetical, "a figural state of suspended meaning," that he has
nothing to fear but fear itself, and that therefore the nonreferential status
of language and literature can be preserved. This at least was the view
of Gearhart, which I hope to complicate as I continue.

Opening Rousseau's text, I find that the opposition de Man relied on,
the distinction between need and passion, is questionable from the beginning, since passions are called "besoins moraux."[12] What happened to
that word *moraux* in de Man's account? The lover of eighteenth-century
moral philosophy immediately recognizes that Rousseau's essay on the
origin of languages is not a treatise confined to linguistics or epistemology, but an example of what David Hume called "moral science," a
large terrain modern people find strangely diverse. By "moral needs"
Rousseau means needs that characterize people's social life, though the
narrower, ethical meaning is not excluded. Rousseau's first two examples
of situations in which the passions require language for expression are
cases of love and fear, "to move a young heart," or "to repel an unjust

aggressor."[13] The ethical determinations of fear were there from the beginning in the definitions of language and passion. In harsh northern nations, Rousseau says, language is motivated by fear and necessity rather than by love. A northern speech is likely to be "aidez-moi" rather than "aimez-moi."[14] The whole essay teaches the lesson that is my main concern, the centrality of politics for the moral philosophy of this period. The essay privileges metaphor not because Rousseau seeks a nonreferential status for the literary, but because he wishes to revalue oratory as the founding verbal art appropriate to societies with free governments. Such societies are not to be found in modern Europe but in the past cultures where "persuasion took the place of public force."[15]

De Man's attack on the literal is a blind, or, to use his terms, a metaphoric substitution for an attack on metaphor or rhetoric. This seems odd in a critic who helped to bring the word *rhetoric* back into American critical discourse. But the best assault on a concept is to appropriate its term for a new use: so rhetoric—persuasive, practically effective arrangement of language—becomes for de Man "rhetoricity," "the rhetorical question which does not even know whether it is really questioning."[16]

The idea of the literary develops in important ways in the essay called "Metaphor," partly because de Man develops the consequences of accepting fear into his story of language. Returning to the example, in Rousseau's essay, of the primitive man who in fear calls other men giants, de Man notes the next stage. After a process of comparison, which de Man reduces to "measurement," primitive man finds other men like himself, so he renames them "men." De Man makes Rousseau's account of the invention of the term *man* a paradigm for conceptualization. The word *man* is not simply representational, and the judgment of equality incorporated into it is not really a simple perception of size: "The invention of the word man makes it possible for 'men' to exist by establishing the equality within inequality, the sameness within difference of civil society, in which the suspended, potential truth of the original fear is domesticated by the illusion of identity."[17] So the political problem of the *Discourse on Inequality*—the cyclical degeneration of civil society— is already understood within the language theory.

De Man captures politics for his theory as the "politicality" of language. Politics is a figure for figuration. These moves, which include the institution of economics through linguistic artifice, are too elaborate to follow here, but they lead de Man to the point of linking Rousseau on the social contract to Rousseau on language theory:

> The *contractual* pattern of civil government can only be understood
> against the background of this permanent threat. The social contract is by

no means the expression of a transcendental law: it is a complex and purely defensive verbal strategy by means of which the literal world is given some of the consistency of fiction, an intricate set of feints and ruses by means of which the moment is temporarily delayed when fictional seductions will no longer be able to resist a transformation into literal acts.[18]

What I think de Man did in this essay is reinvent Hobbes without knowing it, and I do not mean this as a dismissive comment, so brilliant do I think Hobbes. Why doesn't de Man name Hobbes? The connection of Hobbes and Rousseau is well known, partly because Rousseau mentions him, but the Hobbes named by Rousseau or the Hobbes taught in survey courses is not the one I read when I praise Hobbes's work. My Hobbes resembles de Man's reading of Rousseau. Hobbes shows that language is a system of arbitrary signs, that there are no universal entities that correspond to abstract words, that moral words are especially unstable (he called them words of "inconstant signification"),[19] that the understanding that constitutes property is structured linguistically like other moral conceptualizations, and that the social contract is a fragile artifice, motivated by fear, which must therefore be supported by consent and opinion, since universal truths are not available to us and force is always insufficient to the purpose. Most important for my purposes, Hobbes recognizes that human equality (a fundamental of his system) is a fiction of identity, as de Man says Rousseau shows.

For Hobbes, the vain and competitive nature of the passions makes people deny that other people are equal to them. The only passion to be relied on is *fear*, the fear of violent death, as Leo Strauss pointed out in his book on Hobbes.[20] Recognizing that anyone is strong and cunning enough to kill you when you sleep will lead you to sustain the social contract by consenting to obedience on equal terms with everyone else. The relation between fear and the social contract in Hobbes is not merely a "background," it is made explicit; recognizing that there are no natural means of ending the fearful competition in power, all members of society resign their absolute right to protect themselves in any way according to their own judgment and agree to allow one party as sovereign the right to judge and the right to compel. The sovereign is a representative that is not a mimetic copy of the members of the society but explicitly a fictional person, an "impersonation" (I, 16). Under this authority, fear is productive of peace because it is the fear of the sovereign's power, the fear of other citizens, and the fear of anarchy that together ensure obedience.

Continuing my Hobbesian extrapolation, in de Man's chapter on Rousseau's *Social Contract*, the chapter called "Promises," I find a host

of Hobbesian principles. One cannot base a politics on reading the
feelings of individuals nor on the model of family feeling. De Man finds
"the substitutive process" in founding a state "far from harmless," and
he quotes Rousseau's account "to substitute a fragmentary and moral
existence for a physical and autonomous one,"[21] which is reminiscent of
Hobbes's absolute surrender of the right to all things. The sovereign
power that represents a politically constituted people is nevertheless a
state of nature in relation to other sovereigns, and this double structure
illustrates the Hobbesian position on natural law—that there are no stable
moral meanings. Some of the doubleness de Man finds in Rousseau is
missing in Hobbes, because of his monarchical structure, but the position
on law that de Man finds in Rousseau not only applies to Hobbes, but
underlies his insistence on absoluteness in a sovereign government.
Rousseau insists that "there can be no fundamental law that is binding
for the entire body of the people," which for de Man means that "the
text of the law is, per definition, in a condition of unpredictable change.
Its mode of existence is necessarily temporal and historical, though in
a strictly non-teleological sense."[22] And, finally, in both Hobbes and
Rousseau the definition of law entails a troubled, guilty authority for
the theorist of legislation.

Did de Man expect that a theory of indeterminacy or undecidability
would serve the function of suspending literature from worldly action,
when Hobbes used similar conceptions in a theory that politicizes everything and that notoriously refuses to protect literature—not even his own
book—from the supervision of political authority? I will follow de Man's
respect for literature in attributing insight to his blindness. I think that
in *Allegories of Reading* de Man implicitly acknowledges that he cannot
protect the literary from the literal, any more than others he criticizes
can protect the literal from the staining effects of language and metaphor.
That is why the "delay" of the literal acts he wrote about in "Metaphor"
is only "temporary," perhaps no longer than the time of reading his own
essay. I have come to conclusions different from those of Gearhart. I do
think that in *Allegories of Reading* de Man significantly transformed his
conception of the literary, or at least revealed its fragility and pathos.

But is literature conceived as delay a nonviolent concept? For Hobbes
it is not so much that the social contract introduces delay as that it
changes the meaning of delay. The war of all against all is not a state
of continual fighting, but a state of the continual fear of fighting, when,
as de Man says of Rousseau's primitive man who calls other men giants,
fear "is in the nature of a permanent hypothesis,"[23] a hypothesis that
may bring on literal violence at any time. Delay in Hobbes's state of
fearful competition makes room for "anticipation" (I, 13, 184–85), one

of the most important causes of the war of all against all, since it explains why people who are not especially greedy, competitive, or violent nonetheless become violent: to defend by advance attack.

So you need only one restless man, say a Lovelace, to set in motion the endless fearful competition. Delay, the poise between the figural and the literal, itself belongs in Richardson's narrative to the dynamic of violent acts. The stretch of *Clarissa* I began by discussing could be seen as the delay of the literal acts of violence, a time of fictional seductions rather than of rape. But the delay is also delay of the peacemaking contract, the marriage that Clarissa thinks she is moving toward and that Lovelace continues to further by drawing up settlements and seeking a license. In this way Lovelace stretches out a safety net that could, he admits, turn out to be his own marriage trap.

In the sequence I have been scrutinizing, Lovelace and Clarissa each charge the other angrily with "delays." The Sunday quarrel so frightens Clarissa that "in a fit of passionate despair, I tore almost in two the answer I had written to his proposals" (2:379). Lovelace protracts the Monday-night quarrel to distract Clarissa while the women of the house steal a copy of yet another private paper, which turns out to be the almost-torn page containing Clarissa's favorable reply to Lovelace's proposals. Lovelace finds that this text "instantly turned all my resolutions in her favour" (2:397), until he remembers that it has not actually been sent to him. His text is a mere copy, the original still hidden away, perhaps, he thinks, even intended as a decoy to his servant and in any case torn, and so "absolutely retracted" (2:397-98). But, furthering his seduction plot at the risk of furthering the marriage, Lovelace orders legal settlements drawn up before he has officially received Clarissa's approval. Later Clarissa retrieves the torn paper, even though it is somewhat redundant and outdated, and gives it to Lovelace, who is struck by it as if it were "new" to him (2:414).

Is this fiction delaying violence or fiction in the service of violence, de Man's delay or Hobbes's anticipation? In *Clarissa* the undecidability is in the service of violence. Even when the action of the novel proceeds to rape, rape comes in the guise of delays made possible by Lovelace's fictions, delays that also enable him to sustain his project of seduction after the rape. He continues with a new question as his pretext: does once subdued mean always subdued? At the same time he refuses to close off the marriage plot, assuming that now she is ruined, marriage to Clarissa will always be in his power.

Must the delays that are fictions *always* have violent effects? I'm not willing to decide that Richardson's novel or that the criticism written on the novel, or that Rousseau or that de Man's commentary on Rousseau effects the kind of delay that is violent. But I'm not willing to decide that literature is never violent. This decision is not undecidable. It is open to specific determinations.

II

This is more or less where I ended in 1984. Among the many embarrassments caused by the discovery of de Man's wartime writings is this one: my argument that de Man was Hobbesian would from now on appear to have the sort of vulgar practical resonance that I have always combatted in my account of Hobbes. My beautiful comparison between Hobbes and de Man became a trap that seemed to necessitate the commonplace reading I wanted to elude. In short, if de Man was Hobbesian then his collaborationist writings show that Hobbesian principles lead straight to a fascist state. What follows is my effort to get out of the trap. Perhaps in saving Hobbes I will also save de Man, or perhaps I will have to dismantle the comparison and leave de Man to other interpretive machines.

First, I must admit that there is little in Hobbes to reprobate de Man's transfer of allegiance to the occupying powers in Belgium. Since self-preservation motivates obedience, when the sovereign is unable to protect the subject against the victorious power, the subject's obligation ceases, even in the midst of battle (II, 21, 272–74). Like all obedience in Hobbes, the obedience to a new, victorious sovereign is by consent (II, 20, 251–52), which leaves open the possibility of refusing consent. Though Hobbes is usually hypersensitive to problems of individual judgment, he seems to ignore them in the crucial matter of deciding when a war is decisively lost. Perhaps Hobbes leaves this loophole because he wants to make the gamble of war seem very unappealing to sovereigns. From this ragged edge of the theory, we can pull out a pacifist thread running through Hobbes's persistently anti-heroic picture of citizenship and his singular lack of interest in delineating the leadership abilities of the sovereign. Looking back from our perspective on the early 1940s, it seems odd to consider the war over. Yet, as Jacques Derrida has remarked, when we read de Man's journalism we are struck by the impression that "he is already in a 'postwar' period."[24] The decisive matter for Hobbes would have been that the King of Belgium had surrendered.

I could revert to my Hobbesian text, *Clarissa*, for the counterexample of Clarissa's refusal to take the violence of rape as a decisive victory or as an overwhelming motive for sexual submission, whether inside or outside of marriage. Richardson was much criticized for not getting his heroines away from their would-be rapists soon enough, and especially for the outcome of this inertia in *Pamela*, where the marriage is based on the intimacy developed during the attempted seduction and threatened violence. But on the other hand, some readers have always objected that in *Clarissa*, after many failed attempts to turn distrust into trust, the heroine breaks off contracting and repeatedly runs away. Hobbes boasted that he was the first to run away, even when England was merely prerevolutionary. Since he relies so heavily on fear, Hobbes even defends cowards who pay substitutes to serve in their places during war or who retreat in a battle that is not a defeat (II, 21, 269–70). When we evaluate our wish that de Man had joined those who went on fighting, a wish that he had been loyal to "our" side, we might consider Hobbes's distinction. Deserters may be cowards but they are not unjust; they are merely dishonorable. The conflict of values, between the honorable and the just, is not typical of Hobbesian theory, and it shows the difficulty of defining military obligation in his system.

But of course our issue is not just submission or retreat but anything that looks like active engagement in propagandizing the goals of the fascist victors, especially their answer to the Jewish Question. Though Hobbes favors the management of opinion by the sovereign government, he generally develops an exteriorized image of consent and submission. His disapproval of torture recognizes a possibly large range of privacy, not a firm natural boundary of public and private, but a prudential range of tolerance; many things are usually assumed to be of little interest to the state. His definition of liberty as everything not forbidden by law suggests that acts of molding the character of the population will be very limited. This exteriorized, formalized notion of consent has been criticized for being disastrously thin social psychology. But perhaps this thinness can be seen as agreeably weak for a totalitarian use of his system. It is pleasant to find that the Hobbesian theory of consent does not require as much as de Man offered to the fascist regime in Belgium. It is equally pleasant to find that Hobbes's theory of consent would not have required of de Man in his émigré years an elaborate confession and apology, only obedience to U.S. law. A self-protective silence is not a practical danger to the state as Hobbes understands it.

In Hobbes, no amount of acculturation, except religious indoctrination about the afterlife, could induce you to give up your right to defend your life. That is perhaps the reason Hobbes did not imagine the need to provide a protection against the deportation or execution of a large, peaceable section of the population. "Punishing the innocent" violates the law of gratitude and the law of equity. In Hobbes, these are not transcendental laws but theorems about the probable conditions for maintaining peace. It is the good of peace that he intends in saying that punishing the innocent violates "that Law of Nature which, forbiddeth all men, in their Revenges, to look at any thing but some future good" (II, 28, 360). Since all criminals revert to the natural state of war, unnecessarily criminalizing many members of the population creates for the state active risk, which should be avoided. Alas, it seems that consent in modern states can be enforced far beyond the point of self-preservation in ways that Hobbes did not anticipate. In retrospect we can see that self-preservation in Hobbes is a utopian concept of considerable normative weight.

Here I come to a major difference between Hobbes and de Man that seems to provide an exemplary insight into modernity. For Hobbes the passions are always "restless." Though we are not able to read reliably the particular objects of the passions of particular people, we can understand that passions motivate action. Passions are the forces in Hobbes's social physics. There is no state of passionlessness in Hobbes, no depression, we might say. But in de Man, the passions are by their nature in "suspense," a state of inaction, however tense. And that is why it was easy for de Man to accept Rousseau's assertion that language originates in passion. In the chapter of *Allegories of Reading* called "Self," de Man notes the complex internalization of fear in the paralysis of Rousseau's *Pygmalion*, a paralysis he identifies with the sublime. De Man mentions Kant, but of course I think of Burke, whose account precisely discriminates the sublime from fear by the persistent awareness of the fictionality of the threat, an awareness that makes action unnecessary and makes passion the effect of language that cannot be reduced to reference.[25] When I read de Man's wartime journalism, I find him Burkean, in ways more fitting the *Reflections on the Revolution in France*, but in ways not unrelated to Burke's *Philosophical Inquiry into the Origin of Our Ideas of the Sublime and Beautiful*.

The aging Burke and the young de Man elevate a national culture seen in the context of a long-evolving, but suddenly redefined, European history, and both set the values of historical culture against arguments about natural rights. In Burke of 1790 and de Man of the early 1940s, I find a high valuation of literature as a test for the state of cultural health but also as an activity with laws of its own that must not be reduced to literal application. This insistence on a boundary between the literary and the literal that characterized the sublime in Burke reappears in his complaint that the French revolutionaries have been so foolish as to take Rousseau literally. Though Burke is Hobbesian in his basic principles of sovereignty, Hobbes would never have relied, as Burke does, on a redefinition of history or of literature to disarm revolutionary challenges. The contestatory political potential of such writing is never defused in his system.

If I find the later de Man more Hobbesian than Burkean, it may be that he could usefully be seen as dismantling principle by principle his earlier Burkean ideas of history, but perhaps of all these Burkean elaborations on Hobbes, it is the Burkean view of literature that the later de Man was tempted to retain. The de Manian idea of the literary, the unavoidable awareness of fictionality, does not deconstruct Burkean historicism because self-conscious fictionalizing characterizes Burkean cultural theory and Burkean history up and down the line—in his praise for the "well-wrought veil" woven to cover the revolutionary character of the English revolution of 1688–89, in his endorsement of the fictional continuity of the common law, and in his own chivalrous fiction of a united Christian Europe, which amazingly omits or devalues the Protestant Reformation.[26] The powerful ideological construction of the *Reflections*, I would almost say the founding construction of ideology, since I do believe that ideology has a history, is so powerful an ideological tool precisely because it is offered as fiction and prejudice and so withstands exposure of all sorts. It is a text that first and foremost seeks to expose exposures. Similarly, I find de Man's wartime construction of history already ironized, tactical, a fictionalized reflection on other fictions. Naive doctrines of referentiality, totalization, and organicism deserve criticism, but this critical route will not take us everywhere we want to go.

III

Under what conditions does fear appear as what I have called "Hobbesian fear"? I can begin to answer by saying that it appears at times when the necessities of establishing or maintaining a sovereign authority become obtrusive, as they did to Hobbes during the contests over national religious authority and over the division of sovereignty between king and Parliament in the 1640s. By the time of *Leviathan*, civil war and the problems of establishing the authority of the new revolutionary regime made issues of sovereignty paramount. But I have tried to complicate my answer by exploring Hobbesian fear in texts by Richardson and the later de Man in which the structuring role of sovereign institutions seems hardly to be acknowledged. If we accept J. H. Plumb's political historiography, by the time of Richardson's *Clarissa* England had achieved, partly through the ministerial arts of patronage politics, a decisive degree of "political stability."[27] Certainly the presumption of political stability has been entrenched in the United States of the "postwar" era, in which de Man wrote his later criticism. So perhaps the inattention to or back-grounding of the state is a matter of taking its structures for granted. Or it may be that at times significant political power at the level of governmental institutions seems very much out of reach, and writers and even large-scale movements look to other sorts of social power, as in the "antipolitics" of central Europe for most of the 1980s.

Yet the issues of sovereign authority do not ever entirely disappear. De Man's two transfers of allegiance probably have some bearing on his obsessive inquiry into the epistemology of texts. And the problem of allegiance posed by the war in Vietnam partly explains the obsessive interest de Man's arguments inspired in his readers. The disruptive discourse found in *Clarissa* may have something to do with the failure of peaceful national consensus in the Jacobite uprising of 1745. By giving to Clarissa's violent and patriarchal brother the name of James and to Lovelace the scheming traits of the Restoration rake, by giving to Clarissa the claims of religious conscience and of legal right, Richardson could suggest the difficulties of absorbing the seventeenth-century revolutionary past into a general culture, difficulties that Burke later asserted had been successfully "veiled." Persistent armed conflict in Northern Ireland in our time reveals the long-term costs, the causes of instability structural to the "growth of political stability in England." We could read the tragedy of *Clarissa* as an allegory of the social peace that never fully comes into being.

My pursuit of Hobbesian thematics was inspired by the perception that complacency about national stability has long kept citizens of the United States from bringing questions of sovereignty into systematic relation with other kinds of political questions. This barrier is not merely an effect of disciplinary borders or historical ignorance among literary critics. It limits our political understanding everywhere we turn, our understanding both of what we have accomplished and of what we need to accomplish. When the veil that obscures our relation to our own state is torn aside, as when we regard the role of the courts, police, and legislatures in the interplay of violent forces in the abortion controversy, we are painfully surprised and confused. We are astounded that our familiar language of individual rights does little to arbitrate claims of multiply divided and competing nationalities emerging in the breakup of the Soviet Union. And we have been led, in spite of all our knowledge, to fight for a balance of power among the nations of the Middle East, which our own violence must inevitably disrupt in innumerable and unpredictable ways. This is a very frightening conclusion to have reached in January 1991.

Notes

1. "Richardson and the New Literary History: Places of Fear," delivered at the American Society for Eighteenth-Century Studies in Boston, April 1984.

2. Samuel Richardson, *Clarissa; or, The History of a Young Lady*, ed. John Butt (London: 1962), 4 vols., 2:383. This is a corrupt text, but the only complete edition of Richardson's revised novel that is readily available. Subsequent references will be made parenthetically in my text.

3. Carol Kay, "Sex, Sympathy, and Authority in Richardson and Hume," in *Studies in Eighteenth-Century Culture*, vol. 12, ed. Harry C. Payne (Madison, Wis.: 1983), 77–92; later expanded in Carol Kay, *Political Constructions: Defoe, Richardson, and Sterne in Relation to Hobbes, Hume, and Burke* (Ithaca, N.Y.: 1988), ch. 3, "Richardson: Plots of Intimate Knowledge," 121–95.

4. Carol Kay, "On the Verge of Politics: Border-Tactics for Eighteenth-Century Studies," *boundary 2* 12, no. 2 (Winter 1984): 198–99. See also William Beatty Warner, *Reading "Clarissa": The Struggle of Interpretation* (New Haven, Conn.: 1979).

5. William Beatty Warner, "Reading Rape: Marxist-Feminist Figurations of the Literal," *Diacritics* 13, no. 4 (Winter 1983): 27. Warner is reviewing Terry Castle, *Clarissa's Cyphers: Meaning and Disruption in Richardson's "Clarissa"* (Ithaca, N.Y.: 1982), and Terry Eagleton, *The Rape of Clarissa: Writing, Sexuality, and Class Struggle in Samuel Richardson* (Minneapolis, Minn.: 1982).

6. I was delighted to find his reference to the rape of the lock, because in my review-essay I wrote that Warner treats the rape of Clarissa like "The Rape of the Lock." See Kay, "On the Verge," 199.

7. Suzanne Gearhart, "Philosophy *Before* Literature: Deconstruction, Historicity, and the Work of Paul de Man," *Diacritics* 13, no. 4 (Winter 1983), esp. 75–80.

8. Paul de Man, *Blindness and Insight: Essays in the Rhetoric of Contemporary Criticism* (New York: 1971), 134.

9. Paul de Man, *Allegories of Reading* (New Haven, Conn.: 1979), 149, translating from Rousseau's *Essai sur l'origine des langues* a passage alluded to but not discussed in detail in the argument of *Blindness and Insight*.

10. de Man, *Blindness and Insight*, 134–35.

11. *Allegories of Reading*, 151.

12. Jean-Jacques Rousseau, *Essai sur l'origine des langues* (Paris: 1970), 505. Translations from this work are my own.

13. Ibid., 505.

14. Ibid., 527.

15. Ibid., 542.

16. de Man, *Allegories of Reading*, 19.

17. Ibid.,155.

18. Ibid., 159.

19. Thomas Hobbes, *Leviathan*, ed. C. B. McPherson (Harmondsworth: 1968), part I, ch. 4, 109. All further references will be given parenthetically by part, chapter, and page. Thus, in this case, (I, 4, 109).

20. Leo Strauss, *The Political Philosophy of Thomas Hobbes* (1936), trans. Elsa M. Sinclair (Chicago: 1963).

21. de Man, *Allegories of Reading*, 271.

22. Ibid., 266–27.

23. Ibid., 150.

24. Jacques Derrida, "Like the Sound of the Sea Deep within a Shell: Paul de Man's War," *Critical Inquiry* 14 (1988): 608.

25. Edmund Burke, *A Philosophical Inquiry into the Origin of Our Ideas of the Sublime and Beautiful*, ed. J. T. Boulton (Notre Dame, Ind.: 1968), esp. part V.

26. Edmund Burke, *Reflections on the Revolution in France*, ed. Conor Cruise O'Brien (Harmondsworth: 1968), 102–3, 118–19, 170–71.

27. J. H. Plumb, *The Growth of Political Stability in England, 1675–1725* (Harmondsworth: 1973).

CHAPTER 7

Us and Them
On the Philosophical Bases of Political Criticism

Satya P. Mohanty

In a context in which the relationships between our knowledge of and participation in the external world and such criteria as truth, objectivity, and rationality are being reexamined, the claims of a specifically political criticism come to occupy the center of the intellectual stage. Whether inspired by social and intellectual movements such as feminism, Marxism, and anti-imperialist nationalisms or by interdisciplinary academic developments such as deconstruction and more generally post-structuralism, political criticism can be identified by at least a common desire to expose the social interests at work in the reading and writing of literature. It may not always be tied to larger programs or alternative models of cultural practice, but criticism is political to the extent that it defines as one of its goals the interrogation of the *uses* to which literary works are put, exploring the connections between social institutions and literary texts, between groups of people understood collectively in terms of gender, sexuality, race, and class, and discourses about cultural meanings and values. This essay is an attempt to identify, define, and criticize what I see as an unexamined philosophical position latent in contemporary political-critical practice—cultural or historical relativism. Relativism appears less as an idea than as a practical and theoretical bias, and leads, I believe, to a certain amount of historical simplification and political naïveté. My specific contention is that a relativist position does not allow for a complex understanding of social and cultural phenomena since the vagueness of its definition of rationality precludes a serious analysis of historical agency. In outlining the claims of two versions of relativism, an extreme and a more sophisticated kind, I intend to show why we need a more precise definition of rationality than either offers. As I shall argue, it would be seriously debilitating for critical analysis to confuse a minimal notion of rationality as a cognitive and practical human capacity with the grand a priori foundational structure that has traditionally been called Reason. Indeed, as we seek now to understand the colonial encounters that have shaped our historical modernity, and extend or radically revise our current notions of philosophical and cultural "conversation,"[1] the task of elaborating a positive posthumanist conception of the "human" can be seen as tied to this specification of a minimal rationality. I suggest that the need for a basic definition of human agency, and the conception of rationality it implies, should be faced directly by political criticism, and I shall outline the context in which this and related issues might be analyzed. After providing preliminary definitions of political criticism and relativism and delineating some of the relevant contexts in which they can be discussed, I shall offer in the next section of this essay a more specific account of a debate within social anthropology to show the complexity of political motives, alignments, and positions involved in any topic-specific consideration of relativism. The third section provides the primary arguments against relativist positions considered generally, suggesting why they will not serve as useful bases for political criticism. The last section develops my reasons for considering human agency and rationality urgent issues for contemporary criticism and proposes the terms with which such issues might be elaborated.

Framing the Issues: Contexts and Definitions

It would be useful, before going on, to indicate the intellectual context in which relativism can be said to have originated to clarify both its value as a political gesture and its limits as a concept for the analysis of literature and culture. Even though it took definite shape in the course of the nineteenth century, relativism has its origins in the late-eighteenth-century reaction to the universalist claims of Enlightenment thought. Stressing not merely the presence of historical variety but also the constitutional differences evident in human languages, communities, and societies, writers such as J. G. Herder urged that we recognize the changeability of human "nature." Their arguments pointed up the inability of any single faculty, such as what the Enlightenment thinkers called Reason, to comprehend the diverse manifestations of human culture and history. Herder emphasized the creativity of the human mind and argued that we understand its individual creations only by situating them in their particular social and cultural contexts. The development of relativism as a powerful intellectual presence is, as Patrick Gardiner has shown in a useful essay, best seen as a post-Herderian phenomenon that draws on nineteenth-century German idealist philosophy; Fichte, Hegel, and ultimately Dilthey are the convenient individual signposts of this intellectual-historical narrative.[2] Very generally understood, this development underscored the need to define the claims of difference over identity, historical novelty and variety over methodological monism: against the Enlightenment's emphasis on a singular rationality underlying and comprehending all human activities, relativism pursued the possibilities of change, variety, and difference, and began thereby to pose the question of otherness.

This question becomes a basic political gesture in the context of contemporary literary theory and criticism. To situate and illustrate this politics, let me cite as epigraphs three quotations from fairly influential and representative sources that suggest both the present dominant political-critical climate and a possible basis for relativist arguments. These passages are representative of a general tendency in contemporary criticism; indeed, they delineate some of the central features of what one writer has punningly called the post-structuralist *condition*.[3] The emphasis on discontinuity, the celebration of difference and heterogeneity, and the assertion of plurality as opposed to reductive unities—these ideas have animated almost an entire generation of literary and cultural critics. I do not propose to explicate the passages here, nor am I attempting an intellectual history; what I would like to do, however, is identify one issue inherent in some of the large political-philosophical gestures we see in these quotations, and examine its meanings and implications. Let me then begin by underscoring one theme all these passages imply or directly discuss: a sort of epistemic mutation, relevant not only in cultural criticism but in social theory and historiography as well.

> [The] epistemological mutation is not yet complete. But it is not of recent origin either, since its first phase can no doubt be traced back to Marx. But it took a long time to have much effect. Even now—and this is especially true in the case of the history of thought—it has been neither registered nor reflected upon, while other, more recent transformations—those of linguistics, for example—have been. It is as if it was particularly difficult, in the history in which men retrace their own ideas and their own knowledge, to formulate a general theory of discontinuity, of series, of limits, unities, specific orders, and differentiated autonomies and dependencies. As if, in that field where we had become used to seeking origins, to pushing back further and further the line of antecedents, to reconstituting traditions, to following evolutive curves,

to projecting teleologies, and to having constant recourse to metaphors of life, we felt a particular repugnance to conceiving of difference, to describing separations and dispersions, to dissociating the reassuring form of the identical. . . . As if we were afraid to conceive of the *Other* in the time of our own thought.

In the beginning are our differences. The new love dares for the other, wants the other, makes dizzying, precipitous flights between knowledge and invention. The woman arriving over and over again does not stand still; she's everywhere, she exchanges, she is the desire-that-gives. . . . Wherever history unfolds as the history of death, she does not tread. Opposition, hierarchizing exchange, the struggle for mastery . . . all that comes from a period in time governed by phallocentric values. The fact that this period extends into the present doesn't prevent woman from starting the history of life somewhere else. Elsewhere, she gives. . . . This is an "economy" that can no longer be put in economic terms. Wherever she loves, all the old concepts of management are left behind. At the end of a more or less conscious computation, she finds not her sum but her differences. . . . When I write, it's everything that we don't know we can be that is written out of me. . . . Heterogeneous, yes. . . . the erotogeneity of the heterogeneous. . . .

What is now in crisis is a whole conception of socialism which rests upon the ontological centrality of the working class, upon the role of Revolution, with a capital "r," as the founding moment in the transition from one type of society to another, and upon the illusory prospect of a perfectly unitary and homogeneous collective will that will render pointless the moment of politics. The plural and multifarious character of contemporary social struggles has finally dissolved the last foundation for that political imaginary. Peopled with "universal" subjects and conceptually built around History in the singular, it has postulated "society" as an intelligible structure that could be intellectually mastered on the basis of certain class positions and reconstituted, as a rational, transparent order, through a founding act of a political character. Today the Left is witnessing the final act of the dissolution of that Jacobin imaginary.

Common to all three passages is the idea that something of significance has been repressed or left unarticulated in our traditional conceptual frameworks. Though what is left out is variously formulated and named, the political force of these passages derives from a recognition that crucial social interests might be at stake in these absences or repressions, and the challenge for a critical discourse is to create the possibility for their (self-)representation. At the very least these passages urge us to respect the difference between the terms of the dominant framework and those the absent or repressed might use for its self-representation. But even that formulation is a little clumsy for what these passages would like to suggest. Our concepts of "representation" or even of what that "it" might be (is it necessarily to be conceived in the singular, evidencing a unity, for instance?) are perhaps implicated in the very process of this repression or absence. Indeed, what the passages urge us to do is radicalize the idea of difference itself—the other is not us, they insist, and is quite possibly not even *like* us. Herein lies the challenge: how do we conceive the other, indeed the Other, outside of our inherited concepts and beliefs so as not to replicate the patterns of repression and subjugation we notice in the traditional conceptual frameworks? There are large and very difficult issues implied by this question, and much of our understanding of what is crucial to a poststructuralist political and critical climate depends on how we define and specify these issues. More than any synoptic or comprehensive view of poststructuralism, what we need today is greater clarity about what is presupposed, implied, or entailed by our formulation of questions of the "other," which would in effect be an interrogation of proposed agendas through the process of seeking precise definitions. It is with this in view that I would like to ask whether one of the possible extreme implications of these passages—that it is necessary to conceive the Other as a radically separable and separate entity in order for it to command our respect—is a useful idea. Just how other, we need to force ourselves to specify, is the Other? In literary criticism, as I shall indicate more directly toward the end of this essay, such a question arises whenever we discuss unequal relations among groups of people, among languages, and among canons, with their institutionally sanctioned definitions of value, coherence, unity, and intelligibility. In all these instances, the crucial problems arise when we encounter other canons (or the noncanonical), other languages, and other values—in short, when we encounter competing claims and are forced to adjudicate. It is then that relativism becomes a viable philosophical option.

Relativism, as a methodological and substantive thesis, appears in various forms in various disciplinary contexts, but the most immediate context from which contemporary criticism learns to specify its discussion of cultural otherness is anthropology. In fact, the development of poststructuralist ideas in France can be historically located: the trajectory of purely philosophical concerns was influenced by preceding and contemporaneous debates in ethnology. As has been argued in various ways, the institutional history of anthropology is tied to the European colonial expansion of the latter part of the nineteenth century. Naturally, the decline of the formal empires of Europe and the rise of anticolonial movements and independent national states of the "Third World" can be said to have encouraged a greater self-consciousness among anthropologists—from both the international "metropoles" and the "peripheral" countries—

about the politics of studying other cultures. Thus, to put it very sche-
matically, if it was possible to see anthropological description and interpretation of Third World cultures during the heyday of imperialism as
largely complicitous with the exercise of power and the discursive map-
ping and manipulation of powerless others, the self-criticism of Western
anthropology needs to be understood not simply as the natural matura-
tion and intellectual coming of age of a discipline, but rather as the result
of both political challenges presented by these others and the related
demystification of the West's recent history by its own progressive intellectuals. In this context, it is possible to see in the debates within, say,
social anthropology in Britain in the last four decades or so a heightened
concern with methodological politics, an awareness of the historically
entrenched nature of scholarly representations. Unselfconscious—and
interested—misreadings of Third World societies and their values, texts,
and practices, were, it was found, made possible not so much because of
overt and explicitly stated racism (although there was a good dose of that
in scholarly literature for anyone interested in looking), but primarily
because of uncritical application and extension of the very ideas with
which the West has defined its enlightenment and its modernity: Reason,
Progress, Civilization.[4]

In this context—a context so general that it would be impossible to
understand recent developments in most of the social sciences and the
humanistic disciplines without it—the relativist thesis initially becomes
a valuable political weapon. Opposing the imperial arrogance of the
scholar who interprets aspects of other cultures in terms of the inflexible
norms and categories of the scholar's own, the relativist insists on the
fundamentally sound idea that individual elements of a given culture
must be interpreted primarily in terms of that culture, relative, that is,
to that system of meanings and values. Thus there is a clear political
lesson that relativism teaches: it cautions us against ethnocentrist explanations of other communities and cultures. Drawing on the example of
ethnology, the relativist will tell us that texts (or events or values) can
be significantly *misunderstood* if they are not seen in relation to their
particular contexts. The relativist warns against reductionist explanations that use the terms of the familiar culture to appropriate the terms
of the strange one. The central challenge is to the practices of interpretation and the unconscious *evaluations* embedded in them, for relativism
teaches us that interpretation and understanding have historically been
tied to political activities, and that "strong" and "meaningful" interpretations have often been acts of discursive domination. Instead, relativism
urges care and attentiveness to the specificities of context; it emphasizes
the differences between and among us rather than pointing to shared

spaces. What is hoped is that we will, one day, learn to share; that is relativism's utopia.

Relativism in Anthropology: An Instructive Exchange

From this very general account it might be possible to see how the relativist position can hold a geat deal of attraction for contemporary political criticism. Problems begin to appear when we go beyond this general formulation and examine the position a little more closely, articulating its deeper implications and presuppositions. I shall be arguing in a moment that relativism is an untenable—and indeed rather dangerous—philosophical ally for political criticism. But let me first identify the larger scope and potential ambiguity of the issues involved by focusing on two essays, one by Ernest Gellner and one by Talal Asad. Gellner's is a classic, canonized essay, first published in 1951 and included in undergraduate textbooks in Britain to this day; Asad's critique appeared in a recent collection of essays by anthropologists critical of the politics of their own inherited tradition.[5] Gellner attacks the relativist thesis in anthropological theory, associating it with a confused and "excessively charitable" intellectual and political attitude. Asad, in his critique of Gellner's essay, does not so much defend relativism as outline one serious way in which Gellner's attack is misconceived. In Asad's view, the emphasis should be placed on institutions of anthropological "cultural translation," existing as they do in a matrix of unequal languages and asymmetrical access to the institutions of discourse and power. I would like to outline some of these arguments briefly to indicate the instructive complexity of the issues involved in this debate; then I would like to show why despite the cogency of Asad's critique—which is particularly trenchant when it identifies the sloppy argumentative moves underlying Gellner's imperious tone—the problems surrounding the issue of relativism need to be explored more thoroughly.

One of the main points Gellner wishes to make in his essay concerns our attitude toward what we might consider "illogical" or "incoherent" ideas in the culture being studied. If the relativist claim remains that all cultural ideas are to be adequately understood only in their own contexts, that is, only in terms of the systematic beliefs, practices, and values of the culture being studied, is the interpreter necessarily committed to always finding meaning and coherence and giving up all capacity to judge ideas in other cultures as incoherent and meaningless? The contextualist-relativist, says Gellner, errs in adopting this attitude of unwarranted "charity." For often in fact we *need* to grasp the internal incoherence of ideas as they operate within a culture in order to understand their precise function and valence. Thus even though the contextual interpretation claims to be giving us the "real" interpretation of something by situating it in its surrounding world of beliefs and practices, Gellner would argue that in many cases the acontextual—isolated—evaluation of it (i.e., of a statement, proposition, or belief) is necessary if we are to provide deeper accounts of it as a cultural phenomenon. What Gellner calls interpretive "charity" is thus more a kind of sentimental liberalism: it dehistoricizes in the name of contextual analysis and ends up ignoring the deep structural bases of the other culture.

After identifying the extreme form of the contextualist position, which would argue that all ideas are to be interpreted solely in terms internal to the context in which they are produced and used, Gellner insists on the need for a strong evaluative interpretation. Instead of arguing for abandoning the subjective dimension in interpreting others, Gellner wishes to assert the need—if an interpretation is to work at all—for applying criteria that do not derive simply from the object itself but are shared by the anthropologist's own culture. The following passage contains what may be the most succinct statement of his methodological thesis:

> Professor Raymond Firth has remarked in *Problem and Assumption in an Anthropological Study of Religion:* "From my own experience, I am impressed by the ease with which it is possible to add one's own personal dimension to the interpretation of an alien religious ideology, to raise the generalizations to a higher power than the empirical content the material warrants." My point is, really, that it is more than a matter of *ease*—it is a matter of necessity: for interpretation cannot be determinate without assumptions concerning the success or failure of the interpreted communication, and the criteria of such success are not manifest in the "content of the material" itself. One has to work them out as best one can, and it will *not* do to take the short cut of reading them off the material by assuming that the material is always successful, i.e. that the statements investigated do satisfy and exemplify criteria of coherence, and hence that interpretation is not successful until this coherence has been made manifest in the translations. The logical *assessment* of an assertion, and the identification of its nearest equivalent in our language, are intimately linked and inseparable. (33–34)

Building on his claim that "sympathetic, positive interpretations of indigenous assertions are not the result of a sophisticated appreciation of context," and that in fact it may be that "the manner in which the context is invoked, the amount and kind of context and the way the context itself is interpreted, depends on prior tacit determination concerning the kind of interpretation one wishes to find" (33), Gellner introduces here a series of more specific claims. Let me reemphasize some of the crucial ones: the "logical assessment" of an idea we have identified in the other culture is absolutely necessary for interpretation of the idea; an adequate interpretation of an idea in an unfamiliar culture involves a close translation into the "language" of the familiar—that is, the anthropologist's—culture.[6] Charity is less crucial here than we might think; indeed, it might be a conceptual and analytical straitjacket. If Gellner is right, we need to worry more about the internal coherence or logic of the idea in isolation *before* we begin to determine what the appropriate context for interpreting it might be.

This last point is in fact specified by Gellner himself elsewhere in the essay. We evaluate an idea encountered in another culture by apprehending it as an "assertion," for which we then seek an equivalent assertion in our own language. And just as we judge assertions in our own language as either "Good" or "Bad" (Gellner's deliberately schematic terms to cover such polar attributes as true and false, meaningful and absurd, sensible and silly, etc.), we need also to evaluate the assertion/idea in the other culture. The "tolerance-engendering contextual interpretation," however, evades this rigorous process of "logical assessment" by assuming in advance that all assertions we encounter in the other culture are "Good," that is, meaningful and coherent, especially when we understand their own contextual terms and functions. For Gellner, this makes a mockery of the interpretive process itself, which must build on the logical assessment of (isolated) assertions.

The crucial assumption here is that "logical assessment" of assertions can be made only to the extent that we define them in isolation, and we isolate assertions in their (unfamiliar) language exactly the way we do in our (familiar) one. It would seem that for Gellner the identification of an assertion—its definition in isolation from whatever we consider its context—is an unproblematical activity. It is this naive atomism, difficult enough to sustain when we are studying elements *within* our own culture and obviously more complicated and arrogant when we are approaching another, on which Gellner's argument seems to be based. Despite the occasional appearance of terms like *interpretation* and *hermeneutics,* the essay exists in the bliss of prehermeneutical positivist confidence. The liberal relativists in anthropology among Gellner's contemporaries, fueled by a generally Wittgensteinian philosophical climate, need to be attacked, and these are the essential terms with which he counters them. Gellner's terms of analysis, derived from his essentially positivist framework, obscure the most significant issues involved in anthropological interpretation in several ways. Talal Asad identifies one of these quite well; I would like to provide a selective account of his critique before I discuss the inadequacy of Gellner's treatment of relativism. In doing that, however, I will need, first, to develop our understanding of the relativist position by adding another level of complexity to the issues involved; and second, to make Gellner's case against relativism with entirely different terms, challenging the liberals he attacks not for their excessive charity and tolerance but the political apathy entailed by their philosophical position.

Since Asad's critique of Gellner might have significant bearing on contemporary literary-critical theory and practice, it is instructive to look at it in some detail. The most basic consideration Asad wishes to introduce into the discussion is simply that of the context of anthropological interpretation itself: not just the interpretation of, say, the Nuers and the Berbers, but of Anglophone white anthropologists writing in the middle of the twentieth century within intellectually and politically sanctioned hierarchies and codifications of knowledge. For what Gellner is able to ignore throughout his essay is the existence of institutionally sanctioned power relations between interpreter and the interpreted that determine the politics of meaning in the first place. That the following reminder is necessary is itself embarassing, and it might indeed point up the ambiguity of any critique or relativism, including the one I am making in this essay. But Asad, let us remember, is not interested in defending the version of contextual-relativism Gellner attacks; rather, he is at pains to lay out the basic contextual terms with which any anthropological interpretive practice that sees itself performing "cultural translation" must engage:

> The relevant question . . . is not how tolerant an attitude the translator
> ought to display toward the original author (an abstract ethical dilemma),
> but how she can test the tolerance of her own language for assuming
> unaccustomed forms. . . . [T]he matter is largely something the translator
> cannot determine by individual activity (any more than the individual
> speaker can affect the evolution of his or her language)—that it is
> governed by institutionally governed power relations between the
> languages/modes of life concerned. To put it crudely: because the
> languages of Third World societies—including, of course, the societies that
> social anthropologists have traditionally studied—are "weaker" in relation
> to Western languages . . . they are more likely to submit to forcible
> transformation in the translation process than the other way around. The
> reason for this is, first, that in their political-economic relations with Third
> World countries, Western nations have the greater ability to
> manipulate. . . . And, second, Western languages produce and deploy
> desired knowledge more readily than Third World languages do. (157–58)

Asad raises two closely related issues here to contest Gellner's abstract approach. The first questions the adequacy of Gellner's formulation of the problem of interpretation in terms of the logical "charity" or "tolerance," and we shall see in a moment how Asad would extend the meaning of the term by restoring to it its practical context. The second deals with the fundamental model of "translation" itself. Gellner's formulation of anthropological interpretation in terms of "charity" is a convenient abstraction that obscures the practice of Western anthropologists studying other—that is, non-Western—cultures particularly in colonial and postcolonial contexts, since it ignores the basic hermeneutic question about the adequacy of the anthropologist's own cultural language (i.e., its capacity for "tolerance" of new and unfamiliar meanings). The *possibility* that the interpreter and her analytical apparatus might be fundamentally challenged and changed by the material she (and it) are attempting to "assess" is one that Gellner's account of the interpretive process ignores. Whether this account and others like it are naively positivist or whether they trail clouds of ideology and a specifiable political motive is something that needs analysis on its own terms. It may well be that "decolonizing" anthropology will involve writing the discipline's prehistory in the process of developing such analyses, situating these glaring political blindnesses in the context of what may be their limited and skewed intellectual insights.[7]

In our obsessive fear that the typical Western anthropologist might be guilty of excessive interpretive charity, we ignore the more significant fact that in our particular historical contexts the anthropologist, in order to be able to interpret at all, needs to educate herself through cultural and political "sympathy." Indeed, if we deepen our analysis we realize that the model of cultural translation is itself a misleading one: "the anthropologist's translation is not merely a matter of matching sentences in the abstract, but of *learning to live another form of life*" (Asad 149). The echo of Wittgenstein is deliberate, given Gellner's identification of the philosophical enemy, but it raises the important question about the limits of the conception of anthropological interpretation as a translation from one language to another. It suggests that "languages" are not merely "texts" if by that we mean that "translations" can be considered "*essentially* a matter of verbal representation" (160). Anthropological interpretation can be conceived as translation only if we recognize that a successful translation may potentially change our very language; for indeed, as Walter Benjamin has said, the success of the translation of a significant text depends on our very ability to transform our language— that is, our modes and habits of thought and action. By extension, this includes our institutional contexts of interpretation, our "disciplines" and their regimes of truth and scientificity, and the organization of power relations within the global system. An adequate anthropological interpretation must then include not only "translation" but also an account of "how power enters into the process of 'cultural translation' [which must be] seen both as a discursive and as a non-discursive practice" (163). An instance of this *discursive* power—and the nondiscursive power it banks on—is Gellner's very influential formulation of the interpretive process. The model of language and writing here serves to blind us to an entire history that is embedded in the processes of "logical assessment" and decoding meaning. Gellner arrogates to himself the "privileged position" of the interpreter to the very extent that he wishes, as anthropologist, not to interrogate his very real control of the entire operation of this translation, "from field notes to printed ethnography." His "is the privileged position of someone who does not, and can afford not to, engage in a genuine dialogue with those he or she once lived with and now *writes* about" (155).

Gellner's "privileged position" is both theoretically and historically specifiable. The Whiggish tone of the essay betrays more than a simple emotional attitude; it in fact points to a philosophical confidence in a narrowly defined Reason to lay bare the world, a deeply entrenched belief in the adequacy of his "logical assessment" of the "assertion" of the other culture in comprehending its underlying social function. Gellner's "logic" encompasses the entire space of the globe and its meanings; complexity of contextual function and meaning in every conceivable other space is granted only a limited autonomy since its essential terms remain formulated by the terms of Gellner's discursive world. Asad points out the ways in which this view is historically convenient since it blinds social anthropologists to the contexts of power they inhabit; a sophisticated relativist would add to this an account of the ways in which Gellner significantly misunderstands the complexities of his object of study by reducing them to translatable "assertions."

The Political Implications of Relativism

It is important to note that analysis of Gellner's reduction of complex cultural objects to "assertions" should not ignore his legitimate insight that the "incoherences" of assertions and concepts of a given culture can indeed be "socially functional" (42), that they do not need to be logically clear, distinct, and coherent ideas in order for us to be able to study their significance. What Gellner himself fails to recognize, however, is that this is an issue entirely different from the presence of varying criteria of "rational" judgment in different cultures. In other words, the fact that assertions or beliefs may be incoherent in a significant way does not diminish the interpretive complexity of the anthropologist's task in determining the specific terms with which they must be evaluated. And the issue raised by the sophisticated relativist is simply that these terms, these criteria of rationality, may vary significantly from culture to culture. Before we develop our understanding of this position in order to be clear about what exactly is involved in the significant variance of criteria of rationality, it might be best to see what the extreme relativist position involves and why it is more than a bit problematical.

The most extreme relativist formulation of the problem would be that there are no common terms between and among these rationalities, that the spaces different cultures define are entirely different from one another. Reacting sharply to the ahistorical vision underlying Gellner's Whiggery, the extreme relativist would point to the necessity of restoring to our critical perspective the presence of a plurality of spaces and values, the plurality of criteria of judgment and rationality implicit in the different cultural and historical contexts. Gellner's narrow conception of rationality, it would be easy to argue, is predicated on a false and reductive view of modern history as unproblematically One: guided by Reason, obeying the logic of Progress and Modernization, Gellner's model of history is one that should belong to the prehistory of a critical anthropology.[8] For in our "postmodern" world, History is no longer feasible; what we need to talk about, to pay attention to, are histories—in the plural. This position builds on the present pervasive feeling in the human sciences that the grand narrative of history seems a little embarrassing; what we need to reclaim instead, as is often pointed out in cultural criticism and theory, is the plurality of our heterogeneous lives, the darker and unspoken densities of past and present that are lived, fought, and imagined as various communities and peoples seek to retrace and reweave the historical text. In the history of criticism, encountering for the first time the challenge of alternative canons defined by feminist, black, Third World, and other scholars, this is initially not only a valuable critical idea but also the basis for an energizing critical-political project. After all, we have just been learning to speak of feminisms, instead of the singular form that implicitly hid the varied experiences of women's struggles along different racial and class vectors under the hegemonic self-image of the heterosexual white middle-class movement; we have learned to write "marxism" without capitalizing the *m*, thereby pointing to the need to reconceive the relationship to some unitary originary source; we have, in effect, taught ourselves that if history was available to us, it was always as a *text*, that is, to be read and reread dialogically, and to be rewritten in a form other than that of a monologue, no matter how consoling or noble the monologue's tone or import.

Plurality is thus a political ideal as much as it is a methodological slogan. But the issue of competing rationalities raises a nagging question: how do we negotiate between my history and yours? How would it be possible for us to recover our commonality, not the ambiguous imperial-humanist myth of the shared human attributes that are supposed to distinguish us all from animals, but, more significantly, the imbrication of our various pasts and presents, the ineluctable relationships of shared and contested meanings, values, material resources? It is necessary to assert our dense particularities, our lived and imagined differences; but could we afford to leave untheorized the question of how our differences are intertwined and, indeed, hierarchically organized? Could we, in other words, afford to have *entirely* different histories, to see ourselves as living—and having lived—in entirely heterogeneous and discrete spaces?

It will not do, then, to formulate the issue of competing rationalities and histories in the rather simplistic terms of merely *different* rationalities and histories. For the extreme relativist position, despite its initial attraction, seems to be philosophically and politically confused. Every philosopher worth her salt will tell us that this kind of relativism is easily refutable. In fact, she will declare a little contemptuously, such a relativism is *self-refuting*. The argument is summed up rather neatly in the following way: If the relativist position is that there can be nothing other than context-specific truth-claims, that the "truth" of every cultural or historical text is purely immanent to its immediate context, then on what grounds should I believe the relativist? If the relativist says that everything is entirely context-specific, claiming that we cannot adjudicate among contexts or texts on the basis of larger—that is, more general—evaluative or interpretative criteria, then why should I bother to take seriously *that very relativist claim?* The point is that one cannot both claim to hold the relativist position and expect to really convince anyone who does not already believe the position; there is no serious way in which the relativist, insofar as she wishes to be consistent, can ask me to take her serously. There is a self-refutation built into the argument, and it renders relativism less a significant philosophical position than a pious—though not ineffectual—political wish.

The problem is, however, that a refutation of this sort is not quite relevant for the way relativist ideas operate in contemporary critical circles. Relativism rarely appears as an explicit and reasoned position; instead, as I have suggested, it is embedded in our critical gestures, in the kinds of questions we ask or refuse to raise.[9] The more significant challenge would be to see whether there are political implications of the relativist position that the relativist would be interested in *not* bringing along in her baggage. And I think there is at least one rather serious problem that relativism entails. To believe that you have your space and I mine, to believe, further, that there can be no responsible way in which I can adjudicate between your cultural and historical space and mine by developing a set of general criteria that would have interpretive validity in both contexts (because there can be no interpretation that is not simultaneously an evaluation), to believe both these things is also to assert something quite large. Quite simply, it is to assert that *all spaces are equivalent:* that they have equal value, that since the lowest common principle of evaluation is all that I can invoke, I cannot—and consequently need not—think about how your space impinges on mine, or how my history is defined together with yours. If that is the case, I may have started by declaring a pious political wish, but I end by denying that I need to take you seriously. Plurality instead of a single homogeneous space, yes. But also, unfortunately, debilitatingly insular spaces. Thus what needs to be emphasized is that this extreme relativist position—and extreme especially when its implications remain inadequately thought out—is in no way a feasible theoretical basis of politically motivated criticism. It is in fact a dangerous philosophical ally, since it is built on, at best, naive and sentimental reasoning. To the extent that our initial interest in relativism was motivated by a political respect for other selves, other spaces, other contexts, relativism seems now to be an unacceptable theoretical position. It might encourage a greater sensitivity to the contexts of production of cultural ideas, but it will not, given the terms of its formulation, enable the "genuine dialogue" between anthropologist and native, the former colonizer and the formerly colonized, that Talal Asad calls for.

The sophisticated relativist would deny not simply Gellner's kind of claim that the West's rationality can unproblematically evaluate the beliefs and practices of the other culture, but would also wish to distance herself from the position of extreme relativism that commits us all to radically separate and insular spaces. A genuine dialogue of the kind Asad envisions would become possible only when we admit that crucial aspects of the non-Western culture may have a high degree of coherence as part of a larger web of ideas, beliefs, and practices, and moreover that *some* of these aspects may be untranslatable to the language of the Western anthropologist's culture in terms of its historically sedimented and institutionally determined practices of knowing. The classic example is the practice of "magic" and ritual. From the point of view of the modern West, of course, these practices might be seen as coherent and of a piece with an entire form of life, but interpreted more rigorously they could reveal a "primitive" system of belief and an "irrational" practice. Magical rites are patently "unscientific" when the primitive culture pursues them despite a lack of observable or tabulatable evidence that they do have the effects they are supposed to have. Rituals surrounding the planting of crops, for instance, may be practiced because of the belief that they bring about the right kind of weather, and if this were observed to be true, the practice of such rituals would have at least *an* intelligible basis in reason. But what if, as the anthropologist may well note in instance after instance, the practice of this ritual continues despite the absence of any correlation between it and the weather? In that case should the practitioners not be considered irrational in their practice of at least this ritual, and quite possibly unscientific in their use of magic and ritual generally?

The philosopher Peter Winch argues in his famous essay "Understanding a Primitive Society" that it would be wrong to come to even this conclusion.[10] Conducting a debate with Alasdair MacIntyre, who argues something like the above concerning the practices of the Azande, Winch points out how important it is to specify with greater care the details of the context. For it may be that the Zande practice of magic and ritual can go hand in hand with a clear working distinction between practices and knowledges that are technical and those that are magical. In this case—and indeed this is the case according to the anthropological account of the Azande by Evans-Pritchard, which both Winch and MacIntyre are discussing—Zande magic cannot be subsumed into the Western category of the "unscientific." Since Zande practices exist in a larger web that is constituted in part by the magical-technical opposition, Zande magic could be considered (merely) unscientific only if the Azande *confused* it with their technical practices. When a clear distinction exists between magical and technical practices, a one-to-one translation across cultures that ignores the intention of the practitioners is either misleading or at least grossly reductionist. According to Winch, the significant hermeneutical problem in this context can be raised through a kind of dialogue between the Western and Zande webs of beliefs and practices. Thus he considers it important to recognize "that *we* do not initially have a category that looks at all like the Zande category of magic" (102). This is the source of the difficulty but also the beginning of an answer: "Since it is we who want to understand the Zande category, it appears that the onus is on us to extend our understanding so as to make room for the Zande category, rather than to insist on seeing it in terms of our own ready-made distinction between science and non-science" (102). This constitutes the beginning of a *dialogue* because "we" are forced to extend our understanding by interrogating its limits in terms of Azande categories of self-understanding. This dialogue marks the true hermeneutical moment rather than the explanation—or, worse yet, the "logical assessment" (Gellner)—of a discursive object. Two systems of understanding encounter each other to the very extent that both are contextualized as forms of life; this encounter leaves open the possibility of a fundamental change in both. If we recall the basic issues raised by the passages I quoted at the beginning of this essay, it will be clear how this kind of hermeneutical encounter provides at least one solution to the problem posed by the Other.

Winch's achievement consists in showing us that we need to respect other cultures not as insular and impenetrable wholes but rather as complex webs of beliefs and actions. He does this by emphasizing what I have just discussed: that notions of rationality cannot be unproblematically applied across cultures precisely because there are different— and *competing*—rationalities, and one must acknowledge this fact in order to appreciate the specific modalities of actions and beliefs in a given culture. The relationship between cause and effect in cultural practices, for instance, can be understood at different levels. The Zande magical rites performed during the planting of crops need not necessarily be understood by the Azande themselves as leading to (i.e., having the effect of) a certain change in the weather. It would clearly be an improper interpretation, then, to consider these rites as unscientific or irrational, since the Azande have other purely technical practices that are meant to influence conditions related to the planting of crops and the harvest; it would be wrong, in short, to see these magical rites as "misguided" technical practice. The distinction between technical practices and magical ones should alert us to the fact that magic may serve functions that are of a different *order* altogether. Here is how Winch explains the idea of different orders, that is, different levels of human practice:

> A man's sense of the importance of something to him shows itself in all sorts of ways; not merely in precautions to safeguard that thing. He may want to come to terms with its importance to him in quite a different way: to contemplate it, to gain some sense of his life in relation to it. He may wish thereby, in a certain sense, to *free* himself from dependence on it. I do not mean by making sure that it does not let him down, because the point is that, *whatever* he does, he may still be let down. The important thing is that he should understand *that* and come to terms with it. Of course, merely to understand that is not to come to terms with it, though perhaps it is a necessary condition for so doing, for a man may equally well be transfixed and terrorized by the contemplation of such a possibility. He must see that he can still go on even if he is let down by what is vitally important to him; and he must so order his life that he still *can* go on in such circumstances. (103–4; emphases in the original)

The terms with which Winch formulates the discussion in this rich passage make clear that to conceive magical rites as complex practices not reducible to the rational-irrational or scientific-unscientific polarities of the West involves a deeper conception of human practices in general—

that is, in all societies—as complex in their modalities of intention and meaning. As I suggested earlier, the notion of cause and effect is itself one that needs to be intepreted according to its specific modalities. Even within the anthropologist's culture one recognizes the quite different conceptions of causal influence when one speaks of "what made Jones get married" as opposed to, say, "what made the airplane crash" (103). To not acknowledge these differences is simply, as we say in contemporary criticism, to "read" badly. Thus, the most useful lesson that the sophisticated relativist teaches us is that we cannot understand complex cultural acts by reducing them hastily to their propositional content; indeed the reduction often involves basic kinds of misreading and misidentification. And to the extent that we define "rationality" on the basis of such terms as logical consistency or the pragmatic choice of means for our technical ends, Winch's arguments as I have presented them would challenge this most fundamental of our concepts.

Culture, Rationality, and Human Agency: The Limits of Otherness

The key issue is, of course, whether there can be more to the idea of rationality—or culture—than this. For even though he discusses the ways in which different cultures can learn from one another, Winch does not quite face up to the question inherent in his own idea of—competing—rationalities. Difference teaches us not merely new technical possibilities, Winch tells us, but also new and possible forms of life. And he is right in emphasizing this. Criteria of rationality are connected to what we call "culture," the larger moral and imaginative patterns through which we deal with our world. However, content as he is with definitions of rationality and cultural practices at the most general level, seeing cultures only as coherent systems, Winch underestimates the complexity of the question of evaluative comparison among these rationalities and cultures. (The absence of emphasis on evaluative comparison is, we recall, what makes a theoretical position ultimately a relativist one.) But such a comparison would necessarily be more rigorously interpretive, involving specification of the various elements and levels that constitute cultures as *articulated* wholes. Winch's cross-cultural comparison of "forms of life" is pitched at such a high level of generality that his versions of human culture and rationality cannnot register and include significant moral and imaginative practices and choices. If it is to constitute a relevant political interrogation, I would argue, the dialogue across cultures that we envision anthropological interpretation at its best to be conducting must in principle be able to include the levels of ordinary, everyday activity. For this to be possible, we need a minimal conception of rationality that will help us understand human activities—both the grand and the humbler ones—as the actions of agents. Let me explain what I mean.

The Subject of Culture

For Peter Winch, the common point of all human cultures is the presence of a few "limiting notions"—fundamental ideas that determine the "ethical space" of all cultures, the space "within which the possibilities of good and evil . . . can be exercised" (107). The three such notions Winch specifies are Birth, Sexuality, and Death. Together they map the limits of possibility that define our lives and consequently outline our ethical universe. According to Winch, then, it is in this universe that rationality has its moorings. I wonder, however, if we do not lose as much as we gain if we pitch the issues on this high a level. We are, according to Winch, rational creatures and can engage in a dialogue with those who are significantly different from us, but this difference is negotiated at such a level of generality that significant aspects of human life such as, for instance, the conditions in which we work, our struggles to forge political communities, or our varying conceptions of cultural identity and selfhood, remain unarticulated and indeed invisible. Winch's human cultures are individually rational, and they are capable of communicating with one another in a process of hermeneutical self-critique and inter-rogation. But the "rationality" they share is not defined in terms specific enough to register and include a great deal of what we usually consider to be our significant practices and beliefs: it is defined merely as the overall *coherence* of the *whole,* the most general systematicity revealed in the way a culture's actions, beliefs, and intellectual judgments all hang together. Given such a broad definition, *most* of what constitutes our historical life, our humbler acts as social agents and thinkers, remains closed to transcultural dialogue to the very extent that these acts are not ultimately subsumable to birth, death, and sexuality, not registered in the systematicity of the whole. Winch's version of rationality—as inev-itably tied in this way to the large cultural schemes by which we define and live our lives—has gained in moral suppleness over the positivist and the ethnocentric ones, but it seems to have forfeited much of its capacity to judge and interpret; it may have gained in amplitude but it has also become, as it were, tone-deaf. And in matters of culture, as in politics, so much of course depends on the *tone* of things.

   A more specific commonality than the one Winch's definition would posit for all human cultures and societies is the one that is implicit in the very definition of culture as social practice. The perspective of prac-tice, as it has been proposed in several recent developments in social

theory across disciplines and methodological approaches, does not necessarily involve the notion of a unitary and self-sufficient Subject as the
author of its actions.[11] The basic claims would include the following:
humans make their world; they make their world in conditions they
inherit and that are not all within their control; theoretically understanding this "making" involves redefining social structures and cultural
institutions as not simply given but *constituted,* and hence containing
the possibility of being changed. Moreover, in this conception, humans
are seen as individual and collective *agents* in their world; their practices
can be specified for analysis without a necessary reduction to their subjective beliefs and intentions. Of course, the agents' intention and beliefs
about their practices are not irrelevant (since they can be aware of their
purposes and actions), but these beliefs cannot be considered the *sole*
determinant of meaning. "Culture" is thus best appreciated as defining
the realm of human choices in (potentially) definable contexts, choices
of individuals and collectives as potentially self-aware agents; it is constituted *in* (and *as*) history. It is the significance of this kind of agency
that Winch's related definitions of culture and rationality fail to register
adequately. What enables him to hold the relativist position with its
overly general definitions of rationality and culture as large—imaginative
and conceptual—schemes is the absence in his account of any further
specification of the "human," a specification that would make comparative interpretation and evaluation of ordinary human activity possible.
One specification we need to make in literary and cultural criticism, I
would argue, is through the conception of *agency* as a basic capacity
shared by all humans *across cultures.* And in understanding the divide
between "us" and "them," it is this common space we all share that
needs to be elaborated and defined.

   In terms of the problematics of modern social theory Winch remains,
if by default and underspecification, on the side of those who privilege the
role of structure and system at the expense of human agency in their interpretations of social phenomena. In literary and cultural criticism, developments associated with structuralism and poststructuralism have made
us aware of the way language and cultural and semiotic systems, seen as
systems, determine both meanings and subject-positions. The political
agendas of these movements have been tied to a genealogical analysis of
European humanism, and a great deal of attention has been paid to the
deconstruction of one of the hallmarks of modern European history—the
Subject, an effect of specific discursive and institutional forces masquerading as universal Man. In this archaeological critical climate, instances
of positive elaboration of the human have been noticeably absent. This is,
we recognize at first, due to a salutary caution: we are all familiar with

accounts of "the human" that are patently speculative and serve sexist, racist, and imperialist programs. We are also aware of how historical knowledge can be used selectively to construct such accounts, and how these definitions can be made to serve dangerous political ends. But the larger question that a philosophical anthrolopogy pursues (regarding the capacities, tasks, and limits that might constitute a specifically human existence), and its historical-philosophical problematic, will not go away, quite simply because our analyses of social and cultural phenomena often involve acknowledged or implicit answers to this and related questions. To the extent that criticism deals with "culture," that is, to the extent that it engages in the interpretation of texts and contexts in the light of what people—individually and collectively—do, think, and make of their lives, these questions regarding the *subject* of cultural practices will remain to be dealt with explicitly. A thoroughgoing deconstruction of "humanism" and its self-authorizing Subject is less an avoidance of this issue than, first and foremost, a clearing of the ground for reconsidering the problems involved.

It is in the context of political criticism, with its specific concern with other values, texts, and cultures, that the need for a minimal account of the human, defining a commonality we all share, becomes immediate and clear. Donald Davidson has shown us in a series of recent essays the extent to which an interpretation of the Other is dependent on an acknowledgment of common ground. Arguing against the general idea of radical untranslatability (between conceptual schemes, cultures, rationalities, etc.) that an extreme relativist position assumes, Davidson has stressed that we appreciate differences to the very extent that we acknowledge our pool of shared words, thoughts, and ideas.[12] Indeed, "we *improve* the clarity and bite of our declarations of difference . . . by *enlarging* the basis of shared (translatable) language or of shared opinion" (197; emphases added). Davidson concludes the famous essay in which he argues this by saying that there is no "intelligible" basis for the position that all cultures, rationalities, and languages are so radically different that we cannot translate any portion of one to another at all; at the same time, the fond belief that all humankind shares "a common scheme and ontology" (198) is one that is not—yet—convincing either. Winch's "rationalities" are homologous to what Davidson calls "schemes" here, and it is important to recognize the ways in which the competition among rationalities must be conceived, beyond Winch's own account, *by specifying and elaborating shared terms, ideas, and spaces.* The shared ground helps us to situate and specify difference, to understand where its deepest resonances might originate. If (as I argued against the relativist position earlier) we are to deal seriously with other cultures and not reduce them to insignificance or irrelevance, we need to begin by positing the following minimal commonality between us and them: the capacity to act purposefully, to be capable of agency and the basic rationality that the human agent must in principle possess.

But what exactly does a specifically *human* agency imply? It does not involve simply *doing* things, such as fetching a bone or building a nest. Animals and birds are capable of such things, but we do not attribute to them the kind of agency that is so crucial to defining practices and, collectively, cultures. It is not even that our actions are purposive and theirs are not, since animals do in fact act purposefully with an end in view and with varying degrees of organizational economy. But what, by our most careful contemporary philosophical accounts, distinguishes us from animals is that we possess the capacity for a certain kind of second-degree thoughts, that is, not merely the capacity to act purposefully but also to *evaluate* actions and purposes in terms of larger ideas we might hold about, say, our political and moral world, or our sense of beauty or form. This capacity underlies the distinction some philosophers make between the vague generic defintion we might have of a member of the human species and a fuller concept of the human "person": the former is a conceptually unspecific, purely descriptive term, while the latter begins to define the terms and categories with which we act and learn, participate in a community, and are held accountable. It is this capacity for a second-order understanding and evaluation, this potential ability to be critically and cumulatively self-aware in relation to our actions, that defines human agency and makes possible the sociality and the historicality of human existence. It is this theoretical ability in effect to possess a meaningful history that we cannot afford to deny to the cultural Other if we are to interpret that Other.

To go back to the example of the Azande, it would need to be specified that their magical rituals, which do not make sense to "us," are *at the very least* the actions of agents in the sense I have just outline. They cannot, in theory, be unintelligible and meaningless, not simply because they are in accord with the larger cultural and rational pattern whereby the Azande organize their lives and their values (as Winch would point out) but rather because of the more specific point that the rituals are social practices, open to us for analysis (and comparative evaluation) in terms of motives, meanings, and larger goals. But in analyzing rituals as practices, we also understand that the agents do not themselves need to be fully conscious of purpose, direction, and meaning. Indeed, rituals are a specific kind of social practice in which the role of human agency need to be appreciated in its historically sedimented and collective dimension: most of the practitioners of the Zande ritual may now be unaware of the original intention and purpose of these activities, which may have become dense and inscrutable in relation to contemporary individual or collective motivation. Nevertheless, no matter how apparently bizarre their manifestations, these rituals, as social and cultural phenomena, can be understood to the extent that we see them as practices which "they," the practitioners, can *in principle* themselves understand. In a word, "we" have no way of understanding "them" until we allow them a history, that is, grant to their actions the minimum basis of intelligibility that in principle human actions have. Needless to say, this would hold true for their values, their texts, and their languages.

Evaluating Otherness

To return to our discussion of relativism, then, we can see why it is important to go beyond a simple recognition of *differences* across cultures. For "they" do ultimately what "we" do, since they share with us a capacity for self-aware historical agency. If their terms, categories, and solutions are fundamentally different from ours, we have identified not merely a difference but what Charles Taylor calls an "incommensurablity." Incommensurable activities are different, but "they somehow occupy the same space," according to Taylor's useful distinction. "The real challenge is to see the incommensurablity, to come to understand how their range of possible activities, that is, the way in which they identify and distinguish activities, differs from ours."[13] The "range of possible activities" outlines the space of "culture," but in this definition culture is grounded in a specific and important common feature. The centrality of practice in this understanding of culture, emphasizing the social actions of individuals and collectives in definable situations, enriches our notion of difference by historicizing it. Only when we have defined our commonality in this way can the *why* question, about the reason underlying different practices and different choices, become not only intelligible but also *necessary*. For given this essential common space, otherness appears not in the form of insularity or in a relationship of mere contiguity, but as a complex historical phenomenon, available to us only through a process of hermeneutical comparison and specification. Mere difference leads, as I said earlier, to a sentimental charity, for there is nothing in its logic that necessitates our attention to the other. Winch's sophisticated relativism emphasizes the ethical dimension, but to the extent that it too remains underspecified in its conception of rationality, its political implications are at best vague. The rationality a political cultural criticism cannot afford to ignore is implicit in the very definition of human agency sketched above: the capacity all human "persons" and "cultures" in principle possess to understand their actions and evaluate those actions in terms of their (social and historical) significance for the person or culture. It is this issue that relativism, in both the extreme and the sophisticated formulations I have discussed, obscures.

I do not see how political criticism (poststructuralist or otherwise) can afford to deny this minimal rationality that is implicit in human agency or avoid theorizing what it entails. Consideration of the question of rationality is unnecessarily complicated if we confuse the kinds of basic definitional issues I have been outlining here with the philosophical search for large schemes we have traditionally called Reason. Whether in any of its positivist garbs, or the more dialectical "communicative rationality" that Habermas has been seeking, Reason formulated as the grand foundational structure that would subtend (and hence explain) all human capacities and ground all knowledge is now probably best seen as a noble but failed dream. But that does not mean either that there is no rational component to human actions or, more crucially, that we can afford to (philosophically) ignore this rationality. Drawing on cognitive psychological theory, Christopher Cherniak has argued recently against Cartesian attempts to define the ideal epistemic agent, since "the fact that a person's actions fall short of ideal rationality need not make them in any way less intelligible to us."[14] Often, he argues, "we have a simple explanation of why the person cannot accomplish all inferences that are apparently appropriate for him—namely, that he has finite cognitive resources" (20). But that, according to Cherniak, need not be cause for despair; rather, recognizing that human agency can be defined only in the context of this unavoidable finitude is an essential precondition for understanding the rationality of agenthood and for orienting our search toward a "context-sensitive" reason rather than a "highly idealized" one. My attempt in this essay has been to explain why, since for political criticism the concern with agency must be crucial, it would be debilitating at the present moment to confuse the claims of an ideal and comprehensive Reason with the basic capacities we can identify and define only in terms of the minimal rationalities they involve.

Moreover, once we understand that human rationality need not simply be a formal matter as positivists insist, but is instead a fundamental capacity for articulation that underlies our social actions and enables us to be historical creatures, we can begin to realize what else is at stake in all this for political criticism. So long as we base our political analyses of culture on relativist grounds, avoiding the challenge posed by the competing claims of various (cultural) rationalities, we will surrender complex historical knowledge of Others to sentimental ethical gestures in their direction. We might remain wary of ethnocentric evaluation of alterity, but there is a basic evaluation involved in positing connections, perceiving similarities and differences, and organizing complex bodies of information into provisionally intelligible wholes. Central to this process of evaluative judgment, with its minimal tasks of ordering and creating hierarchies of significance, is the understanding of humans across cultural and historical divides as capable of the minimal rationality implicit in agency. This cross-cultural commonality is one limit our contemporary political notions of difference and otherness need to acknowledge and theorize.

The most immediate practical considerations are involved in all of this. In criticism, for instance, the call for respect for alternative canons can be made on the basis of a purely liberal respect for other literatures and experiences, but that will not necessarily comprise a challenge to the dominant order to the very extent that alternative canons are seen simply as coexisting peacefully in a pluralistic academy. If what I have said about the inadequacy of a logic of difference is convincing, the charity evident in institutional pluralism may in fact hide a more fundamental indifference. For in the study of modern literatures, the most crucial political question that arises concerns a history "we" all share, a history whose very terms and definitions are now being openly contested and reformulated. When pluralist arguments are used to support the proliferation of various minority canons and discourses, the question of historical imbrication, indeed the question of this unequal history itself, is obscured by a narrowly pragmatic logic. The study of minority literatures, for instance, can be defended on the ground that an adequate definition of Literature must include all of its variant forms and all the various human experiences they represent. The difficulty with this formulation is that its *vagueness* leaves it open to all kinds of ironic recuperation. After all, when the Moroccan-French writer Tahar Ben Jelloun won France's prestigious Goncourt Prize, President Mitterand found it possible to describe the event as further evidence of the universality of the French language. Ben Jelloun, the first North African writer to win this prize, writes in both French and Arabic and has remained a critic of both the Moroccan regime and the racist practices of the French against North African immigrants. To read—and teach—his works as evidence of the universality of the French language, or even of the rich diversity of the human experience, is precisely to erase the specificity of the postcolonial immigrant writer, ambivalently situated in the belly of the imperial beast. Ignoring the history of colonialism by merely celebrating God's literary plenty, the pluralist critic would be no different here from the socialist president in containing the potential significance of any otherness.[15] One way for criticism to battle such historical amnesia would be to stress the complex agencies of both the colonizers and the colonized that are evident in cultural production and consumption. In fact, it is in the imbrication of these agencies that cultural configurations of colonial histories, of patterns of domination and the resistances to them, can be traced and understood.[16] The academy's eager acceptance of alternative canons—defined often as dehistoricized, formal constructs—suggests the urgent need to go beyond purely *literary-historical* reformulations.[17]

One function of political criticism, as I said earlier, is to identify the social interests that the reading and writing of literature serve. These interests can be variously oppressive or liberating; there is nothing inherent in the texts themselves that can control and limit the uses to which they are put or the meanings and values they are made to deploy. We cannot understand the interests of different social groups or different political visions of the world, however, without historical specification; a general rhetoric of alterity reveals structures and systems, not the terms and conditions in which individual and collective experiences can be identified. Our formulation of such terms and conditions is dependent on a positive elaboration of the varieties of cultural and political practice, and on a theoretical understanding of human agency. For despite the mystifications of the numerous ideologies of the Subject it would be a little too soon to conclude that humans have not acted, believed, and attempted to make and remake their worlds. This has happened in the Third World as much as in the First. To the extent that we specify the common terms on the level of human practice and seek to articulate and understand our contexts, goals, and possibilities, we consider human history potentially intelligible and the individual and collective actions of humans open to rational analysis. Notwithstanding our contemporary slogans of otherness, and our fervent denunciations of Reason and the Subject, there is an unavoidable conception of rational action, inquiry, and dialogue inherent in this political-critical project, and if we deny or obscure it we ought at least to know at what cost.

Notes

1. The allusion is not so much specifically to Richard Rorty, who has been advancing a model of philosophy as an aspect of the continuing "conversation of mankind," as it is more generally to the liberal pluralist politics that might accompany so-called antifoundationalist positions in cultural criticism. This essay can be read as an implicit dialogue with such positions or sentiments; my intention is to depersonalize the issues involved by focusing on underlying arguments and assumptions. Incidentally, while Rorty makes a convincing case against the dominant self-image of academic philosophy as a relentless search for a Truth that would be the foundation for all other forms of knowledge and social practice (*Philosophy and the Mirror of Nature*, Princeton, 1979), he would probably be quite willing to grant that his own alternative account of philosophy engaged in "the conversation of the

West" (394) invites political interrogation. If the forms and protocols of this conversation have developed historically—as they must have, given Rorty's arguments—we would need to be more attentive to the work of those feminist, anti-imperialist, and other radical scholars who have been focusing on the exclusions that have shaped this conversation. In this context, the point of my essay is simply this: the arguments against foundationalism in philosophy notwithstanding, an appreciation of these exclusions is possible only through a great deal of historical specification, and such specification can be done poorly and inadequately if we adopt the basic position of cultural or historical relativism. Indeed, the antifoundationalist position in contemporary philosophy does not *entail* the kind of cultural or historical relativism I discuss in this essay, even though in practice, as *attitudes,* the two might seem to go together.

2. Patrick Gardiner, "German Philosophy and the Rise of Relativism," *The Monist* 64 (April 1981): 138–54. The literature on relativism is voluminous and is probably best approached in terms of specific topics or disciplines. Useful discussions as well as bibliographic leads can be found in the following recent collections: *Rationality and Relativism,* ed. Martin Hollis and Steven Lukes (Cambridge, Mass.: 1982) and *Relativism: Cognitive and Moral,* ed. M. Kranz and J. Meiland (Notre Dame, Ind.: 1982). See also the earlier publication, edited by B. Wilson, cited in note 5.

3. Philip Lewis, "The Post-structuralist Condition," *Diacritics* 12, no. 1 (Spring 1982): 2–24. This is one of the best essays I have read on the relationship between structuralism and what claims to be a *post*-structuralism, and one of the most forceful statements of the case both these movements might make. Lewis argues convincingly that most of the characteristics we usually ascribe to poststructuralism in literary-critical circles do not in fact represent a new theory as much as a radicalization of classical structuralism. Lewis's account of a specifically post-structuralist condition is formulated primarily in Derridean and Lyotardian terms, as that which will resist recuperation by Philosophy or Criticism (see esp. 22–24). Thus "post-structuralism" is deliberately "conditional," involving in part "an impulse or pressure to cultivate artifice, affabulation—an infection, as it were, that pervades philosophic writing and promotes its resistance to the regimen of the *same*" (23). I find this characterization useful, and I would like my essay to be seen as a basic attempt at distinguishing cogent "affabulation" from unconvincing or underdemonstrated claims in contemporary criticism. It is the latter that one finds in great evidence in the guise of a (post)structuralist theory or politics, and it is on one of the underlying problems in such critical discourse that I have chosen to focus. Incidentally, the "regimen of the *same*" is precisely what the current debates between and within feminism, Marxism, and poststructuralism seek to define and specify. This is thus not simply a "philosophical" or disciplinary matter; and its engagement with political theory will probably have much to teach us about the relationship between "writing" or "inscription" as models of human practice and the political "interests" that articulate and mobilize the "social."

I analyze some of the more radical theses of poststructuralism as literary and social theory in *Literary Theory and the Claims of History* (forthcoming from Basil Blackwell, 1992). The present essay constitutes a chapter of the last section of the book. For a critique of a particularly influential version of American deconstruction, that developed by Paul de Man, see my "Radical Teaching, Radical Theory: The Ambiguous Politics of Meaning," in *Theory in the Classroom,* ed. C. Nelson (Urbana, Ill.: 1986). (I use the term *poststructuralism,* unhyphenated and unemphasized, to refer to a general tendency in literary theory, a tendency evident in gestural and stylistic claims as much as in argument or analysis.)

The quotations that follow are taken from Michel Foucault, *The Archaeology of Knowledge,* trans. A. M. Sheridan Smith (New York: 1972), 11–12; Hélène Cixous, "The Laugh of the Medusa," in *New French Feminisms,* ed. Elaine Marks and Isabelle de Courtivron

(New York: 1981), 263–64, 260; Ernesto Laclau and Chantal Mouffe, *Hegemony and Socialist Strategy: Towards a Radical Democratic Politics,* trans. Winston Moore and Paul Cammack (London: 1985), 2.

4. There are several useful studies of this phenomenon, but let me at least mention the following: Talal Asad, ed., *Anthropology and the Colonial Encounter* (London: 1973); George E. Marcus and Michael M. J. Fischer, *Anthropology as Cultural Critique: An Experimental Moment in the Human Sciences* (Chicago: 1986); James Clifford and George E. Marcus, eds., *Writing Culture: The Poetics and Politics of Ethnography* (Berkeley: 1986); George W. Stocking, Jr., *Victorian Anthropology* (New York: 1987), esp. ch. 7; Douglas A. Lorimer, "Theoretical Racism in Late-Victorian Anthropology 1870–1900," *Victorian Studies* 31, no. 3 (Spring 1988): 405–30; and, for a more general account, of course, Edward Said, *Orientalism* (New York: 1978). For a feminist critique of some of the dominant anthropological categories, see Felicity Eldhom, Olivia Harris, and Kate Young, "Conceptualising Women," *Critique of Anthropology* 3 (1977); and for a productive encounter between anthropological concepts and global materialist history, Eric R. Wolf, *Europe and the People without History* (Berkeley: 1982). For an analysis of politically motivated scholarship about the Third World that unselfconsciously reproduces larger patterns of discursive colonization, see Chandra Talpade Mohanty, "Under Western Eyes: Feminist Scholarship and Colonial Discourses," *boundary 2* 12, no. 3/13, no. 1 (Spring/Fall 1984): 333–58; a revised version of this essay appeared in the British journal *Feminist Review* in 1988. (Also see note 8.)

5. Ernest Gellner, "Concepts and Society," in *Rationality,* ed. Bryan R. Wilson (rpt. Oxford: 1985), 18–49; Talal Asad, "The Concept of Cultural Translation in British Social Anthropology," in Clifford and Marcus, eds., *Writing Culture,* 141–64. All subsequent page references to these essays are in parentheses in the text.

6. The fact that the passage I have just quoted is itself question-begging in basic ways is worth mentioning, especially to highlight the contrast with Gellner's imperious tone. How determinate, for instance, does an interpretation have to be? Or: how absolute a conception of success or failure (of "the interpreted communication") do we need to have? These are questions for which Gellner presumes we have self-evident answers, but they seem to me to raise the most crucial hermeneutical issues involved in anthropological— or any textual—interpretation.

7. "Decolonizing anthropology" necessarily suggests a collective and historically specific project. I borrow the term from the special session held at the 1987 convention of the American Anthropological Association; a collection of essays with this title is forthcoming.

8. The theory that "modernization" according to the terms of capitalist development in the West is the telos of Third World societies and economies has been pervasive in the social sciences. One classic text that presents it is W. W. Rostow, *Stages of Economic Growth,* 2nd ed., (New York: 1971); See André Gunder Frank's famous critique of this approach, especially developed in the essays "The Sociology of Development or the Underdevelopment of Sociology" and "The Development of Underdevelopment," in his *Latin America: Underdevelopment or Revolution* (New York: 1969). More adequate historical models than the one modernization theory draws on can be found in such useful anthologies as *Imperialism and Underdevelopment: A Reader,* ed. Robert I. Rhodes (New York: 1970), and *An Introduction to the Sociology of "Developing" Societies,* ed. Hamza Alavi and Theodor Shanin (New York: 1982).

9. One well-known instance might suffice here. The need to base political criticism in a space that is itself an articulation of several, of at least the dominant and the marginal, is what Myra Jehlen emphasizes in her valuable essay "Archimedes and the Paradox of

Feminist Criticism," *Signs* 6, no. 4 (Summer 1981): 575–601. Jehlen uses her central metaphor of an Archimedean point for criticism to argue "that a terrestrial fulcrum, a standpoint from which we can see our conceptual universe whole but which nonetheless rests firmly on made ground, is what feminists really need" (576). However, the fact that she does not examine further the problems of the relativist position she would seem to be attacking here leads to a strange vagueness. Thus, although in her conclusion she talks about "points of contradiction as the places where we can see the whole structure of our world most clearly," she is able to see this as implying "the immanent relativity of all perception and knowledge" (600, 601). If Jehlen means by this that comparative perspectives and analyses reveal the extent to which the different structures of perception and knowledge are produced in specific contexts, and are thus in part understandable in terms relative to these contexts, she has a point, but she seems to want to *suggest* more. For in the very next sentence she sees much larger consequences following from the above point: "Thus, what appears first as a methodological contradiction, then becomes a subject in itself, seems finally to be shaping something like a new epistemology" (601). Accepting the legitimate relativist-contextualist insight about the significance of context helps us fight, say, andro- or ethnocentrism, but since that does not necessarily involve or entail changing the very ways in which we conceive of knowledge and the process of knowing, i.e., seeking a new *epistemology,* I am not sure what Jehlen's suggestion means here. Since she argues an antiseparatist or antirelativist position throughout the essay, I see this suggestion at the end as a confusing vagueness rather than a contradiction in her argument; but it is at least evidence that her position would be clearer and stronger if she thought through the issue of relativism and what it entails.

It might be that cultural criticism is, at least at the present moment, particularly unconcerned about relativism as a problematic position. It would be illuminating to contrast Jehlen's essay with Sandra Harding's recent discussion of the implications of feminism for the social sciences: "Introduction: Is There a Feminist Method?" in *Feminism and Methodology,* ed. Sandra Harding (Bloomington, Ind.: 1987), 1–14. Harding's strictures on relativists include a pertinent political diagnosis: "Historically, relativism appears as an intellectual possibility, and as a 'problem,' only for dominating groups at the point where the hegemony (the universality) of their views is being challenged. As a modern intellectual position, it emerged in the belated recognition by nineteenth-century Europeans that the apparently bizarre beliefs and behaviors of non-Europeans had a rationality or logic of their own. Perhaps the preferred Western beliefs might not be the only reasonable ones. The point here is that relativism is not a problem originating in, or justifiable in terms of, women's experiences or feminist agendas. It is fundamentally a sexist response that attempts to preserve the legitimacy of androcentric claims in the face of contrary evidence" (10).

10. Peter Winch, "Understanding a Primitive Society," in Wilson, ed., *Rationality,* 78–111. The essay originally appeared in 1964 in *American Philosophical Quarterly.*

11. R.W. Connell's recent book, *Gender and Power* (Stanford, Calif.: 1987), provides an excellent summary of these developments, and discusses quite lucidly the implications of this emphasis for social theory in general. The most original and ambitious work with this focus is Pierre Bourdieu's. See especially *Outline of a Theory of Practice,* trans. Richard Nice (Cambridge, England: 1977), and, for a more succinct formulation of his theory, chapters 2–4 of *Distinction: A Social Critique of the Judgement of Taste,* trans. Richard Nice (Cambridge, Mass.: 1984). The idea that social actions are necessarily "recursive," i.e., never entirely original and always a form of revision of existing social meanings, practices, and institutions, is explained quite well by Anthony Giddens in his *Constitution of Society: Outline of the Theory of Structuration* (Berkeley: 1984). I discuss Louis Althusser's conception

of practice as essentially decentered in relation to a self-authorizing subject in "Ideology as Text and Practice: The Subject of Criticism after Althusser," chapter 3 of *Literary Theory and the Claims of History*, and examine in the concluding chapter of that book the relationship between the theoretical conception of agency sketched in the present essay and the need to reconceive what is called the "public sphere."

12. Donald Davidson, "On the Very Idea of a Conceptual Scheme," in his *Inquiries into Truth and Interpretation* (Oxford: 1984), 183–98.

13. The useful distinction between "difference" and "incommensurability" is developed in Taylor's essay "Rationality" (in his *Philosophy and the Human Sciences: Philosophical Papers, Volume 2* [Cambridge, England: 1985], 134–51), which contains a good discussion of Winch and one of the best accounts of what I have been calling a minimal conception of rationality (the quotations are from p. 145). Taylor considers our capacity for "articulation" or laying things out "in perspicuous order" the basic component of human rationality, although it is not quite clear whether he would consider this to be a historically or a culturally universal phenomenon. See also, for an instructive discussion of rationality in relation to language, Jonathan Bennett, *Rationality: An Essay Towards an Analysis* (London and New York: 1964), esp. 86–101. There is a good account of the issues involved in conceiving a postpositivist rationality in Hilary Putnam, *Reason, Truth and History* (Cambridge, England: 1981), and the essay "Beyond Historicism" in his *Realism and Reason: Philosophical Papers, Volume 3* (Cambridge, England: 1983), 287–303. Many of these questions have been debated fruitfully by historians and philosophers of science.

14. Christopher Cherniak, *Minimal Rationality* (Cambridge, Mass.: 1986).

15. The ambivalent relationship between contemporary minority writers and their "metropolitan" audiences is highlighted in the context of Europe's new immigrant populations. At what may have been the first American conference on this subject, "Europe's New Minority Cultures" (Cornell, February 1988), the issue of cultural appropriation and a critical pedagogy that would prevent appropriation became a central issue in both the papers and the discussions that followed. I would like to mention in particular the presentations by Ted Chamberlain on "Britain's New Poetry" and Samia Mehrez on "The Francophone North African Culture Presence in France."

16. Indeed, developments in the historiography of colonialism suggest the extent to which the "imbrication" of the agencies of the colonizers and the colonized is itself an image that demands further specification. In the area with which I am most familiar, South Asia, historical research has moved away from the left historian's primary emphasis on the visible and institutionally organized nationalism of the middle classes in order to trace patterns of resistance in peasant movements and revolts, a kind of resistance colonial historians had been content to characterize as criminal acts or at best unselfconscious and inchoate upsurges of powerful feeling. It would be instructive to compare the pioneering work of such historians of modern India as Bipan Chandra (see esp. *The Rise and Growth of Economic Nationalism in India* [New Delhi: 1966] and the essays collected in *Nationalism and Colonialism in Modern India* [New Delhi: 1979]) with the recent spate of monographic literature that has been redefining Indian nationalism by looking at it, within its own social context, "from below." A basic survey of the latter literature is provided in Sumit Sarkar, *Modern India: 1885–1947* (New Delhi: 1983). Sarkar's study, which is intended to be a synthetic college-level textbook, marks a telling contrast with the popular 1971 high-school text written by Bipan Chandra on behalf of an editorial board of prominent historians appointed by the National Council of Educational Research and Training (*Modern India,* New Delhi). The ongoing work on the role of the peasantry in Indian nationalist struggles can be followed in the pages of such journals as *Economic and Political Weekly* (Bombay), the *Journal of Peasant Studies* (London), and *Modern Asian Studies* (Cambridge, England) as well as in

the series of volumes titled *Subaltern Studies*, ed. R. Guha, published by Oxford University Press, Delhi. Questions of gender in the historiography of colonial India, and the difficult methodological issues raised by other uncoded practices of resistance, are dealt with most cogently by Rosalind O'Hanlon in her recent review essay "Recovering the Subject: *Subaltern Studies* and Histories of Resistance in Colonial South Asia," *Modern Asian Studies* 22, no. 1 (1988): 189–224. Finally, any analysis of a "colonial" formation that emphasizes the historically imbricated agencies of the "oppressed" and the "oppressor" must acknowledge its debt to Eugene Genovese's path-breaking studies of North American slavery, especially *The World the Slaveholders Made* (1969) and *Roll Jordan Roll: The World the Slaves Made* (1974).

The most basic lesson of such historiographical developments for a colonial *cultural* studies is at the very least that we need to be wary of too easily distinguishing "culture" from "history." Even more clearly than in contemporary analyses of metropolitan societies, the challenge for students of the Third World is to suspend the traditional notion of culture as a realm apart, of sweetness and light. The rueful joke that the West possesses a history and a sociology while the Third World merely has an anthropology does have a point, especially about the radical-ideological biases inherent in modern disciplinary demarcations and territories. But we might do well to be wary of the convenient reaction to these biases, which would consist in investing Third World societies with "culture" in the traditional Western mold (after all, that was what both the Orientalists and the early nationalists, in their own ways, tried to do), and be more ready to specify and reexamine notions of "history" and "culture" together. (For an account of "race" as a historical process evidenced in cultural practices and tendencies, see my "Kipling's Children and the Colour Line," *Race and Class*, 1989. I expand and develop the arguments presented in that essay in "Drawing the Color Line" in *The Bounds of Race*, ed. Dominick La Capra [Ithaca, N.Y.: 1991].)

17. For an astute and timely discussion of some of these issues, especially in the context of possible institutional appropriation of minority discourses, see Cornel West, "Minority Discourse and the Pitfalls of Canon Formation," *Yale Journal of Criticism* 1, no. 1 (Fall 1987): 193–201. My essay is in part an attempt to develop some of the issues and questions West raises so well.

Slightly different versions of this essay have appeared in the *Yale Journal of Criticism* and *New Formations*.

Contributors

Jonathan Arac is professor of English at the University of Pittsburgh. Author of *Commissioned Spirits* and *Critical Genealogies,* he has completed a study of mid-nineteenth-century prose narrative, forthcoming in 1992 in the *Cambridge History of American Literature,* and is now working on a book entitled *Huckleberry Finn and the Functions of Criticism.*

Paul A. Bové is editor of *boundary 2* and professor of English at the University of Pittsburgh. He is the author of *Destructive Poetics, Intellectuals in Power, Mastering Discourse,* and *In the Wake of Theory.*

Suzanne Gearhart is professor of French and a member of the Critical Theory Institute at the University of California, Irvine. She is the author of *The Open Boundary of History and Fiction: A Critical Approach to the French Enlightenment,* which was awarded the René Wellek Prize by the American Comparative Literature Association, and articles on historiography, psychoanalysis, literary theory, philosophy and literature, and eighteenth-century French literature. A second book, *The Interrupted Dialectic: Philosophy, Psychoanalysis and Their Tragic Other,* has just been published.

Michael Hays teaches at Cornell University, where he is professor of theater and cultural studies. He has published numerous essays on nineteenth- and twentieth-century European drama and culture as well as on critical theory. His books include *The Public and Performance: Essays in the History of French and German Theater 1871–1900* and the forthcoming *Empowering Aesthetics: The Politics of the New in the Modern Drama.*

Carol Kay is associate professor of English at the University of Pittsburgh. The author of *Political Constructions: Defoe, Richardson, and Sterne in Relation to Hobbes, Hume, and Burke,* she is currently working on a book on eighteenth-century British moral philosophy.

Satya P. Mohanty is associate professor of English at Cornell University. His *Literary Theory and the Claims of History,* which develops the arguments of his essay in this volume, is forthcoming from Cornell University Press in the autumn of 1993.

Daniel T. O'Hara, professor of English at Temple University, is editor of two collections of essays in critical theory and author of four books, including *Lionel Trilling: The Work of Liberation* and *Radical Parody: American Culture and Critical Agency after Foucault.*

Donald E. Pease holds the Ted and Helen Geisel Chair in the Humanities at Dartmouth College. He is the author of *Visionary Compacts: American Renaissance Writings in Cultural Context* and *Deterrence Pacts: Formations of the Canon in the Cold War Era.* He is also the editor (with Walter Benn Michaels) of *American Renaissance Reconsidered; New Americanists: Revisionist Interventions into the Canon;* and, with Amy Kaplan, *Cultures of U.S. Imperialism.*

Index

academe: and the critical agon, vii–ix; and discourse of colonialism, 27, 31–36; Fish on, 40–47; and politics, 25; and *ressentiment,* 39–40

aesthetic, the: and community, 49; and de Man, xiii–xv; and Fish, 44; Hegel on, 62; Lyotard on, 66

agency. *See* historical agency

agon. *See* critical agon

Althusser, Louis: on Marx, 58

American literature studies: and the canon, 3–4; and capitalism, 16; and the critic, 10, 13–15; genealogy of, 11–12; Graff on, 50–51; and internationalism, 11; Poirier on, 51–53; and revisionism, 15; and Wallace Stevens, 53–54. *See also* Bercovitch, Sacvan, the New Americanism

anthropology. *See* social anthropology

anticolonialism, 24–25, 28, 31–32, 36

Arac, Jonathan: on Bloom, 47

Arendt, Hannah, 66

Arnold, Matthew, xxi, 40

Asad, Talal, 121, 129; on Gellner, 123–25

Begebenheit, 67, 69

Bercovitch, Sacvan: on the American dream, 8–9; and the critic, 10; and the jeremiad, 7; and the New Americanism, 2–8

Bloom, Harold, 39–40, 47–48, 53–54

Booth, Wayne, 19

Brewer, Mária Minich, ix

Burke, Edmund: and de Man, 110–11

canon, the. *See* liberal pluralism

Césaire, Aimé, 25

character: and *Bildung* fiction, 83, 85–86, 90–91; E. M. Forster on, 84; and Foucault, 92; and Gothic fiction, 83, 90–92; historical development of the concept, 83–85; and Lukács, 86; John Stuart Mill on, 89; and romantic critics of Shakespeare, 83–85, 88–89; and the subject, 83, 92

Cherniak, Christopher, 138

collective archive, 49–50, 53–55

colonialism: and anthropology, 119–20; and the canon, 139–40; and cultural studies, 144n.16; and linguistic identity, 21–24; and New Historicism, 25–36; and *Othello,* 27, 35; psychology of, 22;